How to Set Up Your
Motorcycle Workshop

Tips and Tricks for Building and Equipping
Your Dream Workshop

C. G. MASI

A Tech Series Book
Whitehorse Press
North Conway, New Hampshire

For Loyd Hall. We all miss you.

Front cover photo by Jeff Hackett.

We recognize that some words, model names, and designations
mentioned herein are the property of the trademark holder. We use
them for identification purposes only.

The name Whitehorse Press is a trademark of Kennedy Associates.

Whitehorse Press books are also available at discounts in bulk quantity
for sales and promotional use. For details about special sales or for a
catalog of motorcycling books and videos, write to the Publisher:

Whitehorse Press
P.O. Box 60
North Conway, New Hampshire 03860-0060
Phone: 603-356-6556 or 800-531-1133
Email: Orders@WhitehorsePress.com
Internet: www.WhitehorsePress.com

ISBN 1-884313-43-4

5   4

Printed in the United States

Table of *Contents*

Preface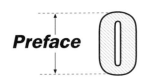

In the seven years since I wrote *How to Set Up Your Motorcycle Workshop,* we've seen a lot of changes. The political pendulum has swung from the Left to the Right. The national economy has gone from boom to bust to kinda schlepping along. Computers have gone from large desktop installations serving a few early technology adopters to laptops, palmtops, and pocket editions whose main function is to plug everyone into the Internet. In a lot of ways, it's like a whole 'nuther world out there.

Most of these changes, however, don't have a heck of a lot of impact on the Saturday Afternoon Motorcycle Mechanic's workshop. You still need tools. You still need a place to put your tools. And, you still need a place to put you and your bike while you use your tools on your bike.

The changes in Motorcycle Workshop Technology (MWT, to be techie-jargony) have been subtle. There are, for example, more women riding and wrenching. The technology on the newer bikes is a tad more advanced. There are, perhaps, a few more goodies you can stuff into your always-bursting workshop space.

Our motivation for bringing out a new edition of *How to Set Up Your Motorcycle Workshop* was not, therefore, to track massive changes in MWT, but to add some things that either weren't available for the first edition, or we hadn't thought of them, yet. By the way, when I say "we" and "our" here, I'm acknowledging the fact that the folks at Whitehorse Press deserve every bit as much credit for this book as I do. In fact, they should get the lion's share of the credit, while I deserve any blame.

Some of the additions we've made, for example, include a description of my multi-purpose workshop. Since we built the house that surrounds that shop in 1999, it was a little hard to take pictures of it in 1996.

Similarly, we couldn't have put in Dave Percival's collector's workshop because, although it might have been in existence in 1996, we didn't know about it. Similarly, the information about Frank Holmes' "Frank's Brit Bike Barn" wasn't available for the 1996 edition.

We've also scrounged up or shot new and improved pictures of a lot of the bits and pieces that can go into your tool collection. I've also learned to use a few more tools over the past seven years. That just goes to show that even an old you-know-what like me can still learn a thing or two.

Of course, we also learned a little from responses to the first edition by motorcycle journalists, mechanics, and jes' plain folks (who are the most important folks of all). We've tried to incorporate their comments whenever possible.

I hope you enjoy this new edition as much as we've enjoyed bringing it to you.

C.G. Masi
March 10, 2003

Determining Your Needs

Lesson 1: Keep Your Plans Loose and Easy to Change

There is no universal plan for setting up a motorcycle shop. What you need to get out of this book is an understanding of how to figure out—for yourself—what you need for your workshop and how to arrange it, and how to do your planning and arranging in an organized way.

Not only is there no universal plan, but a motorcycle shop that will fit your needs today won't fit them a year from now. So, think about what your needs are *right now*.

For example, the other day I stopped by H&H Cycle Works in Needles, California. When I wandered out in the back, there was Tom climbing around on a workbench with boards in his hands. A Skilsaw sat in the middle of the floor atop a pile of sawdust.

"What's going on?" I asked.

"We're making kitty litter," said Tom's partner Loyd, pointing to the pile of sawdust. Half seriously, he continued: "You know, kitty litter is the best thing you can use to sop up oil spills. At least it used to be until the price went up."

"The difference between kitty litter and the commercial clean-up-your-oil-spill stuff is that kitty litter has chemicals in it to deodorize the you-know-what, and it used to be a lot cheaper. Now the price has gone up, though. Sawdust is almost as good, so we're making some of that."

"No, no. I'm putting up some more shelves," Tom said, sliding a pair of enormous leather saddle bags onto the shelf he'd just nailed in place.

Loyd and Tom have been at this location for several years. Yet, Tom had just then felt the need of added storage space right in that corner of the shop. Those saddle bags had been sitting on that workbench for several months since Tom had pulled them off a bike he was rebuilding. It had been his personal bike and they were his personal bags, so he didn't want them to go into the regular stock of used parts and get sold out from under him. Yet, he'd rebuilt the bike and sold it months ago. So, the bags were just hanging around taking up bench space. He needed that space for working on his current project—building a new bike from the frame out. Hence, he felt a sudden need for more shelves.

This planning method is called bottom-up design. With bottom-up design, you futz around with whatever it is that you're making until some aspect or feature proves to be inconvenient. Then you live with it a little longer until you figure out something that would be more convenient. Then you make the change.

Despite seeming very haphazard, bottom-up design is actually the most efficient way to expand or improve something. It only works, how-

Bottom-Up Design Strategy

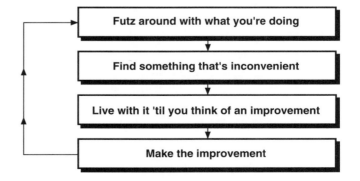

Top-Down Design Strategy

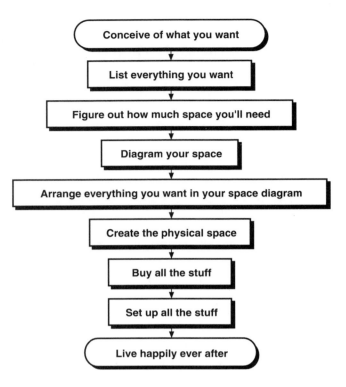

```
Conceive of what you want
        ↓
List everything you want
        ↓
Figure out how much space you'll need
        ↓
Diagram your space
        ↓
Arrange everything you want in your space diagram
        ↓
Create the physical space
        ↓
Buy all the stuff
        ↓
Set up all the stuff
        ↓
Live happily ever after
```

ever, on something that already exists and that you can use. If you're starting from scratch, you have to use the top-down design method.

Top-down design is the darling of detail-oriented management consultants. To use it, you pretend you know everything (that's what management consultants do best!), make a list of all your needs (down to the last spare cotter pin), draw all the plans, buy all the bits, set everything up, and live happily ever after.

What happens if you believe in this method is that you do everything but the "live happily ever after" part. You will find that you (like everybody else) aren't really very smart: You left out more than you put in. Even worse, most of what you did put in turns out to be most inconveniently laid out.

So, you can't use bottom-up design until your shop is laid out. But, only a pathological personality expects top-down design to work. What's a body to do?

The answer, as any Zen Master worth his sandals could tell you (but wouldn't), is to start with top-down design and *expect it not to work!*

Go through the top-down process, but don't get too fancy. Expect to modify it along the way. Expect to rearrange it almost as soon as it's done. And, don't ever expect it to be really finished. It has to change as your needs change.

What I'm going to try to do in this book is to help you get started with that top-down design and get a feel for when and how to modify it.

Lesson 2: Determine Your Needs

What you need is predicated on what you're going to do in the future. Since you don't have a crystal ball with which to predict the future, you're stuck again.

You *can* predict that the future will be something like the past, plus a little room for personal growth and the biker's motto: "Shit Happens." For example, if you've reached the stage where you do your own oil changes, it's a good bet that you'll continue to do oil changes and soon start doing other things, like replacing clutch cables, that require actually taking the bike apart. So, though you may have done all your motorcycle work out in the driveway so far, you should start thinking about setting up an area where you can leave the motorcycle in pieces overnight.

What you will need also depends on what you have for a bike. If you've got a brand-new high-tech BMW, expect to have the dealer do most of your maintenance. State-of-the-art motorcycle technology, like automobile technology, has reached the point where even a talented amateur mechanic is likely to do more harm than good whenever he picks up a wrench.

If, on the other hand, you have the ultimate restored 1967 Norton Commando, plan on a lot of wrenching. Competent Norton mechanics are scarce. The odds are that there won't be one anywhere conveniently near you.

If you want to get started in motorcycle wrenching, don't start with a rare antique with no factory support. Get yourself an old Harley Sportster from the '70s. They were made for tinkering, spare parts for them are available everywhere and there are a kazillion of 'em out there, so if you completely ruin one you haven't destroyed a piece of History.

The things you need to consider when determining your needs are:

• *Your personal skill level.* What you need for a shop depends on what you are capable of doing in it. An expert mechanic needs a fully equipped workshop. A novice just getting started has much more modest needs.

• *Your motorcycle inventory.* Do you have just one bike? Do you have several? Is your bike brand new and likely to need only regular maintenance and installation of the odd custom doodad? Or, do you have an older bike that will likely need serious rebuilding in the near future? Perhaps you own a racing bike, with all the special needs racers have. Perhaps your bike is a show-quality custom job. Maybe you have several machines of different sorts. Your motorcycle inventory—and how many friends and neighbors stop by regularly for advice or help—will heavily determine the size and layout of the shop you need.

• *The space you have available.* Unless you are prepared to construct a whole new building, or are ready to move to a new location, you are going to have to work within the space you have. Go out there and look *right now!* How big is that space? How secure is it from weather and vandals? Especially if you are a renter, how much modification can you do to it?

• *The resources you have.* Your resources include the tools and parts you already have, plus any construction materials you have laying around. You also have to consider how much money you have to buy what you don't already have. The bigger and more professional the workshop you want to have, the more it's going to cost.

• *The professional support you have available.* At one time, I lived two blocks from a shop buzzing with four expert Harley mechanics who not only knew what the heck they were doing, but weren't into gouging bikers. I didn't need much of a personal workshop, then. I did my own maintenance, took care of the little niddly problems and, when I burned a piston or wrecked a wheel bearing—anything major—I wheeled the bike into the shop down the street and handed them money. If I'd lived out in the desert, 45 miles from the nearest gas station, I'd have needed a much more complete shop! You probably live somewhere in between those ex-

tremes. The point is, even professionals figure on getting professional help. Don't tie up your money duplicating resources readily available down the street.

Mother Nature's Plan for Your Bike

Notice that I haven't included an item called "waddaya wanna do?" That is because what you do in your shop is more determined by what Mother Nature throws at you than anything else. You can't say, "I'm going to do only top-end work," and expect the Universe to go along with that.

I once went out and bought a brand new motorcycle because I was sick to death of constantly repairing the old heaps I had. I spent bucks on the extra "we'll take care of everything" maintenance plan the dealership offered. I brought the thing into the shop religiously every 2,500 miles for them to do their expert-maintenance thing. The only time I missed it was when I was in Daytona, 1,300 miles from home, when the scheduled-maintenance-gong sounded. That time I drove it 30 miles to a dealership in Longwood because the Daytona dealership was backed up all week and I wasn't gonna be late for that scheduled maintenance.

After 12 months, the electronic ignition module blew up for no apparent reason. The replacement blew up an eighth of a mile later, also for no apparent reason.

Another 12 months went by and the voltage regulator failed in such a way that the first indication of trouble was the incineration of both my battery and alternator—when I was 200 miles from home. I had to fix that one while camped in a field.

You can run, but you can't hide from Mother Nature! The choices you do have include how much of what Mother Nature throws at you is going to get fixed in your shop and how much you'll leave to a professional. There is, of course, a basic minimum you can't avoid, but most bikers choose to take responsibility for a lot more. Generally, the more experience they have, the more they are willing to tackle.

You can also choose to dive into specialties that, by background or inclination, you feel especially qualified for. For example, in any random group of bikers, you're likely to find two or three who especially enjoy painting. Most, like me, stick to fairly basic color schemes. Some, however, have the talent and inclination to get into fancy custom graphics. To practice that art, they invest in professional-style painting equipment and facilities.

So, although you *must* have some level of workshop facilities to keep your bike healthy, how far and in what direction you expand your facilities is a matter of choice.

What Do *You* Want To Do?

I've talked about Mother Nature's plan for your bike, and the necessity for regular maintenance. I've told you about what you *have* to do and what you *can't* get away with doing. Now it's time to talk about what you *want* to do.

Remember when I said that the way to plan your workshop is to start with a top-down design and expect to modify it as you go along? This is the toppest of the top-down design questions: "What do *you* want to do in your motorcycle workshop?"

In a sense, this is career planning. Even if you aren't saying "I want to be a professional motorcycle mechanic and own my own shop," you should think about what parts of the motorcycling sport interest you. How elaborate your motorcycle workshop becomes and what items you have in there will depend on how involved you become with certain aspects of the sport.

• *How deeply involved do you want to get?* The fact that you're reading this book indicates that you're already pretty involved with motorcycling. You are at least what can be described as a "Dedicated Amateur." But, motorcycling can take up as much or as little of your time as you want it to. And, there are different aspects of motorcycling that you can spend your time on. Motorcycling buffs vary from folks who have a

motorcycle as just one of their many toys, to those who eat, drink and sleep motorcycles.

• *What aspects of motorcycling interest you?* There are touring enthusiasts who live for the next road trip. There are racers who live for the next race. There are bike-show enthusiasts whose every effort goes into getting the next trophy. There are custom-bike builders who think about nothing but their next creation. And, there are mechanics who get off on finding and fixing problems on broken bikes.

Most bikers combine a healthy mixture of all these aspects. Dedicated touring types usually like to have their bikes looking good and want them to stand out from the crowd at the rally. Trophy collectors also like to take their scoots out for a little putt once in a while. Most mechanics like to sometimes put their tools away and make a run to, say, Sturgis.

• *Do you want to become a professional?* It may seem that everyone who gets into the eat-drink-and-sleep-motorcycles ranks would want to become a full-time, professional biker. That ain't necessarily so, however. I am a professional writer and editor. I am an amateur bike builder. People pay me to write and edit the stuff they want written and edited, not what I want to do. Because I'm an amateur, when I build a bike I get to build exactly what I want, when I want it, and I don't give a damn whether anyone else likes it or not.

An amateur does pretty much exactly as he pleases. A professional is selling a service to someone else. People don't pay you to do what you want to do, they pay you to do what *they* want you to do. That's why we have hobbies so we can spend some time doing what we damn well please.

Once you have answered these questions, you are ready to start daydreaming about what you want for your shop. What I hope this book will do is give you a good start on turning your dreams into your reality.

Chapter 2

Types of Motorcycle Workshops

In the course of this book, we'll look at a variety of different types of motorcycle workshops. Each has a different purpose and requires different resources to set up and operate.

The Small Garage Workshop

The simplest permanent installation is what I call the small garage. I define a small garage as a sheltered area big enough to support one bike. When I say "support," I mean that there is enough room to store the bike in the middle of the work area, plus at least one workbench, plus storage for tools, spare parts, and the odd assortment of ancillary materials (oil, grease, chain lube, etc.).

Just because the shop is small, however, doesn't mean it has to be incomplete. In a small garage, you are unlikely to see machine tools much more involved than, say, a drill press. Usually you will pretty much see hand tools. Essentially, you can put anything in a small garage that will fit in it and still leave you room to work.

The small garage is good for a personal workshop for one bike. You can fit more than one bike in such a shop, though. I've had up to four motorcycles in a small garage at once. It was, however, so crowded that I had to move bikes outside every time I wanted to do some work. That is a sure sign that you need to move up to a bigger space.

The Bigger Garage Workshop

The bigger garage gives you more room for more bikes, more supplies, more parts, more equipment—generally more of the same stuff you put into a small garage. The main difference is how you organize that more-of-the-same stuff.

How you organize the space depends largely on how much space you have to divvy up between how many vehicles. There are two ways to organize a fair-size garage devoted to motorcycle repair and maintenance: Assign a work/storage area for each vehicle (Some people own vehicles other than motorcycles. Some people even put those other vehicles in their garage!) or set up a common work space and store the vehicles elsewhere.

Assigned Seating

If you have an overabundance of space, it's often easier to move the tools to the bike than the bike to the tools. You can have a large work space, perhaps including its own separate workbench, assigned to each bike. When you're not either riding or working on that particular bike, it just

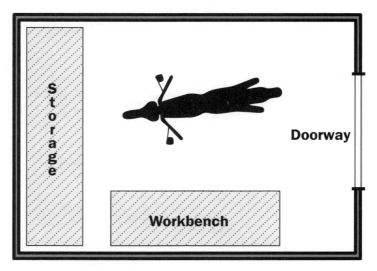

Typically, a small garage has enough room to work comfortably on one, or, at most, two bikes.

sits there (in other words, it's stored) in the middle of its assigned work space.

Common Work Space

If, however, you've got a sizeable bike collection going, you may not have enough space to give each of them that much room. You can then store the bikes together, leaving only enough room between them to pull them in and out safely. When a bike needs work, pull it out into a common work space. When you're not working on any bikes, the work space should be empty. If you find yourself forced to store a bike in the common work space, it's a sure sign that you either need more space or fewer bikes.

With the common work space plan, you have to think about how many bikes you'll be working on at the same time. A bike is being worked on if it's in some state of disassembly such that you don't want to move it. A BSA frame on wheels, with its engine in a box on a shelf waiting for you to find time to rebuild it, is not being worked on. It's being stored. If, after rebuilding, the engine were sitting on the floor next to the bike, with the required nuts, bolts and screws arranged for orderly assembly, all just waiting for you to bolt the motor into place, that bike would be "being worked on."

Most of the time, you want to work on one bike at a time. For example, when going through a regular weekly maintenance routine (check the

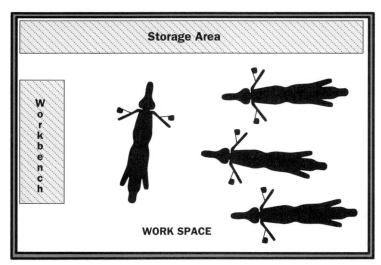

The common work space layout uses space more efficiently than the assigned-seating layout.

oil, service the battery, etc.), you want to go through the whole routine giving one bike your undivided attention. Then, maybe, take a break before going on to the next one. Part of the purpose for that weekly routine is to look for things that are starting to go wrong and attend to them before they affect the bike's operability (e.g., breaking down 70 miles from nowhere). In that situation, undivided attention is the whole idea.

At other times, however, you either want or have to leave the bike in the middle of a job and work on another one. For example, that time the ignition module went out on my almost-new bike, I was pulling out for a run down to Cape Cod and wouldn't be back for a week. Rather than have our vacation ruined, I left that bike in pieces, pulled out an old kick-start Sportster and pressed it into service. Before I could take off with it, though, I had to check the oil, service the battery and lube the chain. In other words, I was working on two bikes at once.

Another example of working on two bikes at once is the long-term restoration. Motorcyclists who get involved in a take-it-apart-so-no-fastener-is-fastened-to-its-mating-part-and-rebuild-it-from-the-ground-up restoration usually have a bike that they use regularly during the months or years such a restoration takes. Obviously, the working motorcycle is still going to need maintenance and repair, even though there is another bike in the shop sitting in some state of disassembly—for a long time.

I could go on and on with more examples. I think, however, it's clear that working on more than one bike at a time is not only possible, but sometimes desirable and, perhaps, even inevitable. When you're working on more than one bike at a time you've gotta have more than one bike's worth of work space.

So, you should organize your work space so that you *can* work on more than one bike at a time. It's simple when you have lots of space in your shop: you just plan work space for more than one bike. If your space is more constrained, however, maybe you can figure on temporarily rearranging what space you do have when you need to put multiple bikes under the wrench at the same time. For example, a bike you're working on is a bike that's not being stored. So, maybe you can slightly rearrange the bikes you are storing to free up a little extra work space.

Aha, you say! You can combine the assigned-seating and common-work space ideas. You have, say, a 1949 Panhead Harley over there without its engine, which is being rebuilt in Cleveland of all places. Panhead tanks, fenders, drive chains, seats, and so forth are arranged all around it so you can put 'em back in the reverse order in which you pulled 'em out. That's assigned seating.

Over there, you've got your '65 BSA Rocket Gold Star, and your KTM Motocross bike, and the Honda Rebel that you ride to work every day. They're all stored together in a neat, compact little line. When you want to work on one of them, you pull it out into a common work area right in the middle.

Yes, that works. People do that a lot. It still uses the two workshop-organizing strategies, however. One part of the shop (the panhead-restoration area) is organized according to the assigned-seating plan. The rest of the shop is set up with a common work area. I call this the "hybrid organization strategy."

Professional Repair Shops

Most bikers, even most of those who develop their mechanical skills to a high degree, do not become professional motorcycle mechanics or open motorcycle shops. On the other hand, I believe all of us who spend a lot of time wrenching on bikes think about going professional once in a while. The step from thinking about it to actually doing it is often just a matter of saying "yes" instead of "no" or "not now." Every novice is a potential advanced amateur and every advanced amateur is a potential professional.

The step into the professional ranks is a major jump. The actual work areas and the tools you need are not that different, but now there is a whole new world of paperwork. Well-organized amateurs like to keep receipts and records of work performed on their bikes. Professional shops absolutely must keep a record of everything that goes on. Mainly, it has to do with money.

Unless you work entirely by yourself (which means you have to be turning a wrench in the

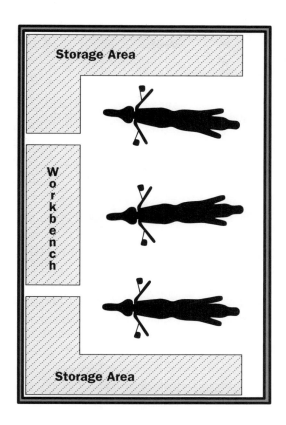

In the assigned-seating workshop layout each bike has its own work/storage space.

back and staffing the counter at the same time), you have to have a payroll. That means keeping a record of hours worked so you can pay the help. It also means payroll withholding tax, social security payments, medical insurance, and on, and on . . .

Whether you have employees or not, you have sales tax, self-employment tax and, hopefully, at the end of the day you have some income to pay tax on as well. You have to file income tax forms whether you make any money or not.

You also have to have insurance for yourself, your employees, your equipment, your inventory and, most of all, your customers' bikes. Remember, a bike falling off a jack can put a mechanic on 100% disability—permanently. A fire in a busy motorcycle repair shop can easily wipe out several hundred thousand dollars worth of your and your customers' property. Ever see what a fire under a full set of five-gallon Fat Bob tanks can do? Not many people can remember seeing it because if they get close enough to see it, they seldom live long enough for it to become a memory!

Crowd control in a professional shop includes passive devices, such as barriers to control access, and active devices, such as having somebody there to monitor what's going on.

To support all these required records, you have to keep track of inventory, work-in-progress, bills you owe suppliers, bills your customers owe you, utility bills, telephone bills . . .

By now you have some idea of the jump in record keeping required to enter the professional ranks. It's a tribute to the persistence of bikers that anyone ever does it at all. Writing wasn't invented so that Shakespeare could write plays, or so teenagers could write love poems to each other. It was invented so that shop owners could keep track of all this crap.

The layout of a professional shop tends to follow the hybrid model. You need a storage area for bikes not being worked on. You also need at least two work areas (by the time you reach this level, it's time to call them "bays" or "workstations") so that you can pull out a second bike to work on while one you've already started is held up waiting for parts. Specifically, you need more bays than you have mechanics.

Your storage area for parts and supplies must be a lot bigger, too. If an amateur has to stop work to wait for parts, it is inconvenient. If a professional has to wait for parts, it's very expensive. Idle hands are hands that aren't earning a living! So, you need to have an extensive stock of nuts, bolts, and other fasteners, plus a good

supply of oil, filters, gaskets, etc. A customer will understand if you have to special order a set of oversize pistons. Nobody'll be happy if you can't supply a plain vanilla tail light lens.

Most repair shops also do a brisk business in new and/or used parts. The parts business and the maintenance/repair/custom business feed each other. The biker you get as a regular parts customer is likely to give you a try when something breaks badly. The customer who brings their bike in regularly for repair or maintenance is a good prospect for upselling into custom parts. Of course, every maintenance, repair, and custom job will include sale of the parts and supplies used during that repair, maintenance, or customization job.

So, the parts business is an important adjunct to the professional motorcycle workshop. You're going to need rows of shelves to keep your stock, display racks to entice customers with the pretty bits, and a cash register to put all their nice green money in. Figure on making change, too.

Another big difference between the amateur shop and the professional is the need for crowd control. You're now dealing with the public. An amateur gets to pick and choose who he or she lets into their shop. Not so the professional. If you aren't going to go broke fast, you have to get hundreds of people wandering in and out of your shop.

The overwhelming majority of those people will be decent folks whom you'll be glad to have around. You'll also get your share of creeps, bums, and riffraff. And, by the time you get to sort out who's good, who's bad, and who's just ugly, it's too late.

You've got to keep them *all* out of your parts bins and away from your mechanics. If you have people fingering your stock, it will at best get all mixed up and at worst disappear. If you have people pestering your mechanics, then at best they'll never get anything done and at worst someone or something is going to get very badly hurt. Crowd control includes both active and passive devices.

Active devices generally amount to having somebody sitting around all the time. That person has three jobs. First, they are there to make the customers feel welcome and to help them find what they need, whether it's service or parts. Second, they are there to watch everything. Third, they have to throw something at the thieves, whether it is a verbal warning, something heavy, or a call to the police.

Passive devices includes counters, display cases, gates, and "employees only" signs. The recommended layout is infinitely variable. The general principle is to define separate areas for storage, work, and customer travel. Use some kind of barriers to separate the customer-travel area from the rest of the place.

When you're an amateur, you want to keep your workshop well hidden from anyone but those you invite in. The professional shop must announce itself to every passerby. That means outside signs, parking, etc.

Most maintenance/repair/custom shops I know of also do a more or less brisk business in new and used motorcycles. They are in an excellent position to buy good stuff cheap and turn it around at a profit. Without a dealership franchise, it's not likely that they'll get to stock new bikes, though. To get a superior used machine (including fairly late model ones) or a spanking new custom bike, an independent shop is often the best place to go.

We should also mention boutiques. What has a boutique got to do with motorcycle workshops? Well, those goggles hanging from my mirror came from an independent maintenance/repair/custom shop. So did the bandanna hanging from my belt, as did those gloves. So did that T-shirt. So did those chaps. Enough said?

Depending on the area, the clientele, and the stock they carry, an independent shop can pull in a fair bit of change by selling motorclothes and accessories. Generally, the motorclothes and accessories can be handled by the same system that deals with parts and supplies. The general principle is to treat the boutique stuff like you treat the pretty chrome bits that you display most visibly.

Dealerships

The differences between an independent shop and a dealership come down to basic thermodynamics: pressure, volume, and temperature.

Pressure comes down from the factory to invest more time, money, and effort than you can muster to sell as much stuff as they can supply. Note that I said "more than" rather than "as much as." That's because the best way the factory can help you grow your business is to push you as hard as they can. I'm always hearing dealers complain about what "the factory" demands and how they'd like more support. I've never heard, however, a reliable story about a dealer voluntarily giving up their franchise to become independent. Something must keep them coming back.

What keeps them coming back is *volume*. Dealerships sell more stuff for more money than independents. With more money and more volume, they have better access to more money for expansion. A bigger shop with more stuff and more employees attracts more customers. More customers inside park more bikes outside, and that attracts even more customers! It is a cycle that is vicious only to the competition. In the end, this cycle pressures the dealer into taking a larger volume of money to the bank.

You may think that what I mean by *temperature* is the heat of all those customers' bodies feverishly trying to bring money in and take stuff out. Not so! There's one thing that factory sup-

The step to the professional level puts you into a whole new world of paperwork.

port can supply that very, very few independents have access to: an army of marketing professionals. You wanna see what marketing support can do for dealerships? Just take a close look at the Harley-Davidson phenomenon!

Factory support can also include access to and training on advanced business information systems. A dealer no longer has to rely on Gladys the part-time bookkeeper for their inventory control system. The Factory is gonna make sure you have the best systems they can come up with. And, they're gonna make sure all their dealers know how to use them. There's a lot to be said for being a cog in a corporate machine.

As for the layout of the dealership's workshop (now a Service Department), the principles of setting it up are exactly the same as for an independent shop. The difference is that a dealer no longer needs me to tell them how to do it! They've got that army of factory consultants to draw on.

Special-Purpose Shops

You end up with a special-purpose shop when you set yourself up for certain jobs that require a good deal of specialized equipment. The most obvious example is a professional spray painting setup.

To consistently get the best results, spray painting requires ultimate cleanliness (drying paint sucks up airborne dust and shows it off conspicuously in the finished product), excellent ventilation (to prevent damaging the painter's brain with toxic fumes), and careful temperature and humidity control (to assure proper curing of the paint). It's also messy as hell! While you *can* do general motorcycle maintenance and repair in the same space you spray paint, both activities will suffer badly if you try.

Spray painting should be done in a special-purpose shop because you need a special room. Other special-purpose shops exist because the equipment needed is bulky and/or extremely expensive. Machine-shop equipment is both bulky and expensive—as well as requiring a fair amount of skill to operate. Sheet-metal fabricating equipment is certainly too bulky to stick in a corner of a general-purpose motorcycle shop.

The decision to set up a special-purpose shop involves a number of considerations. Now, don't just skip over this part saying, "I haven't even started changing my own oil, so why should I think about special-purpose shops?" Deciding *not* to set up such a shop is still a decision, and should, like any other decision, be made consciously.

The first consideration is whether you will need the services of a specialized shop.

Sandy is a dedicated touring enthusiast. He typically puts 30,000 miles per year on the old odometer. By the time a bike has lived with him for a year, it's usually ready for a less arduous life with somebody else. He seldom keeps a ride for more than two years, and fancy custom work is simply not part of his game. He buys stock bikes off the showroom floor, maybe bolts on a new carburetor, custom pipes, and his favorite style of seat, then runs it to death. Then he trades it in for another new bike off the showroom floor. I doubt that he has ever caused custom paint to be applied. Unless he drastically alters his riding habits, he never will. He has absolutely no use for a paint shop.

Guy, on the other hand, spends as much time fussing over his bike as he does riding it. Among his gentle ministrations is a new coat of paint just about every year. Among the colors I've seen on his '74 FX over the years are a stock Harley blue paint job (before he replaced the tanks), white, and burgundy. Guy has his own spray booth.

Assuming that you regularly need the services of a specialized shop, the next consideration is whether, and at what price, the service is available in your area. I've made a lot of money by designing custom equipment for people, then hiring someone else to fabricate the parts. Despite having been a regular customer at machine shops over the years, I've never invested in the space and equipment needed to set one up because the service is readily available almost everywhere. Why spend thousands on a used lathe, when you have a riding buddy who owns a machining business?

The third consideration is whether you have the skill to use the tools, or have the time, talent, and desire to learn to use them. Once you acquire a skill, such as welding, acquiring the equipment and setting up a space to use it are sure to follow. If, on the other hand, you barely know how to install a bolt, don't go running out to buy a computer-controlled milling machine.

Finally, there's the resource question. I know how to paint a bike. In fact, I've put together some noteworthy custom paint jobs. And, I really should repaint that Sporty because it's now finished in three mismatched colors of chipped and cracked paint. However, at the moment I have neither the space or the equipment, nor am I willing to spend the bucks to set up a paint shop. That bike's going to continue looking like the swap-meet special that she is until I plunk the sheet metal down in somebody else's paint shop.

If you pass the tests of need, lack of availability, skills required, and resources available, then and only then should you set up your own special-purpose shop.

Temporary Workshops

Some people say that you can tell the *real* bikers because they're the ones working on their bikes in the dealer's parking lot. All the tourists wearing leather are inside buying logo T-shirts while the dealer's mechanics install their new chrome luggage racks. The "real" bikers are out front installing their own carburetors.

This attitude is, of course, a little extreme. There are lots of good reasons to let somebody else do a job that you could very well do yourself. It all depends on how urgent it is, how complicated or fussy it is, how anxious you are to have that new part on your bike, and how much you want that logo T-shirt. But, there is an element of truth to it as well.

Why would anyone think of working in a parking lot as the badge of a "real biker?" For the answer go back to the section labeled "Mother Nature's Plan for Your Bike." Motorcycling experience teaches you to be ready for anything, especially unpredicted mechanical work. As you gain experience with mechanical work, you tend to become quick to pick up a wrench at the drop of—anything.

At a cocktail party some years ago, some yuppie asked me when I would quit riding motorcycles. I simply said, "When I'm dead." The yupster, who had apparently gotten the same an-

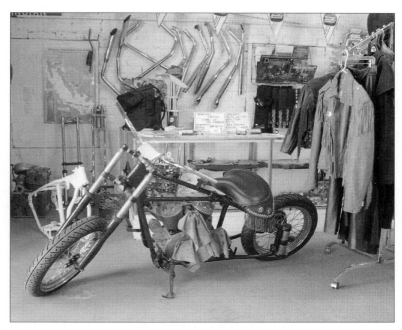

Independent motorcycle repair/maintenance shops can do a brisk business in new and used parts as well as motorclothes and accessories.

swer before from bikers, asked why motorcycle people get so involved with their sport. While I stood there with my mouth open, my non-biker father, who was standing nearby, surprised me by jumping in to say: "It gets into their blood."

Dedicated motorcyclists have bikes in their blood. Over time, dedicated motorcyclists learn to carry a full tool kit everywhere and to set up a temporary shop anywhere. When you're always ready to handle emergency mechanical repairs, installing, say, a new air cleaner is a dawdle. If you have a "new and improved" dingus, why leave it in its box, strap the box onto the bike, and ride home using the "old and yukky" dingus, and only then make the swap? If you've got the tools and you've got the talent, you can swap it out right there! All it takes is a temporary workshop. And, that temporary workshop should be part of the permanent running gear on your bike.

The temporary workshop has two components: tools and a work area. For a temporary shop, you carry the tools in a separate pouch that is best mounted somewhere on the bike. Some folks carry their tool kit in their saddlebags, but saddlebags are best kept for luggage. Some components of your tool kit, such as a shop manual or

Your temporary workshop consists of a tool kit you carry with you and whatever work space you can find.

a spare quart of oil, are too bulky and have to go into your saddlebags. The actual wrenches, screwdrivers, etc. should be stored separately.

The work area is something you simply can't carry on a bike. You have to make do with what you find around. It consists of some kind of floor (don't think of it as the ground—it's a "floor"), lighting and, if necessary and available, shelter.

Floor

For a temporary shop, your first consideration is to look around for the best available floor. It could be the pavement you're parked on, the shoulder of the road or a supermarket parking lot.

A couple of years ago, I was tooling along Route 27 in Sherborn, Massachusetts. Route 27 is a backwoods two-lane road and Sherborn is so small that it's practically invisible. Suddenly, my engine quit. From the way that it quit, I suspected ignition failure. The roadway was so narrow that I didn't dare stop on the side to diagnose the problem, so I pulled in the clutch lever and coasted while looking for a likely spot.

Just ahead, I spotted the entrance to a small country graveyard. That's where I stopped. I coasted into the graveyard, stopped, and pushed the bike to a level spot where the gravel roadway was hard-packed. Half an hour later, after finding and reconnecting the broken wire, I was off again.

I chose that entranceway to that graveyard because it was the closest spot where I could find a flat, hard, clear area larger than the bike and safe from speeding trucks.

Lighting

Lighting for a temporary shop is catch-as-catch-can. In full daylight, natural light is perfectly adequate. At night, you've gotta try to find a streetlight or illuminated parking lot. Then, there's also working by the light of your buddy's headlamp. I've even done repairs by the light of my own headlamp reflected off the sides of buildings, trees, shrubs . . . (these memories are making me feel sick!). Woe to non-smokers who get stuck with an electrical problem out in the desert on a cloudy night without a cigarette lighter! Lighting is something we don't think about until we don't have it.

Surprisingly, a flashlight is only slightly better than no light at all. Because it gives an intense narrow beam, the light a flashlight gives makes it very hard to look for anything unless you know just what and where it is. Once you locate the problem, a flashlight can help guide your fingers as you make the actual repair. You can sometimes reflect the flashlight's beam off something else to provide a wider area of illumination.

Shelter

Shelter is usually not much of a problem. On a bike, you're out in the open anyway. When you're stopped for a breakdown, the only thing missing is the wind. That can be good or bad, but it's not fatal. All you really need to worry about is rain.

Rain is a pain in the butt. Touring folks, who are the most likely to get stuck out in the boonies, are also the most likely to be out in the rain. If you're putt-putting to the store, or headed off for a toy run, or just blowing the cobwebs out, you can always pull out the car or cancel the trip. If you're out on Michigan's Upper Peninsula,

1,500 miles from home and it's a rainy day, you're going to don your rain suit and ride anyway. If you break down, you've broken down in the rain. You'd better find something to put between your bike and the rain while you sort the problem out.

It's nearly impossible to fix a breakdown with water falling out of the sky onto your bike. First, everything feels different, so problems you normally would notice first by touch go unnoticed. Second, everything looks different, so you've got to have a piece obviously broken and hanging off before you'll even see it.

Finally and most importantly, although motorcycles are designed to function perfectly when there's lots of water outside, they most definitely aren't supposed to have water on the inside. If you start opening things up and taking this and that off while out in the rain, you'll get water in there and damage more than you fix. Maybe you are a tough guy and can stand to work on your bike in the rain, but the *bike* can't stand it.

Okay, if your bike can't stand being repaired in the rain, whaddaya do? There are three strategies you try: not breaking down in the first place, getting lucky, and knowing when to quit.

The first, and usually the most successful, strategy is not breaking down in the first place. There are two components to this strategy: proper maintenance and using common sense. By keeping your bike in good operating condition at all times you greatly reduce the chance that you'll break down. Also, check the whole machine over very carefully before starting out for the day. If there's anything the least bit suspect, stay put! Remember, Mother Nature favors those who have a healthy respect for Murphy's Law. She goes stalking those who don't.

If not breaking down in the first place doesn't work (and once in a while it doesn't), it's time to get lucky. Getting lucky is not something you just wish for. You work at it, and start working at it long before you start your engine. The point is that luck is a commodity that you have. You build up your supply by being aware, careful, and thoughtful, and by looking ahead. You use it up fast every time disaster could strike, but doesn't.

Getting lucky starts with being very aware of what's around you. How far is it between overpasses? Are you going through a populated area where there are building overhangs to shelter under? What about trees? What are the weather patterns that are moving through that day? Showery? Steady rain? Clearing in the afternoon?

At the first hint of trouble, look for a nice sheltered area to break down in. Depending on how early you detect trouble and the speed you're going when you detect it, you usually have at least a quarter mile, and often much more, of mobility left before your bike coasts to a dead stop. Use that distance to get under cover, or at least to a downgrade where you can push the bike under some shelter. And, grab the first shelter you come to. Don't use up more luck by trying to stretch for someplace better.

Another way of getting lucky is to have whatever breaks be easy to fix in the rain. Electrical wiring problems, for example, are usually pretty easy to fix in the rain. Don't try to replace a blown head gasket, though. The main consideration is what will happen if water gets to the exposed parts or into exposed openings. If nothing serious will happen, you've gotten lucky. If rainwater would jeopardize your repair, your luck has run out.

When your luck runs out, it's time to pull out the third strategy—knowing when to quit. Yell, swear, shake your fist at the sky, and generally give vent to your frustrations. Then look around again for a way out.

If that doesn't work, sit down, look glum, and wait for a good Samaritan. What was that ancient Chinese saying? "If you sit by the river long enough, you'll see the body of your enemy floating by." The Zen Master would say something like, "If nothing can be done, then nothing is the best thing to do."

What you don't want to do is leave your bike. There are few places where motorcyclists go where they'll have to wait more than a few hours before someone comes by to take pity on them. Usually, it's much sooner. If you're sitting brokenhearted by your bike, the good Samaritan is more likely to stop than if you're striding purposefully toward the horizon.

An open-air workshop will provide plenty of light during the day, but can create a cleaning problem.

Open-Air Workshops

An open-air motorcycle workshop is essentially a small- or medium-sized shop without walls. It is *not* a temporary shop with a roof.

The difference is that, with a temporary shop, you pretty much work with whatever you can find. If you're lucky enough to find a concrete wall, that becomes your workbench. The only tools you have are the tools you have: what's on your bike supplemented by borrowing from whomever is around with tools to lend.

An open-air shop is a permanent installation. You arrange your lighting. You arrange your toolboxes and workbenches. You arrange storage.

What you don't arrange is walls. That leaves you with two problems to consider: weather and security.

Since you don't have walls, you have to protect whatever you leave in your shop from the elements. Your workbench needs to be made of metal, plastic or, at least, pressure-treated wood.

You really need to have a leak-tight roof. I've never seen anyplace that it doesn't rain. Right now I live in the desert. It rains here. If you leave stuff out, it gets rained on.

Don't blithely arrange your storage shelves around the outside edge of your open-air workshop the way you do in a building. Rain doesn't fall straight down. It comes in at an angle because rain is often (though not always) accompanied by wind. That wind will blow the rain several feet into your shop area. Put the storage in the middle of the shop, and work on bikes farther out.

Another thing the elements provide for your outdoor-workshop enjoyment is dust. Anything oily or greasy, such as motorcycle parts, is a magnet for dust. Thus, cleanliness is more of a concern in an open-air shop than in a fully-enclosed shop. You can't go away for a week, then come back and expect the shop to be clean. It won't be.

Then, there's security. Depending on where you are, this may or may not be a problem. If you set up an open-air shop in a New York City alley and leave it open and unattended for, say, a minute, something is likely to disappear. You'll have folks stealing from you just to teach you to beware of thieves (how's that for logic!).

On the other hand, I have a weekend place out in the middle of the Mojave Desert. The nearest dwelling is a mile away and it's someone's vacation cabin. The nearest town is 15 miles away and it doesn't even have a store. I don't get out there much—leaving the open-air shop unattended for months at a time.

In the past two years, I've had one break-in: some rainwater collected in a bucket and a cow walked through to drink it.

Security is not a big item out on The Ranch!

In between those extremes, you do need some security. At least, put locks on toolboxes. Lock all the bikes at night. If you can, put a fence around the place. Don't leave stuff out to tempt the neighborhood kids. You don't want to be responsible for some kid coming in and putting a hole through his thumb with your electric drill, now do you?

Chapter 3

Basic Principles

The Importance of a Good Floor

Substrate is a word engineers use to denote a solid, nominally immovable, usually flat surface that they build everything on. When you're building a house, it's the foundation. If you're building a semiconductor chip, it's a single crystal of silicon. If you're working on a motorcycle, it's the workshop floor.

In the film *Monty Python and the Holy Grail,* one of the characters describes the tribulations he had in building his castle. The problem was that he chose to build it in a swamp. Everyone told him he was crazy to build his castle in the swamp, but that's where he wanted to build it, so build it there he did. Predictably, it sank into the swamp. He built a second castle on the same site. That one fell over and sank into the swamp. The third one burned, fell over, and sank into the swamp. But the fourth one stayed up!

Why would the fourth one stay up? It stayed up because it used the first three as a substrate.

The quality of the substrate determines the quality of your workshop. That is true of every workshop, from a temporary shop by the side of the road to the largest, most established dealership's maintenance area. There are five characteristics that make (or break) the workshop floor's quality:

• *It must be hard.* You're going to bring in a motorcycle weighing several hundred pounds and lean it on its kickstand on the floor. Then you're going to jack that bike up, shake it, rattle it, and roll it using wrenches, hammers, and other implements of destruction.

Then you're going to drop things on the floor. Then you're going to rest heavy parts such as

generators and engine blocks on it. If that floor isn't hard, you'll be constantly dealing with sinking kickstands, wobbling jacks, material gouged out of the floor getting all over and into the bike's innards, not to mention a badly damaged floor.

• *It must be flat.* Slopes make it hard to position the bike so it's stable. Certain operations, such as changing the oil and adjusting the steering damper, require you to set the bike level. That's very hard to do on a sloping floor. Bumps and hollows make jacks wobble, stools tilt, front-ends flop, and bikes roll. Adjusting a drive chain or belt is dicey at best on an uneven floor.

• *It must be strong.* Weak floors bounce. You don't want your floor bouncing while, for example, the bike is up on a jack, or you're trying to

If you work on a concrete floor a lot, be sure to get yourself a stool. Your knees will hate you if you don't!

A workshop substrate must be hard, flat and strong. Concrete is the best.

Asphalt pavement also makes a good workshop substrate.

Gravel and dirt are often the best you can do for a temporary workshop floor. Unfortunately, kickstands sink in and dropped parts have lots of good places to hide.

perform a delicate operation. Even indelicate operations, such as connecting a rear-brake return spring, are ten times harder if the floor is bouncy. Of course, with all that activity around a heavy motorcycle, a weak floor is eventually going to fail.

• *It must be clean.* Cleanliness is next to a well-maintained motorcycle. The dirtier the floor, the more crap you'll get into your motorcycle's guts. Crap destroys motorcycle guts.

• *It should be a light, even color.* Who cares what color the floor is? You will the first time you drop a carburetor float spring. No matter who you are or what you do, the only way to keep from dropping tiny, difficult-to-replace motorcycle bits is to never work on a motorcycle. Once that irreplaceable part hits the floor, you have to see it to find it. Motorcycle bits are almost always black, brown, or silver in color. The best color for the floor is beige. It contrasts with almost everything small enough to get lost.

Absolutely the very best floor for a motorcycle workshop is a concrete floor at least four inches thick painted with a light beige, non-slip floor paint.

Second best is an unpainted concrete floor. It is hard, flat, strong, and the light grey color typical of cement contrasts decently with the darker parts that land on it. The problem is that bare concrete cannot be thoroughly cleaned. Yes, you can shovel off the trash you've dropped, but you can't get it dirt free the way you can a painted concrete floor.

Try sweeping a concrete floor clean. It doesn't work. Every stroke of the broom pulls up microscopic bits of the concrete, making amazing amounts of gritty dust. The very act of sweeping up the dust creates more dust that you then have to sweep up, creating more dust in a cycle that ends only when you wear through the concrete or give up and paint the floor.

My father, in an effort to clean his concrete garage floor without making dust, once tried wetting the floor down before sweeping it. He didn't make dust, he made mud—which later dried into dust.

Most motorcycle workshop floors are of the unpainted concrete variety. Most folks are more willing to put up with the dust than go to the trouble and expense of painting the floor. You have to move absolutely everything off the floor, put down an amazing amount of paint, then put everything back. Then, depending on how much traffic you have through your shop, you'll have to do it all over again in a year or so when the paint wears through.

The only thing that keeps unpainted concrete up to number two on the list is that everything else is worse.

Linoleum makes a really nice-looking workshop floor, but it isn't hard enough, and quickly gets torn up under the gentle influence of a kickstand. Torn linoleum is, of course, a magnet for dropped parts, especially washers. They love to snuggle down under the edge like a two-year-old under a blanket with a teddy bear. Even if you find the #%@&* thing, you'll have the Devil's own time trying to dig it out.

Physics research labs, where they fool around with all sorts of ridiculously heavy, sharp, fussy equipment that's slid around on the floor by scientists who don't give a damn about anything but getting the results of the next experiment, tend to favor asbestos tile. If properly laid down, it has all the characteristics of a painted concrete floor, but wears like iron.

The only Achilles' heel asbestos tile has is that pressing a sharp edge or point into the tile cracks it. Of course, that's exactly what happens when you put a motorcycle kickstand down. Even the flat blade-type kickstands usually rest slightly on edge. If you put asbestos tile down on a motorcycle workshop floor on Monday, it starts breaking up by Thursday. So, don't do it!

I rather enjoyed working on the wooden floor in a horse barn that I once used for a couple years. A wooden floor in a horse barns needs to support beasts that weigh two to five times what a motorcycle weighs, and to support them when those beasts get excited and start jumping around. Horses are big, and horses aren't any more placid than the average collie dog. So, wooden horse-barn floors are built to be amazingly strong and solid. If they're made of wood, they clean well and are moderately hard. Unfortunately, although level, they tend to be uneven. They also suck up dropped parts like crazy! The phrase "dropped between the cracks" comes from adventures on horse-barn floors.

Good workshop practice dictates that the floor is clean and parts that have been removed from the bike are contained in parts trays or boxes. Although tools are out on the bench along with parts, they aren't mixed together. Finally, there's plenty of light coming from all directions (notice there aren't any shadows except under Dale's feet).

A common temporary-workshop floor is asphalt pavement. Pavement in good condition can have all the advantages of an unpainted concrete floor. Dark-colored parts, however, are a lot harder to spot when dropped on pavement than on concrete. Even things the size of a 3/8-inch bolt can disappear when dropped on pavement.

Be careful to look for a spot that is clean, dry, flat, and level. Low-lying paved areas often collect sand and gravel. If you plunk your kickstand down there, you're effectively working on a dirt floor. Always look for the higher spots that get swept clear of dirt by wind and rain.

The same caution goes for highway breakdown lanes and shoulders. There, you have to compromise between getting off into the dirt and sand, or being clipped by the next tractor-trailer doing seventy miles an hour.

Sometimes, the best thing available is packed earth or gravel. That graveyard entrance road I mentioned in the last section was packed earth. It's OK in a pinch for diagnosing a problem in an emergency, or for tightening a loose bolt or nut. Do not, however, take anything major apart on a dirt floor. Even taking a step kicks up dust. And, the dust you kick up is made of microscopic rocks. I don't want microscopic rocks in *my* engine, do you?

Do not ever, ever, ever work on a motorcycle parked on grass! Nothing dropped in the grass will ever be found. Murphy's Law requires that you will drop an irreplaceable bit in the grass, should you ever be so stupid as to work on your bike in the grass.

I once installed a luggage rack on a Heritage Softail parked on the pavement two feet from a freshly cut (in other words, short) lawn. I dropped a brand new, brightly chromed flathead screw that bounced to the edge of the lawn. I saw it land. After searching for an hour, I gave up and got a replacement for the screw. Every day for two months after that, I looked in that grass for that screw because I couldn't believe that something that easy to spot could disappear so completely. A thousand years from now, some future archaeologist will find that screw and say, "Dumb biker!"

A final word for those who spend a lot of time in their workshops. Concrete floors are hard. If you stand on them day in and day out for years, you'll start having foot, knee, and back problems because of the constant pounding from walking on that concrete. This won't be a problem for the weekend mechanic who spends the rest of the

time in a carpeted office. For the professional, however, this is a serious consideration. Pull off those bike boots and slip into some padded running shoes. You'll feel a lot better at the end of the day and be a lot taller when you retire.

Guy Petagna gave me a great tip for the serious amateur motorcycle mechanic: put short-pile scatter rugs in your workshop. They give you a soft, clean place to put yourself while the bike stands over its preferred concrete surface. If the pile is short, it stops dropped parts from scattering to the four corners of the globe. When bits snuggle under the rugs' edges, it's easy to lift the edge and find the part. Of course, they're not recommended for the heavy traffic and time pressure of a busy shop. Every time you move a bike, you have to rearrange the rugs. But, they make working a lot more pleasant for the amateur.

And be sure you keep 'em clean!

A Tidy Shop Is a Happy Shop

Whenever you do something, you make a mess. That's the First Law of Thermodynamics: The entropy of the Universe always increases. Entropy is the word physicists use for disorder. Whenever anything happens, disorder is the necessary result. Cleaning your house results in a mountain of trash outside. Maintaining or repairing a motorcycle results in containers of used oil, piles of discarded bits, torn up packaging material, puddles of spilled fluids, tools all over the place, dirty hands, and grimy clothes. Unless you do something about it, the mess on the floor simply gets deeper and deeper until you can't work in there anymore.

I learned the advantages of a tidy shop the hard way—by letting my work area get messy. Eventually, I couldn't find my tools because they were buried under a leaf litter of dirt, old packaging material, scraps of electrical wire, and discarded parts. When I couldn't walk across the floor because at every step I was slipping on a lost tool or tripping over a worn-out part, I yelled "Enough!"

The only way to get rid of the mess is to invoke the *Second* Law of Thermodynamics: You have to do work to reduce entropy. Of course, you can never reduce the entropy of the Universe. You can only shift it around. When you

A convenient trash can is as important to a well set up motorcycle workshop as a good toolbox.

clean your shop, you reduce the entropy inside by making an even bigger pile of entropy in the trash bins out back. That pile of entropy then contributes to an even bigger pile of entropy in the nearest landfill. Archaeologists learn more from excavating ancient landfills than from unearthing temples and palaces.

So, since a necessary result of maintaining and repairing motorcycles is making a mess, a necessary part of working on motorcycles is cleaning up the mess. When you take a tool out, put the tool back. When you open the box your new Bosch regulator came in, throw the box in the trash bin. Consider that trash bin as important a piece of equipment as your workbench. And, put the trash bin within easy reach of your workbench. Kitty litter and a container for storing used oil are as necessary a part of performing an oil change as the wrench you use to open the drain plug. You can't run a shop without a broom any more than you can run one without a toolbox.

Beyond the inconvenience of working in a messy place, there's the problem of junk getting inside your motorcycle. Dirt is a word for nonspecific unpleasant material. Being nonspecific, you can never be sure what it will do if it gets into your bike's innards. Grease will turn electrical connections into disconnections. Sand will turn a transmission into shrapnel. Metal shavings can turn a fuel delivery system into a fuel nondelivery system. Almost anything getting into the motor will turn it into a rebuild project.

Since entropy also increases as a mess spreads out, messes spread out. If you open up a bike within inches of a dirty messy workbench or floor, the dirt and mess will quickly (instantly, in fact) spread into the bike. You can't say, "Here is where the mess ends and the clean part begins" because the mess will simply flow downhill into the clean part.

Ben Franklin, whom I stuck with the epithet "Father of Modern Workshop Practice," gave this advice: "A place for everything and everything in its place." In other words, organize your shop. Each tool has its place in the drawer of its toolbox. The toolbox goes there. The workbench goes there. The bike to be worked on goes there. The trash goes in the trash can, which goes there.

Loyd will be mad at me for showing you this picture. I took it when the shop at H&H Cycle Works was shut down for a couple of weeks this summer and things got a bit messy.

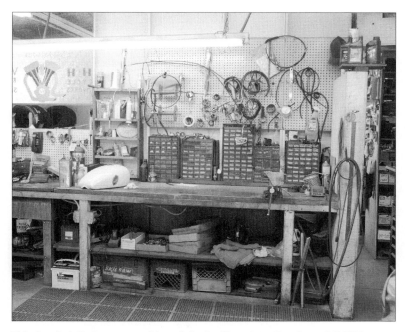

This is what that same workbench looks like when the shop at H&H is operating. There's a lot of stuff there, but, true to Ben Franklin's dictum, there's a place for everything and everything is in its place.

The new carburetor parts go there. The used carburetor parts go in a separate section (separated by some sort of wall) there. The oil, grease, etc. go there. The new headlamps go in their little

What's that you say? Your shop is never this clean and neat? Well, Jim Hamilton admitted that he'd spent hours cleaning the place up just for this picture. It usually looks a lot more worked in.

Usually, the only thing out of place is a copy of the sponsoring book or magazine plopped on the workbench as if whoever owns the shop just got done reading it.

In a real workshop with real mechanics (amateur or professional) doing real work on real motorcycles, there is a real mess. The more work, the more mess. What you have to do is keep a dynamic tension between making a mess and shoveling out the mess.

If you're going to loosen eleven chrome acorn nuts so that you can remove the primary cover on a 1972 Sportster, you ain't gonna take the wrench out of the toolbox, loosen the nut, then put the wrench back in the toolbox, remove the nut, then get the wrench out again for the next nut, and repeat the process eleven times! You'll take the wrench out, loosen the first nut, then put the wrench down where it will be handy for the next nut. In fact, you'll probably leave the wrench on the floor while you lift the primary cover off and do whatever it was you removed it for, so that the wrench will be handy when you want to tighten the nuts after putting the cover back.

Workmanlike practice says you'll put the wrench back in its toolbox after you're done.

At the end of the day, when all the jobs are done and all the bikes are buttoned up and everything put away, your shop might vaguely resemble the pristine type-A dream shop in the photo. But not likely, because you probably won't refinish the workbenches and repaint the floor every night!

cubbyhole in the light bulb section of the electrical-parts section of the new-parts storage area. And so forth.

I'm beginning to sound like a type-A bozo. I'm not a type-A bozo. You can tell by looking around my office. It doesn't look neat. It could use a dusting.

If you look at a photo of what purports to be the "dream workshop," it will be immaculately clean and perfectly neat. Every tool will be in its proper place, workbenches will be clear, the floor buffed and polished, and the trash emptied.

A Small Garage Workshop Profile

Any building big enough to store a car is big enough to set up as an amateur's motorcycle workshop. Shown on the next page is the layout of a shop I used quite comfortably from 1990 through 1994. It had all the basics: a workbench, space for tools, shelf storage for small parts and consumables, an area for long term storage of used parts, a bay for working on one motorcycle, and room to store at least one more.

The garage was built into a New England split-level house, and intended to house the family car. Obviously the main door was plenty big enough for moving a bike in and out. A second door opened directly into the house's foyer.

Heat, a definite consideration in New England, came mainly from leakage through the uninsulated partition separating the garage from the rest of the house. It was adequate to keep the shop well above freezing even on the coldest nights. If it got too cold to work comfortably, I could simply open the door leading into the house to bring the shop up to room temperature. I also kept a 1,200-watt electric space heater in the shop for times when I wanted to close the door or to get a quick shot of extra heat.

The 24 x 96-inch workbench was more than adequate. It included open storage shelves underneath for power tools and shop rags, and plenty of space on the end for an assortment of spray lubricants, pencils, notebooks, paper towel roll, and so forth that you always want handy.

The workbench top was made of 3/4-inch plywood sheathed in stainless steel. That made it ideal for doubling as a welding bench. Not only did it provide good electrical grounding, but it wouldn't burn when spattered with molten slag.

There was even a great spot to store the welder and associated paraphernalia underneath.

I mounted the vise on the right-hand corner where it could swing either to the side (off the right-hand end of the bench) or forward.

Shelf storage consisted of one five-shelf metal unit and a metal storage cabinet that also

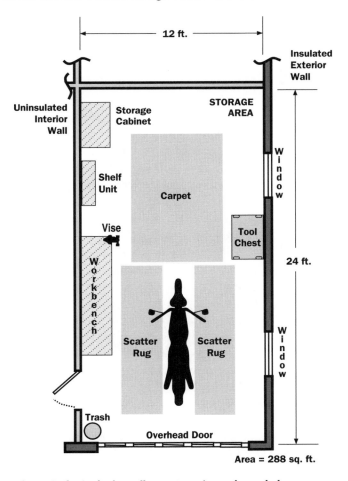

Layout of a typical small-garage motorcycle workshop.

had five shelves. Spare gas tanks and old Honda seats went on top of the metal cabinet along with pans for draining motor oil and primary fluid.

I stored my stock of wooden blocks, boards, and pieces vertically against the wall between the workbench and the shelf unit. That way it was handy to the workbench, which is where I usually needed it, but was out of the way as well.

Large stored items, such as fenders, front ends, tires, and even an old Triumph frame graced the back of the shop. At its peak, this storage area contained, in addition to that Triumph frame, a whole BSA waiting for restoration and an almost completed trike. There was still a fair amount of free space in the back part of the shop.

Free space is important, especially in a small shop. For example, suppose you start working on your primary chain. First you have to remove the primary cover. Now, whaddaya do with that pretty chrome piece? You need a safe place to put it while you work on the primary chain. I had a nice, free (not "unused!") space to put it down in.

A 6 x 9-foot rug graced the floor of that free space. In winter, it insulated that big chunk of floor area to keep the shop a lot warmer and it helped control dust. But, its most important function was protection of shiny chrome parts I temporarily stored there. Without the rug, I would have had to constantly worry about whether those parts would be scratched by contact with the concrete floor. There's less worry about damaging chromed parts when you know that you have this major piece of shop real estate covered with a soft carpet.

I always like to keep some kind of cart or small wooden bench around to use as a light portable workbench. Mainly, it serves as an extra little spot to lay out parts trays and put tools down. The best place to store that auxiliary bench is against the wall on the side of the work space opposite the main workbench.

Of course, ya gotta have a stool. What I used in this shop was a 9 x 6 x 18-inch wooden box. It didn't look like much, but it was actually more useful than the typical stool. When working on something low on the bike, I could lay the box down to get a seat six inches off the floor. If I wanted to work on something higher up, that same box became an 18-inch high stool. It even

had a handle on one end, so I could pick it up and turn it easily with one hand.

Nasty stuff, such as gasoline cans and used motor oil, lived in the corner against the outside wall near the main door. My big bag of kitty litter, the trash can, broom, dustpan, and brush made their homes in the other corner, between the main door and the door into the house.

As is typical with any shop intended to support one bike, the bike's assigned parking spot was the middle of the work area. For all the same reasons that I had for putting a rug down in the free space, I put a long scatter rug down on each side of the motorcycle. Actually, there's an additional reason for putting rugs down beside the work space. That added bit of cushioning over the cement floor makes the tired old joints feel a whole lot better at the end of the day.

There were two areas where this shop was inadequate: lighting and power. Lighting consisted of one naked light bulb in the middle of the ceiling, but there was plenty of light during the day from two windows in the exterior wall and glass panes set into the overhead door. At night, the light from a 150-watt bulb in the ceiling fixture did a credible job of area lighting because the ceiling and walls were painted white. There was enough reflected light so that no part of the shop was in deep shadow. I used a drop light to brightly illuminate whatever I was working on at the time. Power consisted of one lonely outlet in the middle of the interior wall, not far from the ideal spot for the workbench. So, I mounted a six-outlet strip on the workbench and plugged it into the wall outlet. Whenever I needed power on the side of the bike away from the workbench, I used the outlet on the drop light. I never once ran out of places to stuff a plug.

I did, however, run out of amperage. Despite having an ideal welding bench and all the stick-welding equipment I needed, I couldn't do big projects because the 20-amp outlet couldn't pump enough juice through the welder to handle thick structural steel.

I used this shop for about three years. It was adequate for all the regular maintenance tasks and most of the repair work an amateur motorcycle mechanic typically gets into. Bolt-on custom operations went well, also.

Guy got tired of storing his Hog in an 8 x 10-foot metal shed and hauling it up and down the cellar ·stairs every year to store it for the winter. So, one day he decided to build himself a big garage. When I say a big garage, I mean a BIG garage. He built a garage that's thirty feet deep, fifty feet wide, and two stories tall! Most automotive shops aren't as big as the motorcycle workshop he had room for—even after letting Peggy park her Camaro on the left side.

Living in New England, he had to worry about heat in the winter, but not air conditioning for summer. Summers just don't get that hot (although sometimes they *feel* hot). In his area the trick is to get plenty of air flow through the building. As long as you can keep the air moving, you're OK. Of course, with those big garage doors open and some windows in the back wall, there's plenty of air flow.

Once creature comforts are taken care of, the next order of business is lighting. When the doors are open in the daytime, natural light fills the work area. Remember that reflected sunlight is one of the best lighting systems you can have, all you have to do is let it in. Sunlight reflecting off the outside pavement, lawns and trees, and the neighbors houses across the street, not to mention the huge expanse of bright blue sky, provides plenty of light flooding in through those doors. The large windows in the back let in enough light to adequately illuminate the workbench.

On cloudy days, days when it's too cool to keep the garage door open, and at night, overhead fluorescent fixtures do the job. Eight-foot ceilings leave room to suspend these fixtures by

chains from the rafters and still have them high enough to be well out of the way.

The arrangement of the fluorescent tubes is shown on the next page. Note that the roll-up garage doors block the light from two fixtures (each) when fully open. Thus, to get proper illumination at the door-end of the work area, Guy has to close that garage door. On the few nights

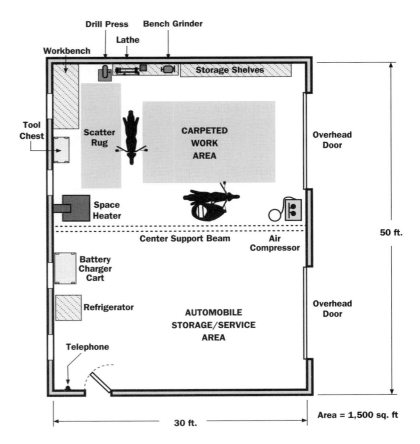

Layout of Guy's large garage motorcycle workshop.

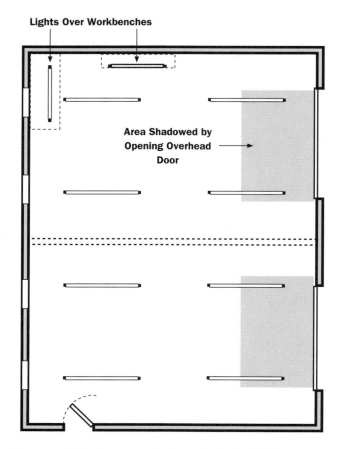

Lights Over Workbenches

Area Shadowed by Opening Overhead Door →

Fluorescent tube lamps are the best choice for lighting any large motorcycle workshop. Arrange them carefully to provide diffuse light for all parts of the shop.

only provides power for tools used on the workbench, but gives a convenient spot to plug in cords to bring power out to the work area when necessary. There's an additional power strip mounted on the wall at the back. That's for a wall clock, additional pinup lamps, neon bar signs, or anything else Guy might want to hang on the wall and power up.

The second workbench really houses a mini-machine shop, including a small lathe, a drill press, and a bench grinder. Since these machines stay plugged in, the power strip supplying them with electricity is mounted on the wall at the back of the bench. Each tool also has its own gooseneck lamp for additional spot illumination.

Spot lighting and power when needed at the bike are provided by two drop lights hung from the main beam that runs front to back down the garage's middle. They're hung in the middle so that each can be used on either side of the garage. There are two of them so that more than one person can work on more than one vehicle at a time.

With so much space available, it's not surprising that Guy uses the hybrid scheme of allocating space to motorcycles. Each of his bikes has its own assigned parking spot. He keeps a large space clear for the work area. In other words, he doesn't park bikes there unless they are being worked on.

The floor is beige-painted concrete. For comfort, aesthetics, and insulation, he lays light-colored carpeting down over most of the work area. The insulation value is not to be taken lightly. In a climate where the temperature stays below freezing for months at a time, and typically dips into the teens most winter nights, bare concrete gets very, very, *very* cold. You can get frostbite by leaning your bare hand on a New England concrete floor in late January.

On any given Saturday, you can stop by Guy's shop and find at least one other person working on a bike (besides Guy). Often during the summer, two or three bikers will stop by to help out or get help, or more often just to chat. The main topic of conversation is usually motorcycle maintenance and repair, so it's a great place to learn the art.

per year when it's too muggy to work with the door fully shut at night, Guy can leave it as much as half-way open without blocking the fixtures.

Following good practice, Guy has an added fixture set up directly over each of his two workbenches. Separate switches control these workbench lights.

The tool chest is set up handy to the main workbench. The tool chest is on wheels, but its location is so convenient that he almost never moves it. Drawers (actually, an ancient mahogany three-drawer dresser shoved under the workbench) provide additional tool storage.

The workbench itself is a butcher-block bench top set up on two very sturdy sawhorses. A power strip at the front edge of this bench top not

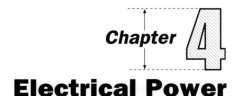

Chapter 4
Electrical Power

Power, in the form of electricity on tap from an outlet in the wall, is not necessary but at times it's really nice to have. Most of the mechanical power needed for motorcycle work comes from your muscles. I guess I could go into things like nutrition and body building, but that would be a little bizarre for a book on setting up a workshop. I'll concentrate on the main auxiliary power source available to motorcycle mechanics: electricity. The main use for electrical power in motorcycle repair is for lighting, which I'll cover in the next chapter.

Other than for lighting, electrical power is needed in relatively small quantities for operating power equipment, such as welders, air compressors, and drills. In my experience, the second most common use for electrical power around a motorcycle (after turning on the lights) is to run a battery charger.

The first thing to think about when planning for electrical power is the total amount you will need. Remember that electricity flows.

Ben Franklin was the one who came up with the idea of thinking of electricity as a flow, and he dubbed the rate of flow *current*. These days we measure electric current in *amperes* (usually abbreviated *amps*).

If you have three light bulbs, each drawing one amp, you need to supply a total of three amps. If you then press the button on an electric drill that uses five amps, your requirements will jump to a total of 5 + 3 = 8 amps.

Every electrical device should have marked on it something that will indicate how much current it will draw. Some devices, like drills, list their current requirements directly in amps.

Devices that produce light or heat, however, usually specify watts rather than amps. For normal house current, 120 watts translates into one amp. A 60-watt light bulb draws one-half amp. A 300-watt soldering iron draws 300/120 = 2.5 amps. To figure the amps you need, take the watts specified and divide by 120.

Table 4.1   List of Electrical Power Needs

Item	Watts	Amps
LIGHTS		
■ **Fluorescent light over workbench**	15	0.125
■ **Overhead room lights:**		
Incandescent light 1	75	0.625
Incandescent light 2	75	0.625
Incandescent light 3	75	0.625
Incandescent light 4	75	0.625
■ **Drop light**	75	0.625
ELECTRIC HEATER	1,500	12.500
AIR-CONDITIONER		12.500
POWER TOOLS		
■ **Hand electric drill**		5.000
■ **Drill press**		15.000
■ **Air compressor**		25.000
■ **Battery charger**		1.000
■ **Arc welder**		30.000
■ **Soldering iron**	240	2.000

Manufacturers of electrical equipment that produce heat or light tend to list the input power required. This soldering gun draws 100 watts or 140 watts depending on how far the trigger is depressed.

Manufacturers of electrical equipment that produce something other than heat or light tend to rate their products by the input current required. This electric drill draws 2.2 amps.

Table 4.2   Calculation of Likely Maximum Draw

Item	Watts	Amps
LIGHTS		
▪ Fluorescent light over workbench	15	0.125
▪ Overhead room lights (total)	300	2.500
▪ Drop light	75	0.630
ELECTRIC HEATER	1,500	12.500
POWER TOOLS		
▪ Drill press		15.000
▪ Air compressor		25.000
TOTAL		55.760

The smartest thing to do is take a sheet of paper and make out a list like that in Table 4.1. List every item in the shop that uses electricity. Even the little items add up.

Suppose that you just turn on the overhead lights and the one over the workbench, hook the drop light on the handlebars, and solder a lug onto an ignition wire. In the meantime, you'll probably take advantage of having the battery disconnected to throw a charge in it. The total current draw is 6.38 amps—more than one-third of what's available from a standard 15-amp outlet strip—even though the only item drawing over one amp is the soldering iron, and that only draws two amps.

Once you have your list in hand, you need to figure your maximum likely needs. Don't just add everything up. You'll end up with a whacking great total that is far more than you'll ever use! The list in Table 4.1 adds up to over 100 amps.

Look for the maximum that you need to use at one time. You have to figure that you'll always have the lights on and the heater or air conditioner (but not both) going whenever you're in the shop. The worst single load on the system is the welder, and you probably won't need any other power tools while you're running it. Most amateurs run the air compressor only when it's needed. However, there's a fair chance that sometime you'll run it at the same time as another tool, such as the drill press. So, your likely maximum draw is shown in Table 4.2.

You have to plan in a generous reserve capacity. If you don't, you'll find yourself with sagging voltage (flickering lights and brownouts) when you have peak use, and your circuit breakers and main fuses will degrade over time.

Your electrical service equipment—the wires, outlets, and breaker panel (traditionally known as the "fuse box," although these days it should contain circuit breakers not fuses)—should effectively last forever. Running them at near capacity, however, will cause them to fail in just a few years. As they begin to fail, you'll find the breakers popping more and more often for no apparent reason; insulation on wires will degrade, creating the danger of electric shock or fire; and, finally, when the system gets so cranky and dangerous that you have to replace it, the electrician's bill will be higher than what it would have cost to install ample components in the first place.

Generous reserve capacity is a factor of two. That's the reason you don't just add up the items in Table 4.1 as if you were powering everything at once. If you did, you'd find yourself putting in 240-amp service!

Table 4.2 tells you to put in 120-amp service, which is much more reasonable.

OK, now you have 120 amps coming into the wall through a main fuse. You have to distribute that throughout the shop. You do that by splitting your service among several separate circuits with a circuit breaker on each.

It's a good idea to have your overhead lights on one circuit and your workbench light and drop light on another. That way, if one breaker goes, you'll still have some lights while you fumble around the shop trying to remember where the breaker box is.

You want to keep your big-load items on separate circuits and segregated from the lights. Figure on a 45-amp circuit just for the welder. If you rig it so you can't run the air compressor at the same time, you can put both welder and compressor on the same circuit.

How can you rig it so you can't run the compressor and welder at the same time? Simple. Make sure they have to use the same outlet. Instead of installing a standard 3-prong, double-outlet box, use one of the several standard high-current plug configurations and a single-outlet box. With only one outlet in the shop that will fit the plugs on those devices, you can't have them both plugged in at the same time.

Yes, it's a pain in the butt to have to unplug the air compressor every time you want to run the welder. But, that's the price of having a safe and reasonably cost-effective electrical system. How often do you use your welder? How often do you use compressed air? More importantly, how often do you switch from one to the other?

So, we now have a 45-amp circuit for the welder and compressor. We can put in a 15-amp circuit just for the workbench power strip. The light over the workbench and the drop light can both plug into it. That leaves 60 amps, which we

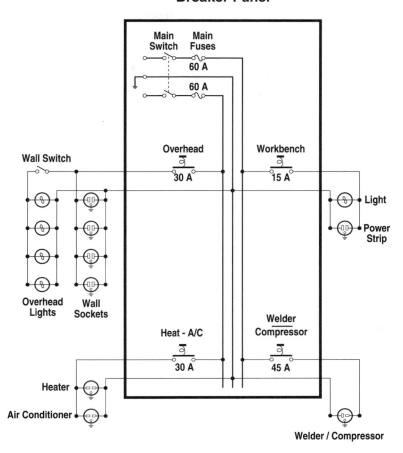

Wiring diagram for a typical amateur shop electrical system.

High-current electrical outlets with various plug patterns are available to help prevent overloading electrical circuits. All these outlets are designed to restrict which high-current 120-volt appliances can plug into which parts of the circuit.

Use outlet strips attached to your workbench to give you lots of sockets to work with. Outlet strips should have built-in circuit breakers (on this one, the circuit breaker is a small button on the end near the cord) and on/off switches.

can divide between two 30-amp circuits for wall outlets around the shop.

As for placing outlets, the rule of thumb for setting up your living room is to put outlets six to nine feet apart because standard cords for table lamps, televisions, etc., are about six feet long. Placing the outlets six to nine feet apart means that there will always be an outlet handy no matter where you want to put your TV. Happily, you almost never need electrical power at the bike.

For example, wise mechanics always try to do their cutting and drilling at the workbench, then attach the cut or drilled piece to the bike. If you do your cutting and drilling over the bike, you almost surely are going to get bits of whatever you were cutting or drilling into the bike in places where they shouldn't oughta go.

If you have to mark the location of a hole with the piece on the bike, mark the location, then take the thing off the bike and drill the hole over at the workbench. It takes a little extra time, but less extra time than trying to dig metal shavings out of your drive belt. And you also, then, don't need outlets in the middle of the work area.

You do, however, need outlets right at the workbench, and a lot of them. Use an outlet strip there with at least six outlets. You don't need to

have a switch or breaker on the strip, but it doesn't hurt. If you have a 15-amp strip on a 15-amp circuit, a breaker on the strip is redundant.

You need outlets near enough to the work area so you can conveniently plug in a drop light or an extension cord when you need light or power right at the bike. When you do need it, you gotta have it! But, you can use drop lights with pretty long cords.

Always install three-prong outlets. You can always stick a two-prong plug in a three-prong outlet. But, if you've got a two-prong outlet and a three-prong plug, it's off to the hardware store for an adapter. Or, if you're a little more foresighted, you have to rummage around trying to find where you left your stash of three-prong adapters.

All that I've said so far assumes that you're setting the power system up from scratch. That makes sense for you solid types that buy a house and live in it for 25 years, or for anyone setting up a professional shop.

Gypsies like me, however, blow into town and rent whatever's available. You don't spend a lot of time and money setting up a shop when you figure you'll hit the road soon. You work with what you've got.

The principles are the same, though. Figure out what you'll need, then try to match it up with what you've got. That's why all my outlet strips have breakers. Most of the time, those 15-amp strips are plugged into 30-amp circuits. Without their own breakers, they'd be a fire hazard.

The trick, when working with an existing system, is to find out what you've got and don't exceed its limits. You may think you can get away with it, but you can't.

I once had a place that didn't have an outlet fused for more than 20 amps. That's about what my welder draws. I was able to run a bead of weld about four inches long before the breaker would pop. Needless to say, I only pulled the welder out for emergencies.

Lighting

Aristotle, the ancient Greek thinker so idolized by medieval European scholars, taught that our eyes somehow sent out some beam that "felt" objects and returned with a scouting report to the eye. If that were true, what th' heck would we need light for? We'd see just as well in the dark as in bright sunshine.

Your eyes see an object because light from some source reflects from the object into your eyes. Everything is dark until you light it up. If you want to be able to see something, you'd better install a light to illuminate it. If you don't light it, you won't see it.

Thus, your need for lighting is just the opposite of your need for power. Whereas most operations around a motorcycle don't need any power at all, you can't do a lick of work on a bike without light.

It can't be just any old light, either. The *quality* of the light makes a big difference. The best possible light for working on a motorcycle is to be found in a small patch of shade on a bright, sunny day, although the light in the middle of a parking lot under thin clouds is of about equal quality. The idea is to get lots of light flooding in from all directions.

Single bright sources, such as direct sunlight or a single light bulb, are horrible. Your eyes will be dazzled by all the light reflecting off those expensive chrome doodads—blinding you to that rat's nest of wires in the shadows between the chrome doodads. Your assignment, whether you choose to accept it or not, is to figure out which of those wires goes where by reading their color codes.

If you've ever tried to look at your bike's wiring in direct sunlight, you know exactly what I mean. With a single, bright source (in this case our friend, Mr. Sun), your wiring is in deep, dark shadow. When you move the scoot into the shade so that the only light is the diffuse reflection from the ground, neighboring buildings, and so forth, the wiring suddenly, magically becomes visible. It would stand out even better if you shoved a drop light right in next to it!

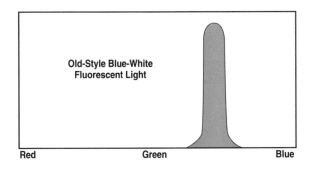

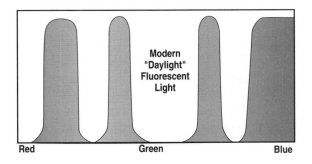

Old-style fluorescent lights gave a hideous blue light in a narrow color band. Modern fluorescent lights use a mixture of phosphors that add color bands to make the light they give more natural looking.

Natural sources of light are sunlight, skylight, and firelight. Evolution has matched the color response of our eyes to that of natural sunlight. Incandescent lights give an orangy light. Quartz-halogen lights run hotter to give a more natural looking light than standard incandescent lights. The light we normally see outside on a sunny day (in other words, daylight) is a combination of direct sunlight and diffuse skylight.

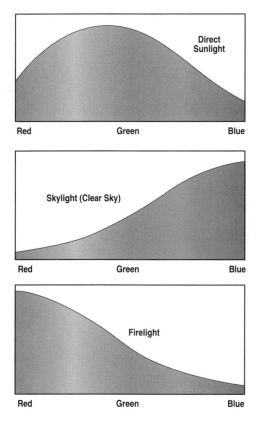

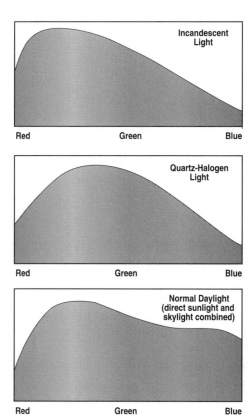

Table 5.1 on page 37 gives the characteristics of different light sources. The type of source is very important. I've classified them as "point," "beam," and "diffuse."

Point sources radiate in all directions. They create sharp shadows. The direction of the shadow, however, varies with where the source is in relation to the part of the bike you are looking at. An overhead bulb, for example, may throw shadows to the right near the front of the bike and to the left near the rear. On the other hand, since point sources also illuminate objects around the bike, they usually provide some diffuse reflected light to partially fill in shadows.

Beams, on the other hand, throw deep, dark shadows. The deepest, darkest shadows come from using a single spotlight as the only illumination in a dark shed. The essence of a beam is that light rays are all parallel. If you're using only a beam source, you have to go, literally, out of your way to get your shadow off your work. I've been seen hanging over the saddle to work—upside down—on the opposite side of a

bike because the only illumination was from somebody's headlight beam.

Of course, whenever that happens, some idiot wants to stand right in the beam to watch what you're doing! Moving that idiot out of the way calls for the utmost in tact—something bikers with broken motorcycles in the middle of the night have in short supply.

Instead of a gentle "Please stand over there so you're not in my light," it's usually "Get out of the way, you idiot!"

The light blocker, who is already several feet away, has no idea what they're doing wrong or they wouldn't be doing it. Repeated nighttime motorcycle breakdowns can escalate to broken friendships and divorce proceedings unless some perceptive and kindly brother or sister quietly shows the offending party how to watch where their shadow falls.

Diffuse light sources are much easier on mechanics and their relationships.

When setting up a permanent motorcycle workshop, one of your first considerations has to be lighting. Unless you are *extremely* budget constrained, don't skimp on it.

Your two choices are incandescent and fluorescent. The older style blue-white fluorescent lights provide more light per watt than incandescent, but they're ugly as sin. The lights are ugly and the light you get from them is ugly. It is harsh and it is blue. The newer, more expensive fluorescent tubes give a warmer (i.e., more red) light than the awful things we used to be stuck with. Those things gave people headaches and made everyone look like they had just died of asphyxiation.

The culprit is the basic physics by which fluorescent lights work. The light that you actually see comes from the white phosphor coating on the inside of the tube. Different phosphors produce different colors of light. Some produce a narrow band of blue light, some a band of red, and so forth; but they all produce light that has a restricted color range. The old tubes used a single phosphor that produced light in a color band that looks blue-white.

Lighting manufacturers have improved fluorescent light by using a mixture of phosphors so that you get several bands of light of different colors. It's a big improvement, but it's still not the natural-looking continuous spectrum you get from incandescent lights. That's why most people put incandescent lights in their living rooms and fluorescent lights in their workshops.

An advantage to fluorescent lights is that they're much less expensive to operate. Watts of power consumed translates pretty directly to dollars per hour and a 25-watt fluorescent tube produces about as much light as a 75-watt light bulb. That's the same illumination for one third the price. If you've got a big shop that operates all day, that's an important consideration.

However, if you run your lights for only a few hours per week, power cost is not a big item. Consider using incandescent bulbs. The choice will come down to initial purchase cost and aesthetics.

Not that incandescent lights are perfect. They produce an orange-yellow light. We like it better because it reminds us of the warm yellow glow from a fire. It may not be perfect light, but at least it somehow seems "natural."

Table 5.1 Characteristics of Common Light Sources

Source	Distance	Color	Type of Light
NATURAL SOURCES			
▪ Sun	infinite	yellow	bright beam
▪ Clear sky	infinite	blue	dim diffuse
▪ Hazy sky	infinite	white	bright diffuse
▪ Cloudy sky	infinite	white	dim diffuse
▪ Reflected sun	tens of feet	varies	bright diffuse
ARTIFICIAL SOURCES			
▪ Drop light	less than 6-inch	yellow	bright diffuse
▪ Drop light	more than 6-inch	yellow	beam
▪ Overhead bulb	several feet	yellow	point
▪ Multiple bulbs	several feet	yellow	bright diffuse
▪ Fluorescent tube, blue-white type	several feet	blue-white	diffuse
▪ Fluorescent tube, "daylight" type	several feet	warm white	diffuse
EMERGENCY SOURCES			
▪ Street lamp	infinite	varies	bright beam
▪ Multiple lamps	infinite	varies	bright diffuse
▪ Flashlight	few inches	yellow	bright point
▪ Flashlight	few feet	yellow	beam
▪ Direct headlamp	several feet	yellow	beam
▪ Halogen headlamp	several feet	white	bright beam
▪ Reflected headlamp	several feet	yellow	diffuse
▪ Moonlight	infinite	white	beam
▪ Starlight	infinite	white	dim diffuse

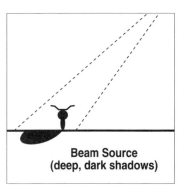

**Beam Source
(deep, dark shadows)**

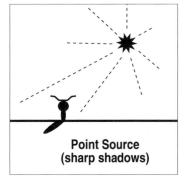

**Point Source
(sharp shadows)**

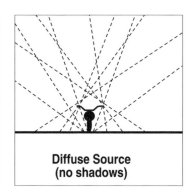

**Diffuse Source
(no shadows)**

Light seems "natural" when it mimics one of the two sources of light humans have used since humans have existed: sunlight and firelight. We have evolved to associate sunlight with doing outdoorsy stuff on a bright summer day. We have evolved to associate firelight with being warm and cozy in our own little cave at night.

Sunlight has a continuous spectrum of colors with two peaks. One peak, in the yellow color range, comes directly from the sun, which has a yellow color. Since direct sunlight consists of parallel rays, it is a beam-type source—so watch where your shadow falls. The second peak in the sunlight spectrum is blue and comes from sunlight reflected off the air. It is, therefore, diffuse.

The best *color* light comes from quartz-halogen bulbs. All the great things quartz-halogen lights have going for them come from running the filament at a higher temperature. Higher temperature means a brighter, less-orange light.

You can't run a regular bulb that hot because the tungsten filament literally evaporates. The "halogen" part of the name "quartz-halogen" comes from filling the bulb with halogen gas at a relatively high pressure so the filament doesn't evaporate.

They use quartz instead of glass to make the bulb because, at the higher operating temperature, glass has a tendency to soften like warm butter. Then your bulb explodes. I've seen it happen. It's not a pretty sight. Quartz, however, is even clearer than glass (which is green, by the way) and doesn't soften until the temperature gets much higher.

If quartz-halogen lights are so great, why don't I recommend using them to light your

motorcycle workshop? Because it'd be like cracking a walnut by attaching the nut to a concrete retaining wall with duct tape and hitting it with a 1958 Buick Roadmaster. Lighting your shop with quartz-halogen bulbs would cost a lot of money and you'd have to wear sunglasses to work on your bike.

The top two illustrations on the next page show the right way to light the work area for a single motorcycle. One figure shows how to do it with fluorescent lights and another with incandescent lights. The long fluorescent tubes fill the shadows better than incandescent bulbs but either will do the job nicely.

The idea is that you want to have light coming in from all directions, so you don't have to worry about *any* shadows. No matter where you stand, sit, or squat, or what part of the bike you work on, what you're looking at will be directly illuminated and the shadows will be filled in.

If you know anything about lighting for, say, professional photography, right about now you are scratching your head and saying: "But, we're always told that having shadows is important. It's supposed to keep things from looking flat."

When you're making great art, or lighting a living room, or trying to make that model look voluptuous rather than fat, you need shadows. Shadows make things look nice. Shadows carry information about the three-dimensional shapes of what you're looking at. That's not what you want in your workshop.

What you want in your workshop is fast, easy-to-get information about what's going on in that machine. When you're trying to diagnose, disassemble, or assemble a motorcycle, you have enough to worry about without messing around with dramatic shadows.

This book is about setting up a workshop. What you want in your workshop is light wherever you point your eyes. Remember, if it's not lit, you can't see it.

You want the main lighting to come from overhead. Unless you are extremely deformed or have very bizarre posture, your head is higher than your hands. Having the light high puts the light where you can see and the shadows of your arms where you can't. Those portable halogen work lights that you set on the ground will do a great job—if you prefer standing on your head to work on your bike.

If your workshop is properly illuminated, you will have very little use for a drop light. Have one on hand, however. There are sneaky places inside and under the seat that are hard to illuminate from above. Also, a drop light is useful for working under the bike, for example when looking for an oil leak. Besides, a drop light makes a great extension cord when you need electricity at the bike.

The diagram on the next page shows how to light storage shelves. There are two considerations: shadows from shelves and shadows from parts seekers.

You need enough vertical distance between each shelf and the one above it, so that light reaches all the way to the back. The lower the overhead light and the farther out from the shelf it is, the farther back it will reach into each shelf.

You need a line of sources, or at least more than one, so that when you are looking for a part, you aren't looking into your own shadow.

In most amateur shops, the shelving units are lined up along the wall. In that case, the light you use to illuminate the work area will probably be perfectly situated to illuminate the storage area as well (unless you've bought expensive reflectors to concentrate the light on the bike, thereby robbing light from the shelves).

When your parts storage gets so extensive that you have rows of shelves, it's time to worry about how one row of shelves interferes with its neighbors. To minimize shadows, use multiple lights or fluorescent tubes, and center them over

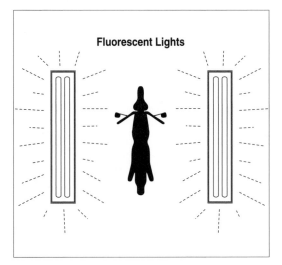

When lighting a motorcycle work space with fluorescent tubes, arrange them on either side of the bike with the long axis parallel to the bike. Make sure the tubes are somewhat longer than the bike.

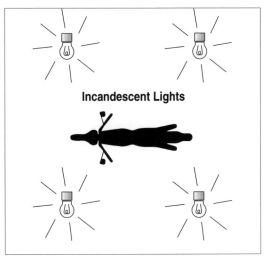

When lighting a motorcycle work space with overhead incandescent bulbs, use four bulbs—one in each corner of the work space.

In a large shop, arrange lights in between work areas.

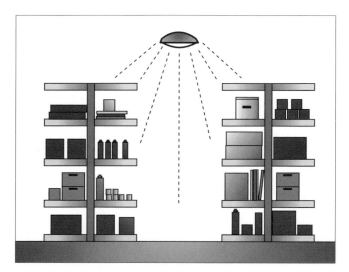

Light rows of shelves with lines of fixtures centered over walkways.

Painting the walls and ceiling with flat white paint fills the room with diffuse light, even if the main light source is a single overhead bulb.

the walkway between the shelves. Hang them as low as practical.

Whether you know it or not, the paint on your walls, ceiling, and floor are part of your shop-lighting system. Rich, dark paneling looks great in your den. Don't put it in your workshop. Paint everything white or beige.

White paint scatters a fair fraction of the light that falls on it back into the room. If you paint the ceiling and walls white, shadows disappear. It's the best diffusing screen you can find. A single naked light bulb in a white room gives more even light than the most ornate (and expensive) lamp housing—with complicated diffusers and reflectors—in a dark-walled room. Flat white paint works better than semi-gloss or (horrible thought!) gloss white paint.

You get the same effect by painting the floor. Overhead lights reflect off the light-colored floor to fill in all those nasty shadows under the seat and even under the bottom of the bike.

Don't, however, paint the floor white. When the paint is fresh, it'll reflect so much light that it'll give you headaches. In no time, though, it'll

get ultra-grimy and look really awful. You would have been better to paint it beige or grey. Beige is better because it gives color contrast to help you find most of the parts that you'll drop on it.

Illuminating a larger workshop is the same as illuminating a small workshop. You should have lights on both sides and in front and in back. A light can illuminate the right side of one motorcycle and the left side of the one next to it.

The planning procedure is to first decide where you want to put what and then plan lights to illuminate it. Lay out your work areas and storage areas, then pick locations for lights to illuminate those areas.

When your shop gets really large—over, say, 50 x 50 feet—you simply arrange a whole lot of overhead lights all over the place in a regular pattern. The idea is to evenly illuminate the entire floor area so that no matter where you put anything, it gets light from at least two sources that are spaced widely apart. Then, when you experimentally find dark spots (such as storage areas with rows of shelves too closely spaced), you can fix them with a few strategically placed lights.

Chapter 6

Heating and Air Conditioning

Bikers are more tolerant of environmental conditions than, say, librarians. They have to be. They simply have to put up with more crap from the atmosphere than people who aren't stuck outside for hours, and sometimes days, at a time.

I hate riding in the snow. I hate riding in the rain. The only thing worse than riding in the snow and rain is not riding. Sailors have the same problem. So do construction workers.

What you need in your motorcycle workshop depends a lot on what the environmental conditions are in your part of the world. For example, Canadian workshops don't have a lot of use for air conditioning. In southern Florida, they don't need much heat. In Utah, they need a generous supply of both.

When motorcycles were first invented, folks used heat to keep things from freezing and they didn't have air conditioning at all. My grandmother, who lived nearly all her life in Massachusetts, used to turn the heat off at night and open her bedroom window about an inch to let in that crisp, clear air blowing off the dry, powdery snow. As late as the 1950s, garages and barns were unheated.

Even today, expect your motorcycle workshop to be cold in the winter and hot in the summer. The main reason is heat leakage through the main door.

You need a pretty substantial-sized door to accommodate wheeling bikes in and out of the shop. You don't want to be pushing bikes through a door that is less than four feet wide. It probably should be at least eight feet wide if you want to accommodate a sidecar or a trike.

Yes, I have on occasion brought a bike in through the front door so I could strip down the engine in the front hall. I've even taken off the handlebars to do it. But, we're talking about recommended practice here, not some of the ridiculous things we did as kids.

So, if you're going to have anything that resembles a motorcycle workshop, it needs a big door and big doors let in heat in the summer and cold in the winter. Trying to keep too fine a control of your workshop temperature is going to be expensive.

Let's say it's 40 degrees outside and you want to keep your workshop temperature at an even 70 degrees. You open the door and wheel your bike

An electric space heater is a clean and convienent way to heat a small space.

in. This is not as quick as prancing in all by your-self. The door will be open for at least 30 seconds and quite possibly much longer. By that time, the workshop temperature has dropped to 50 de-grees. So, your heating system has to chug along until it pumps out enough heat to boost the shop temperature back to 70 degrees. All that time, you're cold anyway.

By the time the shop gets up to 70 degrees, you've finished replacing the spark plugs, changing the oil, and checking the battery. Now, you have to take the bike outside to lubricate the drive chain (better to dribble chain lube on the pavement than on your nicely painted shop floor). So, you open the door and wheel the bike out. Again, the shop temperature drops to 50 de-grees and, again, your heater chugs away to bring it back to 70. You've just heated all the air in your shop by 20 degrees—twice! Wouldn't it be better to leave the shop thermostat on 60 de-grees? Then, you'd have heated it twice by only 10 degrees. You'd cut your heating dramatically.

OK, so I've convinced you to minimize your heating bill by letting the shop get a little cold. Keep the shop at or above 50 or 55 degrees. Wear a sweatshirt. Wear a hat. You won't die. Be glad you're not trying to do this job by the side of a deserted highway!

A permanently installed gas space heater takes a little more effort than an electric heater, but can produce more heat.

What kind of heater do you need? Again, that depends on how big your shop is and how much heat you need. Shops the size of a one- or two-car garage should use space heaters.

Yeah, your garage is one of those built-in af-fairs that takes up half of your basement and bor-rows heat from the house. But, do you really want your house's furnace chugging away every time you open the garage door?

The exception is, of course, when your house has zone heating and your garage has its own zone. Then, you just have to walk over to the thermostat, set it somewhere between 50 and 60 degrees and forget it.

Everyone else: Get a space heater. A space heater is a box that you install in a corner. It gets hot and radiates heat to the space around it.

Your choices come down to what you get the energy from. You can power the heater with wood, coal, gas, or electricity.

I do not recommend wood or coal. Wood stoves are popular in places like New Hamp-shire, where there are a lot of trees around. How-ever, it takes about an hour to get a decent-sized wood stove cranked up. Then, the place gets too damn hot!

You also have to have a wood pile right handy and that takes up half the space in your shop. Then, every hour or so, you have to drop what you're doing and throw some more wood in the stove.

It's a bad idea to store all your wood outside because it's cold out there. When you bring in an armload of that cold wood and shove it into the fire box, it's like throwing in a block of ice. The firebox cools down, the fire damps out, not to mention you had to open the door to get the wood, and you have to spend an hour warming everything up again.

If you *insist* on heating with wood, plan a wood-storage space inside the shop that's big enough for a day's supply. At the end of each day, put enough wood aside to get the stove cranked up in the morning, and then refill the woodbox.

In the morning, use the set-aside pile (which is as warm and dry as it's ever going to be) to start the stove up. The stuff in your inside wood bin will have had all night, plus a couple of hours, to dry out and come up to workshop temperature. It'll burn a lot better than that stuff still outside under the tarp.

What actually happens if you heat with wood is that you're busy doing what you're supposed to do in your shop—wrenching on your bike—and you forget to feed the stove. Then the fire goes out and the stove gets cold. Then the shop gets cold and it finally dawns on you to feed the stove. Now, you have to heat the stove up all over again. It's messy, takes up a lot of space and time, and generally is a pain in the butt.

Coal stoves aren't any better, just dirtier.

That leaves you with gas or electricity. Both are safe, easy to operate, and don't take up a lot of space. Which you choose depends on how permanent your installation is to be and how much heat you need.

Gas space heaters are relatively inexpensive to operate, but need some careful plumbing. Installation is not cheap. If you are putting in a permanent installation, gas is a good choice. Don't go renting a garage and installing a gas space heater, then expect to take it away when you move.

The plumbing gas heaters need are for gas supply and exhaust.

Gas bottles need to be kept outside. They don't leak often, but when they do, they're fire bombs that'll demolish the building. Also, if you have a fire in your shop, the fire guys will want to run over and pull the gas bottle off to get it away from the building. They won't be happy if they have to cut a hole in your burning building to get to the gas bottle. So, the bottle has to be outside with a metal gas line running through the wall to your space heater.

If you have gas piped into your place, you don't have to worry about the bottle. But, hooking up to the gas main is no less of a project. In essence, the gas company has one big gas bottle off in the boonies somewhere. They take care of piping it into your shop. So, it's their responsibility. Don't even think of messing with their pipes—accidents involving gas mains typically demolish entire neighborhoods! Just pick up the phone and call them in to do it.

Gas heaters need an exhaust vent as well. If you don't vent them outside, they'll dump car-

LP gas bottles have to be installed outside with a gas line leading into the shop.

bon monoxide into your shop. First, you'll get a headache. Then, your pet canary will die. Then, you'll die. Then, they'll write newspaper stories about what an idiot you were. They'll probably point out that you were a biker to reinforce the public's belief that bikers are congenital idiots.

I can see the headlines now: "Dumb Biker Gasses Self in Garage!" The first paragraph will also mention that you weren't wearing your helmet at the time.

The details about how to install gas space heaters are contained in various state and municipal building and fire codes. It's not a do-it-yourself project. You buy one of these suckers from a gas-appliance dealer and pay them to put it in. That way, you don't gas yourself, or blow yourself up, or burn your house down, or void your homeowner's insurance.

Electric heaters are a lot easier (and less expensive) to install. They are, however, expensive to run.

Electric heaters come in two styles: baseboard and free-standing. To heat anything big enough to fit a motorcycle in, you'll need 1,200 watts at a minimum.

To really guesstimate what you need, measure the floor area of your shop and multiply by it by the ceiling height to get the volume of air you have to heat. If you live someplace with severe winters—anything north of, say, Kansas City—figure on about a watt for every cubic foot. So, if your shop is a typical one-car garage size of 15 x 25 feet, the floor area is 15 times 25 = 375. If you've got an 8-foot ceiling, you can figure the volume as 375 x 8 = 3,000 cubic feet. You'll need 3,000 watts of space-heater power. That'll draw 25 amps.

What about elsewhere? It depends on where elsewhere is and how much you use your shop. At the time of this writing, I'm living in Arizona. There are about four days a year when I need *walls* on my workshop, never mind heat.

As for air conditioning, unless you're a professional motorcycle mechanic, I'm here to tell you that you don't need it. You're a biker, for chrissakes!

OK, it's 95 degrees in the shade, so what? After you get done changing your oil, you're gonna put on a helmet and a leather vest, then go cruising the interstates where there ain't gonna be any shade! You're gonna be sitting on an engine that can boil water! If you weren't wearing thick, tall boots and heavy pants, you'd burn your leg on an exhaust pipe when you stopped. Then, you'd have a lot more to worry about than a little sweat running into your eyes!

In the Southwest you need shade. The heat won't kill you, but the sun will. In the Southeast, however, the heat won't kill you, but the humidity will.

Ventilation is generally more important than air conditioning. In most parts of the world, there are only a few hours a day when it's too hot to work in the shade. If you can get air flowing through your shop, you'll be OK. If you can't, it'll become an oven.

You have to have ventilation anyway. How're you gonna start up your motor with no ventilation? Ever degrease a carburetor in a closed room? Gets you high, doesn't it? That "high" comes from your brain cells winging their way to heaven as they die! Gotta have ventilation.

Open that big door. Open any other doors you might have available. Open some windows. If you have summer where you live, have an open-air shop area.

Professional mechanics, however, don't usually have the option of slipping into the shade with a piña colada when it gets too hot in the shop. The only thing they can do is close the big door and crank up the A/C.

If you're setting up a professional shop and believe that you'll need air conditioning, call your friendly neighborhood air conditioning guy. He's in the phone book.

If you live someplace that's reasonably dry in the summer, you can opt for a swamp cooler, known more formally as an "evaporative cooler." A swamp cooler works by sucking air through a big, wet sponge, called a "cooler pad." The water in the sponge evaporates, cooling the air. The air then blows through your shop, cooling you.

The up side of swamp coolers is that they are relatively inexpensive to operate and work best when you have that big door open. They like to have good air flow. The down side is that as the humidity goes up, the swamper's effectiveness goes down. You see, it only works if the water evaporates. If the humidity is high, the incoming air can't hold more water, so the water in the sponge fails to evaporate. Then, instead of blowing cool air around the shop, you just get hot fog. Swampers work great when the relative humidity is below 30%. When the humidity goes above 40%, forget it.

Swampers can also be dirty. The problem is that, since swamp coolers' best feature is their low cost, people don't run expensive distilled water through them. They run the cheap stuff that comes out of the water mains. It contains minerals. The minerals don't evaporate with the water. They turn into dirt. The dirt gets blown all over the shop with the cool air.

Actually, most of the swamper dirt ends up on anything that's right near the swamper's outlet. So, don't store your custom motorcycles right where the swamper blows, and figure on cleaning the swamper and the area around it fairly regularly.

Chapter 7

Work Space

Work space includes storage, space around the bike, your workbench, and miscellaneous space.

Storage

Plan to have a lot of stuff. Since you're going to have a lot of stuff, plan to make places to put it. Even more important, plan some way of finding where you put the stuff when you need to get it out again.

In Chapter 3, I talked about entropy: the amount of disorder. Your storage is not just a hole into which you push your stuff when you're not using it, it is a system to control the entropy of the stuff you're not using.

Whatever is in your shop is either being used right now, or being stored. At least half of the space in your shop is given over to storage. That toolbox is storage for tools when you're not using them. The box of clean rags under the workbench? In storage. The unopened case of 50-weight oil: storage. The cans of penetrating oil, chain lube, fork tuner, and so forth that are pushed back against the back wall on your workbench are in storage. The container of parts sitting by the back wheel of the bike you're working on right now is storage. In fact, everything in your shop but what you have in your hands right now is in storage.

Stuff in storage has certain very important properties:

• *It is out of the way.* Don't leave stuff lying all over the place. Activity creates entropy. If your stored stuff is too close to where you're moving around, it will get mixed up, damaged, and trip you when you're moving from point A to point B.

• *It is easy to get to.* You shouldn't have to climb over stuff to get to other stuff. See the first important property.

• *It is easy to find.* Being easy to find is different than being easy to get to. Who cares if what you want is easy to get to if you have to hunt through forty-seven easy-to-get-to places before you find what you're looking for. Not being easy to find negates being out of the way and being easy to get to.

• *It is safe.* That means don't store your stuff on the sidewalk in Times Square. It also means don't store an open box of chrome doodads under your swamp cooler. If your storage area is in a leaky basement, don't leave the stuff on the

A toolbox is just a storage place for tools when you aren't using them. Note the newspaper covering the bench. It's an inexpensive way to keep your work area clean.

floor. When you go looking for it six months later, it should be right where you left it and in nearly the same condition as when you left it.

Everything you store should be stored in some kind of container. Recommended containers are boxes, shelves, hooks, and drawers.

Boxes are the least desirable storage containers. I list them first because they are the preferred containers for us nomadic gypsies. The only reason we like them is because they save time packing and unpacking. We get our stuff out of them as soon as possible and put it on shelves, hooks, or in drawers. Sometimes "as soon as possible" runs into months of working out of boxes.

The main problem with boxes is they aren't compartmentalized. That makes it hard to find the stuff that's in them.

The exception is your toolbox. Toolboxes have nice compartments so you can separate your open-end wrenches from your socket set. Metric tools go there. Screwdrivers go there. And so forth.

Boxes can, however, be useful for keeping a lot of stuff together in one place. For example, when I take a bike apart for a complete reconstruction, I tend to haul out a bunch of boxes. Engine innards will go into one box. The fuel system (carburetor, air cleaner, fuel lines, petcocks, etc.) will go into another. Other boxes will systematically house parts for other systems. When I finish that bike, the leftover parts either go into the trash bin or go to more general storage. For example, I have a certain spot for all the old Bendix and Keihin carburetors I have left over from the bikes I've upgraded to S&S carburetors.

Shelves are great for most of your stuff. Shelves keep stuff off the nasty, dirty, unsafe floor, where you'd rather have your feet, anyway.

Storage shelves are, of course, the ultimate in convenient, space-efficient, easily-organized, and useable storage. Unfortunately, they always look like hell.

Many amateurs love the glass-jar system for storing small parts. The main advantage is that you can see what's inside without having to open the jar.

They change a storage area (where stuff is just scattered around a two-dimensional floor) into a storage volume that can store four to six times as much stuff.

Shelves have height, width, and depth. Height is the vertical distance from the shelf to the shelf above it. Width is the horizontal distance between the left and right ends (when you're facing the shelf). Depth is the distance from the front (near) edge to the back (far) edge.

Make the height of lower shelves bigger than the height of the upper shelves on the theory that big stuff tends to be heavier than little stuff. You always want the heavy stuff lower down than the light stuff. That makes the whole shelving unit more stable. It also keeps you from dropping a Harley engine block on your head when trying to put it in or get it out of storage.

Big, heavy things, like cast-iron engine blocks, go at the bottom. Big, lighter things, like gas tanks and fenders, go above them. Small heavy things, like carburetors, go next. Then, finally, put all the relatively small bits, like manifolds and clutch levers, up around eye level. Especially, put all the chrome bits that you don't want damaged when you drop something else on them at these higher levels.

Don't put anything above eye level if you ever care to see it again. Above eye level is the last place anyone is ever going to look for anything because to look there, they have to go hunt up a stool.

I've been known to stash tanks and fenders on top shelves because they are among the few things that are large enough to be seen there, and they aren't too heavy. Things stored on top shelves, however, tend to get dropped more often because of the awkwardness of getting them down. A tank dropped from six feet onto a concrete floor gets pretty well trashed. I don't recommend it.

Hooks are for flat things like gaskets and cables. Drawers are for the piles of anonymous parts, like screws, washers, nuts, and bolts. A neat variation on the drawer theme is the glass jar. Peanut butter jars are especially good. That's where you keep your assorted fasteners. I've got one jar for small American-thread fasteners, an-

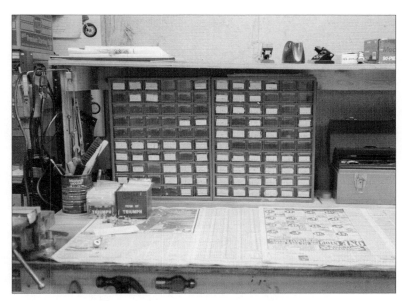

For small parts, storage bins combine the advantages of shelves and the keep-the-stuff-under-control properties of boxes.

Compartmentalized trays are a less formal alternative to storage bins for small parts.

other for up to half-inch fasteners, and another for metric things.

The nice part about glass jars is that you can see what's in the jar without opening it. If you don't let it get more than two-thirds full, you can just pick the jar up and roll it around to get a quick look at every part in there. If you see what you want, you open the jar to get it.

The glass jar system is not recommended for professional mechanics! They should do things a little more, well, professionally. Their time is too

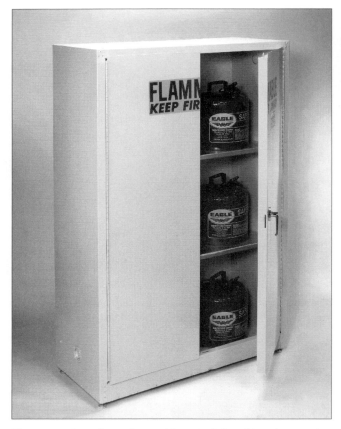

The reason for using a flammable-materials cabinet is to make it easy for the fire-department to figure out what to hose down first. *Photo courtesy of Eagle Manufacturing Co., Wellsburg, W.Virginia.*

Ziplock bags are ideal for protecting shiny bits in storage. They are even more useful for storing especially grungy bits (such as gears or sprockets) that are better off not being degreased. A sprocket covered with grease will rust a lot less than one that you've just cleaned. Naked greasy bits, however, are unpleasant to deal with in your storage area.

valuable to spend hunting around for odd, mismatched parts stored in glass jars. I don't want to see a mechanic I'm paying $40 an hour spending 10 minutes poking around looking for a five-cent screw. Professionals should have a large stock of carefully organized fasteners and other bits. All the hex-head bolts that are 3/4-inch long should be separated from the hex-head bolts that are one inch long, and so forth. The difference between a professional and an amateur is that amateurs have the luxury of wasting time ditzing around. Professionals have to get in, get the job done, and get out in the shortest possible time consistent with having the job done right. Because having well-organized storage (so that stuff is *really* easy to find) saves so much time, it is the hallmark of the professional shop.

Another variation on the drawer theme for fasteners is the tackle box. It is compact and por-

table, and has all these little bins to separate different sized fasteners. I keep meaning to get one.

Flammable fluids are another problem. Motorcycle shops have everything from gasoline to cleaning solvents laying around. Your flammable liquid storage should go into a closed cabinet marked FLAMMABLE in big, obvious letters. The reason is to let the firefighters know what to hose down first. It's not a bad idea to put your flammables cabinet someplace where it's easy to see and hose down from the door, but not so close that it'll fry anyone trying to use the door when it burns.

The best way to get an appropriate cabinet is to trot down to your local hardware, building supply, or automotive supply store and ask for one. Tell 'em what you want it for, and they should be able to supply it.

You shouldn't just pick up any old metal cabinet and print FLAMMABLE on it in magic marker. That would be better than nothing, but, since a new metal cabinet is likely to cost you $200 anyway, it's better to get one that is guaranteed to meet fire codes.

Of course, a storage cabinet is nothing but a set of shelves with a door and walls to completely enclose it. A good storage cabinet is the ultimate in safe storage. Items in a storage cabinet don't get dusty and dirty. Items in a storage cabinet don't get shoved aside, stepped on, or picked over. Potential thieves can't see what's in there when they case the joint.

Unauthorized riffraff can't surreptitiously check that stuff out because, even if the cabinet isn't locked, opening and closing the doors announces to everyone in the shop that someone's poking around in there. Watch what happens whenever a storage cabinet door opens or closes. Everyone within earshot looks over at that cabinet. They aren't just nosy. It's a natural human reaction to the sound.

Being the ultimate in safe storage, however, means it is the ultimate in "out of sight = out of mind" storage. Just as potential thieves can't quickly scan over the shelves in a storage cabinet to see what's there, the mechanic can't scan them either. That's why storage cabinets are not a major feature of professional shops. They waste too much time.

Work Space Around the Motorcycle

OK, more than half of the space in your shop is devoted to storage. Most of the rest of that space is devoted to work space around the motorcycle.

Never put a motorcycle you're working on in a corner! A big touring motorcycle is some 3 feet wide and 8 feet long. To work comfortably on that bike, you need at least three feet clear on either side and a similar amount in front and in back. In a pinch, you can work with as little as two feet of work room, but that's only in dire emergencies and for extremely simple tasks.

So, you need a space nine feet wide and fourteen feet long to work on a bike. If you don't have that much clear space in your shop, you don't have a shop.

I once met a guy who had three Harleys in a 9 x 12-foot shed. He also had a lawnmower, two bicycles, a barbecue grill, three bags of fertilizer, and a kiddie pool in that shed. This guy did not work on the bikes in the shed. To work on a bike, he had to spend half an hour unpacking the shed

and wheeling the bike out to the driveway. If it rained, he didn't work on any bikes. He had a storage shed, not a workshop!

What if you've got two motorcycles in the shop at the same time, sitting side by side? Does that mean you need six feet between them or only three feet?

That depends on how many mechanics work there. If you're the only one working in the shop, you only need space for one of you. When you're facing bike A to work on it, you won't be also facing bike B at the same time. So, you need three feet between them.

If, on the other hand, there are two people working in the shop at the same time, you have to leave enough room for both to work between the bikes without bumping into each other. Leave six feet between the bikes.

So, what're you going to put in this space around the bike? Of course, you're going to put yourself there. The dimensions are set up to fit a human being actively moving around and fixing things on the bike. You also need a place to put parts that you take off the bike.

At this point we have to differentiate the haves from the have-nots. Those who have a hydraulic lift set up their work space differently from those who do not.

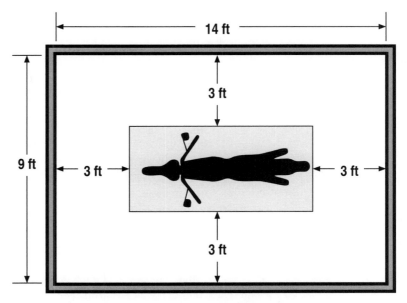

You need three feet of room in every direction around a bike you're working on. That makes a "standard" motorcycle work space nine feet wide and fourteen feet long.

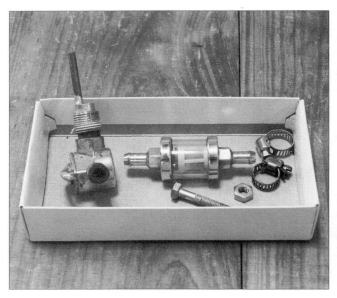

Any small open box can be used as a parts tray for controlling hardware and little bits while working on a bike.

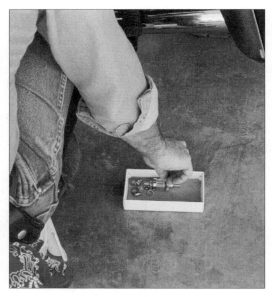

Three useable locations for your parts tray: (a) on the floor next to your stool,

Let's start with the have-nots. The bike is sitting on the floor. Most of the time, while working on a bike, your hands will be within 18 inches of the floor. The only way that's gonna happen is if you sit or squat to get your hands down there. Get yourself a stool!

If you don't, your knees will last about an hour. When you're young, the pain starts at somewhere between fifteen minutes and a half hour into the job. As you get older, it starts sooner. I'm now good for about a minute and a half!

After an hour the pain will affect your performance. You'll be thinking more about how much you hurt than about what you're doing. If you push yourself much beyond that, it'll take days for you to recover. If you don't learn your lesson, plan on knee-replacement surgery when you reach fifty years old. By then, arthritis will have crippled you. I'm not kidding about this!

Next, you'll need some trays to put parts in. My favorite source for parts trays is the boxes checkbooks come in. After you've burned up all those checks paying for your bike, and the mortgage on the shop building, and the tools, and the spare parts, and the whatever, you'll be left with the little boxes the checks came in. Don't throw them away. Separate the tops from the bottoms and you get two parts trays from each box.

Parts trays are for temporary storage only. Don't let worn out, broken, or otherwise extraneous parts collect in the bottom of the tray. When you're done working on your bike, your parts trays should be empty. Clean 'em out and put 'em away!

If you, for example, replaced your battery and saved the little 6-mm bolts and nuts that go on the terminals because you just didn't have the heart to throw away perfectly good nuts and bolts, don't just leave 'em in the bottom of the tray. That changes it from a parts tray to a storage tray.

The characteristic that makes something a parts tray is that it is small: no more than four inches wide, twelve inches long, and two inches deep. Any bigger than that and it will be getting in the way as you work around the bike.

You use a parts tray to hold (not store) all the itty bitty items you pull out of your bike that will get lost almost instantly if left on their own. Unlike most fasteners, washers, and carburetor jets, a parts tray is visible enough so that, with only a modest awareness of your surroundings, you can avoid stepping on it or kicking it into a corner.

If you, say, remove a 10-32 screw that's 3/8-inch long and lay it on the floor, when you go to put it back in the bike half an hour later (after doing to the bike whatever you took the screw out

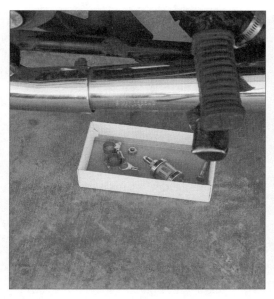 

(b) under the frame or behind the rear wheel,   **and (c) nestled in a convenient nook on the bike.**

in order to do) it simply won't be there. Even if it happens to have avoided being kicked into a corner, you'll have the Devil's own time relocating where you put it. Put everything small enough to fit into a parts tray into a parts tray.

What if you end up pulling off so many itty bitty parts that you fill up your parts tray? Get out another parts tray.

What about all the parts that are too big to fit in a parts tray? They're big enough to take care of themselves. I've never seen anyone fail to re-locate a chrome outer primary cover that was left out in plain sight. It's the little stuff that gets lost.

Where do you put the parts tray while you're using it? I've found three usable locations. All have their advantages and disadvantages.

The first location is on the floor next to your stool or even right under whatever you're dismantling. The advantage is that you don't have to move your hands much to get the bits from the bike to the parts tray. That minimizes the odds that you'll drop them along the way. The disadvantage is that when you stand up to get another tool from the toolbox, or a replacement part from the workbench, you've got a good chance to knock over the parts tray.

The second location for your parts tray is directly under the frame or behind the rear wheel. The advantage is that the tray is readily accessible and is almost impossible to kick over. However, if you forget it's there and move the bike, whammo!

Finally, you can nestle the parts tray in some nice nook or cranny on the bike itself. Putting it on the seat is not too hot, however, because it's too easy to knock off accidentally. If you've got those big, flat-topped saddlebags, laying the parts tray on the right-hand bag (the opposite side from the kickstand) works great. It kinda nestles in next to the fender.

Don't try putting your parts tray on the workbench or anyplace else that will force you to turn away from the bike. If you do, you'll have to turn around to move the part to the tray. Usually, dismantling anything is a two-handed (at least) operation. If you have to turn away from the bike to put that last fastener into the tray, something always slips.

That takes care of the have-nots: the folks who have not got a lift.

Those who do have a lift should organize their space entirely differently because, instead of the bike being within 18 inches of the floor, it's now a couple of feet or more in the air. Folks who have a lift don't need a stool. They do, however, need something that they can bring in to support, say, a rear wheel while removing it to change a tire.

Another major difference with a lift is that parts tend to go on the workbench rather than in a parts tray on the floor. Maybe the parts tray sits in a cranny on the bike, but more likely it sits on the workbench or, even better, on a roll-away cart that can be brought right in next to the bike.

When the bike is up on a lift, the penalty for upsetting a parts tray is severe. Instead of simply

A workbench should be about three feet deep and six feet long. The work surface should be at about belt level.

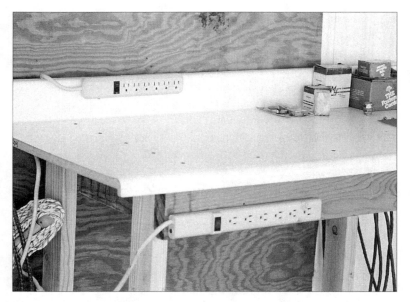

Outlet strips on a workbench can be mounted at the front or at the back. Each location has advantages and disadvantages, so putting strips in both places may be the best choice.

spilling over an area a few inches across, parts hit the floor with enough kinetic energy to carry them almost anywhere. I've seen washers dropped from workbench height that have rolled thirty or forty feet across a shop floor before disappearing behind a cabinet. Imagine a whole tray of parts scattering across the shop floor. Not a pretty sight, is it? For that reason, folks who work with a lift tend to arrange their small parts carefully on the workbench, rather than collecting them in parts trays that can then be overturned.

Workbench Space

You don't need a helluva lot of workbench space around motorcycles. That's because most of your work will be done right at the bike. Workbenches are needed for:

- Temporary storage of large parts removed from the bike;
- Temporary storage of replacement parts prior to installing them;
- Laying out of small parts while working on a bike on a lift;
- Working on subassemblies, such as carburetors, generators, and cylinder heads that have been removed from the bike.

A table is not a workbench. Tables are too low, too flimsy, and their surfaces can't take pounding.

Workbenches are solid. You and your partner of choice should be able to dance on it without it wobbling. You should be able to drive a Harley over it without seeing it flex.

Does this sound like overkill? Nobody's gonna dance on it. Nobody's gonna drive a Harley over it. Wanna bet?

You may not intend to dance on your workbench or to drive on it, but you do intend to work on it. If it's not solid enough, it'll let you down when you need it most.

The surface should be tough. The best surface I've had on a workbench was a stainless steel sheet supported by marine plywood. The second best was two-by-fours glued together and planed flat. Formica over a plywood base is way down the list. Figure that the thing will be pounded, scraped, gouged, oil soaked, and acid bathed.

That's today, and you want it to be ready to go again tomorrow, and the next day, and the day after that . . .

The ideal workbench is six feet wide and three feet deep and pushed back against a wall. The bench top should be at about belt level. Since belt level varies considerably depending on who's wearing the belt, I can't be much more specific. For most people, though, it's between 32 and 40 inches from the floor. The best compromise level is about 36 inches.

Generally, it's better to have the top a little low than too high. If you spend a lot of time working at the bench, too low means you'll get a pain in your lower back. If the bench is too high, it gets you more in the shoulders.

You don't want the bench to be more than three feet deep because your arms aren't that long. Most folks have arms around two and a half feet long. They tend to keep their work within 18 inches to two feet of the front of the bench. That leaves six inches to a foot of space for all those temporarily stored parts, and another six inches for cans of WD-40, Loctite, penetrating oil, ashtrays, and so forth that you want when you want them.

The items you want to store at the back of the workbench are those that you use for a couple of seconds at a time. You don't want to have to walk over to a storage shelf, get it, walk back, then repeat the round trip so that you can spend two seconds going sssst!

The workbench needs to be about six feet long so that you can lay out the big items, such as tanks and primary covers, on the workbench and still have room to rivet that kick-starter ratchet assembly together.

But you don't want your workbench to be more than about six feet long. Why? Because, if it is too long, you'll start using the ends for permanent storage. Workbenches collect junk. If you don't have too much space on the bench, you're more likely to clear the junk off it. Put the junk in your storage area or in the trash.

Now, you're going to look at all the shops that I've profiled in this book and notice that most of them have a lot more than six feet of workbench space. Notice, however, that those workbenches also service more than one bike. Each shop is di-

Roll-away carts are great for giving you a convenient flat surface to put just about anything while working on a bike.

vided up into work areas and each work area has a workbench (or section of a workbench) devoted to it, and each such workbench (or section of a workbench) is about six feet long. Even the 22-foot workbench that graces Jim Hamilton's shop is divided into four work areas, each about five-and-a-half-feet long.

A workbench needs a vise. The best location for the vise is the front right-hand corner (unless you're left-handed) with at least a foot and a half of space between the right-hand side of the bench and the wall. That gives you room to hang something that needs hacksawing over the right side of the bench and hacksaw it.

Notice that vises designed for benchtop mounting all have mounting holes at three corners of a four-hole pattern. That's because they are designed to be mounted just this way.

If you're left-handed, mount the vise on the left instead of the right.

Now, your workbench has some short-term storage for large and small parts, permanent storage for certain supplies, and a vise. To see what you're doing, you'll need an overhead light. And, to do most of the operations you bring to the bench, you'll need power.

You can set long-term project bikes up on stands to get them up to a convenient working height.

A lot of workbenches have under-bench storage, either as shelves or even drawers. I, personally, never went in much for drawers under the workbench. Somehow, whatever I'm working with on the bench seems to interfere with getting the drawer open. I'd rather have drawers in a storage area nearby than built into the bench. Other people, however, sometimes seem to have other ideas.

The overhead light is best supplied by a fixture specifically set up to illuminate the bench. Ideally, it is a fluorescent tube at least three-quarters as long as the bench. You can use at least two incandescent bulbs, but that gives you more of a shadow problem.

The overhead light should be just that: over your head. It should be at least a couple of inches over your head so that you aren't bonking your head on it when you lean over to peer into whatever you're working on. Given a choice, it should be four to six feet above the top of the workbench. If it's too low, you'll still hit it with sissy rails, fork tubes, and all sorts of elongated parts while you're trying to do something useful to them. If it's too high, you won't get good illumination.

The center line of the fluorescent tube should be over the bench, between three and six inches from the front edge. That way the shadow of

your head falls behind you (where nobody will ever care about it) while the shadow of what you're working on falls toward the back of the bench, where it won't be in your way.

Electric power for the workbench is best supplied by outlet strips. You never know what part of the bench will need power next, so you want to arrange outlets all along its length. The best way to do it is with outlet strips.

There are two places you can mount your outlet strips: at the back or at the front. If you mount the outlets at the back, your cords end up draped over the bench, interfering with what you're doing. On the other hand, if you put the strip at the front, the cords and plugs are right at your belly and interfere with what you're doing.

The first time I worked at a bench with outlet strips on the front, I was doing a lot of electronic soldering. We used soldering pencils, which stayed plugged in and stayed hot. So, there were all these cords hanging off the bench that went from the outlets along the front to the soldering pencils on the bench.

Every once in a while (actually, more than once a day) one of those cords would get caught in my clothing. Any motion would yank the hot soldering pencil off the bench right at me. It would then do a half-flip on its way to the floor.

The natural reaction when a tool starts heading for the floor is to catch it, which I would do without thinking. Of course, Mother Nature made sure that the time required for the pencil to do its half-flip equaled the time it took for me to catch it. So, I'd end up grabbing the hot end. I got more burns that way! Made me not want to plug soldering irons into the front of the bench, it did.

So, sometimes you want things plugged into the front, and sometimes you want them plugged into the back. I submit that you might want to put strips in both places.

Try to keep your toolbox off the workbench. Those who have a lot invested in tools go for those tall, multi-drawer toolboxes that roll around on carts. If you have one of those setups, you're safe. You won't be tempted to put it on your workbench.

If, however, you have one of those portable, carry-around, throw-it-in-your-trunk toolboxes, you first thought will be to stash it on your workbench. Don't do it. It's too big. It'll take up too much space. When you open it, you'll knock over everything on the workbench. Get yourself a cart, a small table—anything to keep it off the workbench. Put it on the floor if you have to. Just keep it off your workbench.

Miscellaneous Space

There is no miscellaneous space in a workshop. I've been in scores of workshops over the years, and I've never seen any space that could count as miscellaneous space. I've seen unused space. I've seen spaces set aside for walkways. I've seen space taken up by junk piles in the corners. I've never seen "miscellaneous space."

The word "miscellaneous" was invented to give a name to things that you couldn't think of a name for. When people start categorizing things, they pigeon hole all the big items first. Suppose you're categorizing the parts of a motorcycle. You'll start with all the parts of the motor and lump them into a category called "Engine Parts." Then, you might go to the tanks, fenders, and other sheet metal parts and call them something like "Sheet Metal." Then you lump the wheels, forks, brakes, and so forth into "Running Gear."

Eventually, however, when you get down to things like mirrors, hand grips, tassels, and chrome headlight visors, you begin to run out of steam. You see the number of categories heading off toward infinity and the number of items in each category approaching one. At that point, you'll be tempted to quit and throw everything left over into one category called "miscellaneous." It means, "All the Stuff Left Over That I Can't be Bothered to Categorize." I suspect that Ben Franklin would have yelled, "Quitter!" It takes just a little more effort to sort through what's left and put it in a *real* category.

In management circles there's a saying: "Work expands to fill all available time." There's a similar principle at work regarding workshop space: "Stuff expands to fill all available space."

Basically, what happens is that any empty space that's not being used for something else gets co-opted into storage. It gets filled with junk. Then it can't be used for anything else until you clear out the junk.

Most of the advantages of a hydraulic lift can be had by building a roll-away platform.

If you have enough money and spend enough time working on bikes, a hydraulic motorcycle lift makes work go a lot faster and easier.

The moral of this story is to plan a use for every cubic inch of space in your shop. Call it work space, storage space, walkway, or whatever. Just call it *something!* If you're blessed with space that you don't have immediate need for, label it "Storage" and leave it empty. Come back in a week and you'll find something stored there.

Don't forget the fire extinguisher. With all the flammables around a typical motorcycle shop, no sensible shop owner should be without a decent unit capable of dousing a small fire. Don't use water to extinguish an oil- or gasoline-based fire—it will only spread it further.

So, if every bit of your space is planned for, categorized, and in use, waddaya do when you get more stuff? If all the space that didn't have something else in it was earmarked as storage space and your stored stuff has expanded to fill all the storage space, what happens when you get another bike to work on?

You re-plan your plan. Remember back in Chapter 1, where I told you to start with top-down design and *expect it not to work?* This is one of the times it doesn't work.

I notice that the Zen Master has just placed his sandals on the top of his head and walked out the door, smiling and giggling.

Go through the top-down design process to lay out all your space. Don't worry about having the perfect arrangement for all time. Realizing that you don't have to be perfect—that in reality there is no "perfect"—frees you to do a good job of taking care of right now. Then, when things change, you can do a good job with that right now, and all the right nows after that. Strive to take care of right now, and the future will take care of itself.

The Zen Master just peeked around the corner and winked at us.

One last thing to remember when thinking about planning space: The fact that stuff expands to fill the available space implies that it can also be compressed. You can rearrange your shelves, throw out all the stuff that you shouldn't have kept anyway, and generally pack everything more tightly.

If, after you have compressed everything as tightly as it will go, you still need more space, it's time to get more space. Invest in a storage shed. Build that addition. Move to a bigger place. Or, take a booth at a swap meet. If the stuff you've got is too trashy to sell at a swap meet it's too trashy to keep—throw it away.

A Multi-Purpose Workshop Profile

Some of us just don't know what we want to do when we grow up. Sometimes we want to build motorcycles. Sometimes we want to play with hot rods. Sometimes we want to rebuild an antique Beechcraft airplane engine. If you have that problem, as I have, you need a multi-purpose workshop.

The watchword for a multi-purpose workshop is *reconfigurability.* You've gotta be able to move things around to share space among your various activities. That means most of the stuff in your shop has to be portable.

There are two ways something can be portable: First, it can be light enough to pick up from where it's no longer useful, and put it down someplace more useful. Second, things that are too heavy or bulky, but still need to move around, can go on wheels.

Some tools, like all benchtop power tools, need to be bolted down so they don't move while you're using them. Bolting stuff down kinda defeats the reconfigurability theory, though, so you have to make compromises. Make things as reconfigurable as you can, then stop.

Another item that stays bolted down is the drill press. A drill press is one of the most often used power tools you can have. It's more useful than a lathe and a milling machine. But it vibrates too. So it needs to be bolted down.

Reconfigurable Shop Features

Space

You can't move things around if you don't have room to move around. Reconfigurable shops tend to use space inefficiently.

Lots of Storage

Different activities require somewhat different tool sets, different supplies and components, and leave different boxes of spares in their wake. With different activities, you're more likely to have multiple projects going on at the same time. Since each project needs storage for its own stuff, that's just another reason for needing more storage.

Lots of Power Outlets

Electrical power is not a huge item in a motorcycle shop, but when you need it, you need it. In a reconfigurable shop, you never know where you'll need it, so you need it *everywhere*. In a

Tool*boxes* are portable because one person can pick up and move them a reasonable distance. However, a tool*chest* may be packed with 100 lbs. of tools or more. There's no way I can pick it up and move it. That's why it's got wheels. It rolls like a dream.

This scroll saw on a work table is a space compromise. It's unusable unless bolted down, but bolting this scroll saw down permanently on the benchtop may not be space-efficient. Clamping it to the work table means it and the clamps can go back to its little storage spot after you're done working with it.

The countless little drawers in the rack to the right carry nuts, bolts, and washers. Nails, rivets, and other fasteners go in the drawers on the upper left. Electrical wiring supplies go on the lower right. All the special tiny motorcycle bits like ignition points, condensers, and in-line fuel filters go in the middle right.

fair-sized shop area, mounting outlets in the ceiling with pigtails dropping down is a very good idea.

Permanent Fixtures Along the Walls

Put the fixed items, such as machine tools and storage shelves, along the walls. Leave the center for moveable items, such as rolling toolchests and portable tables.

Lots of Lighting

Just as with power outlets, you never know where you'll need light next, so you have to ensure adequate illumination everywhere. Having lots of windows is part of the plan.

Moveable Equipment

Other than the toolchest and portable toolboxes, the rollaway cart gets the most use in this shop because I can move it beside whatever I'm working on.

Tools like a table saw, unlike most pieces of equipment, are small enough to move around but big enough to stand still in use. When I need it, I pull it out. When I don't, it goes back against the wall, out of the working space.

A Place for Everything

Reconfigurability doesn't cancel Ben Franklin's first principal. In fact, reconfigurability makes it more important. When your shop is basically fixed, you just find a place for everything once and put it back in the same place. Reconfigurability makes you rethink your space every time you reconfigure. Everything still has a place, but it's not always the *same* place.

Permanent vs. Temporary Storage

You need some permanent storage and some reconfigurable storage, so there are several permanent-storage places around this shop.

In one corner there's a permanent storage cabinet. The top of the cabinet stores bulky but fairly light items, such as gas tanks and jack stands. Its top shelf is for motorcycle helmets, gloves, goggles, etc. The second shelf stores supplies like a spare paper towel roll, a stash of light bulbs, ziplock bags for organizing parts during a long-term restoration project, and so forth. The third

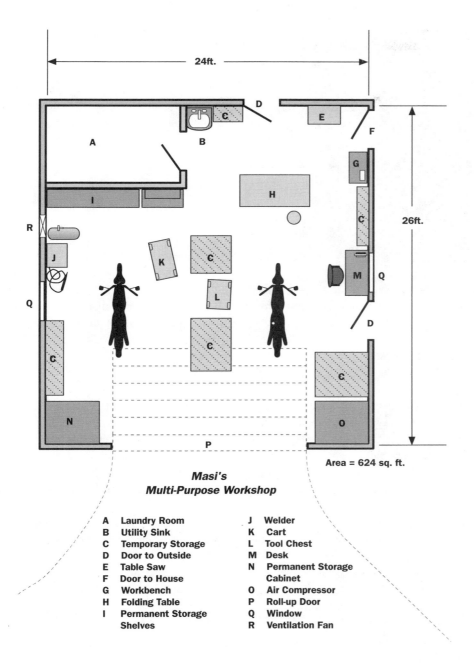

**Masi's
Multi-Purpose Workshop**

A	Laundry Room	J	Welder
B	Utility Sink	K	Cart
C	Temporary Storage	L	Tool Chest
D	Door to Outside	M	Desk
E	Table Saw	N	Permanent Storage
F	Door to House		Cabinet
G	Workbench	O	Air Compressor
H	Folding Table	P	Roll-up Door
I	Permanent Storage	Q	Window
	Shelves	R	Ventilation Fan

shelf stores hand-held power tools like a portable drill and a chain saw. The near future will see a second cabinet going up there. The bottom shelf stores dangerously flammable stuff like paint thinners and solvents. That's also where my ammunition stash goes. I told you this is a multi-purpose shop.

These materials are all dangerous in the event of fire. So, I store them in a location that's near an access door (the roll-up garage door) so fire-men can get to it easily without having to crawl through a smoke-filled, burning building. At the same time, they don't have to edge past it if it's on fire. They can get in through the regular door in the other corner and open the garage door without getting within six feet of the flammables cabinet.

Of course, next to that cabinet hangs the ubiquitous key rack. I know where my keys are when I need 'em. It's right next to the door through

A sturdy desk can also be a permanent storage area, especially for storing paperwork. This one has a bench grinder bolted to the edge where it doesn't interfere with writing or working on small, sit-down projects.

which vehicles (or at least the motorcycles) go in and out, and next to the cabinet with the helmets and goggles.

The tall, gray, rectangular wooden box next to the cabinet, by the way, is a homemade 10-inch astronomical telescope. Giving me a place to play telescopes is another purpose for this multi-purpose shop. Telescopes are bulky, fairly heavy when they get to that size, and easy to damage. They need a permanent storage space that's out of the way.

The second permanent storage space is along another wall in open-shelf storage. Most of this is general storage, but some areas are set aside for nuts, bolts, and other hardware that are part of the general supplies every shop needs.

Each drawer in the three-drawer cabinet has its own storage function, too. The top one carries specialized model-airplane tools such as heat guns and irons for stretching fabric over the frames. The second drawer is filled with electrical house-wiring components for that whole separate long-term project. The bottom drawer is more general storage.

The third major permanent storage area is the drawers in the desk pictured. The lower left drawer is a small hanging-file cabinet unto itself. You want the warranty card for that paint sprayer? It's there, enshrined in its very own manila folder. How about the title for that Suzuki? It's there in its folder along with the repair records going back to the day it left the dealer—twenty-four years ago. The top left drawer stores all the air tools and fittings for the compressor. The top right holds micrometers, calipers, and other assorted machinists' measuring instruments, as well as note books for several construction projects.

The middle right drawer is for electronics wiring. Soldering guns and irons go there, as well as rolls of wire in various sizes and colors. That's also where you'll find crimpers, wire strippers, digital multimeters, and so forth. That makes them right handy for wiring stuff up at the desk. The illuminated magnifier is there 'cause I can't see the dang little holes in the circuit boards anymore!

The bottom drawer is for all kinds of tape: appliance tape, electrical tape, masking tape in various widths, and, of course, duct tape.

Temporary storage fills in the areas that are not needed for working and not needed for walking between the storage areas and the work areas. That's a lot of territory. It also gets reconfigured with each reconfiguration of the shop.

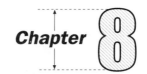

Chapter **8**

The Basic Tool Kit

The two things you must have to work on a bike (aside from the bike itself) are a work space and tools. We've pretty much covered what you need for a work space. It's time to turn to the tool kit.

The contents of your toolbox, and even the size and shape of your toolbox, will vary greatly on your skill level and the kind(s) of bike(s) you are going to work on, as well as your personal taste. You will need at least two tool kits: your emergency tool kit and a full set of tools that you keep in your shop.

I divide tools into two classes: basic tools and specialized tools. Basic tools are the assorted general purpose items that are so useful in so many situations that you simply can't do without them. Screwdrivers, wrenches, and pliers are basic tools. Specialized tools are those that you need to do specific jobs. You can't install a clutch in a Harley-Davidson without a clutch-spring compressor. I've installed clutches in some other makes without such a tool, but it ain't easy.

As you become more adept at working on your motorcycle, you will want to try more involved projects. That is the time to invest in more specialized tools.

Don't try to assemble a basic workshop tool kit one item at a time. Basic tools come in sets. In this chapter, I'm not going to talk about individual tools, I'm going to talk about sets. Table 9.1 lists the basic tool sets you need to acquire before you do anything else—even before you get a toolbox.

Combination Wrenches

Fixed-size wrenches can have open ends or box ends. Which you need depends on what kinds of

contortions you need to go through to get the wrench on the thing you're wrenching and swing it through enough of an arc to make the exercise worthwhile. Combination wrenches have a box-

---

Table 8.1   Basic Tools

- Combination Wrenches
- Socket Wrenches
- Adjustable Wrenches
- Allen Wrenches
- Slot Screwdrivers
- Phillips Screwdrivers
- Pliers
- Hammers

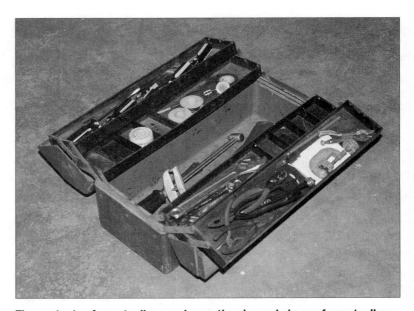

The contents of your toolbox, and even the size and shape of your toolbox, will vary greatly depending on your skill level and the kind(s) of bike(s) you work with, as well as your own personal taste.

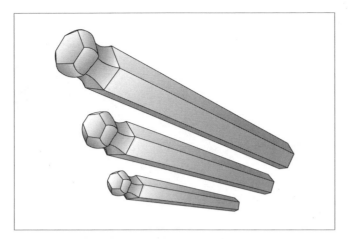

The ball-end hex key is another variation of Allen wrench. The ball end allows you to fit the key into a socket-head bolt even when you can't line up the wrench axis perfectly with the bolt axis. They are especially useful when working under fenders and other places where you can't see what your fingers are doing.

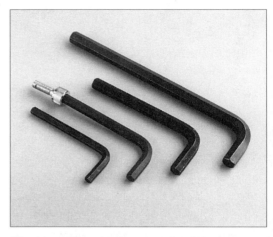

Allen wrenches, also known as hex keys, are especially useful around a motorcycle because the bolts they fit (called "socket head cap screws") have a more compact head than hex-head bolts.

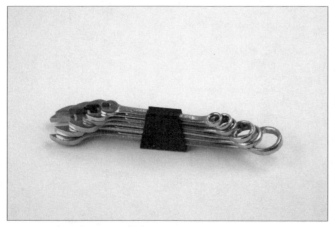

Combination wrenches sport a box end and an open end on each tool. Expect the box end and open end to be the same size.

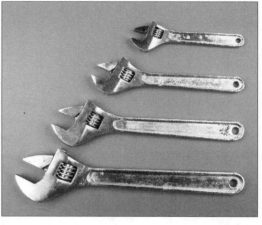

Crescent wrenches are the adjustable version of the open-end wrench.

end wrench at one end and an open-end wrench at the other. Therefore, they are the most useful sort of wrenches to have. The most useful American standard wrench sets give you a range from 3/8-inch to 1-inch. Typical metric sets span 8 mm to 19 mm.

Socket Wrenches

The most useful socket set size has a 3/8-inch drive, whether the sockets themselves are metric or American standard. A 3/8-inch drive socket set spans the same size range as combination

wrench sets. The other drives you'll eventually find useful are 1/4-inch and 1/2-inch. But, to start with, get a 3/8-inch drive set. In any socket set, expect to find (at least) a set of various size sockets that includes a spark plug wrench. Also expect to find a ratcheting handle and an extension to go between the ratchet and socket.

Adjustable Wrenches

The type of adjustable wrench you want for motorcycle work is a crescent wrench. They come in various sizes according to the length of

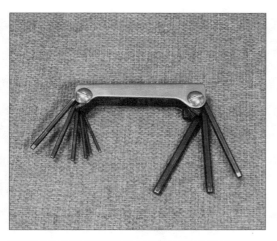

Some hex key sets have multiple keys that jackknife into a common handle. Surprisingly, they are not particularly useful for an emergency toolkit because each key tends to be considerably weaker than an equivalent-size individual hex key.

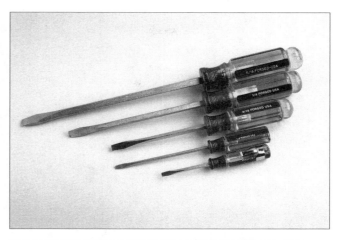

Slot screwdrivers have the flat-tipped blades Mom used to have in her kitchen drawer.

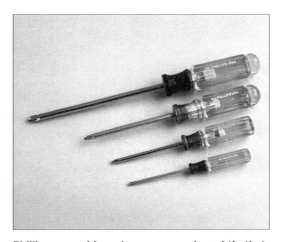

Phillips screwdrivers have a cross-shaped tip that comes to a point.

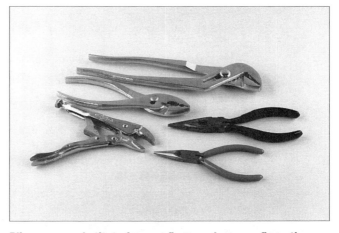

Pliers are a substitute for your fingers when your fingertips are either too weak or too big and clumsy to do the job.

the handle. In your basic tool kit you need only one or two. I've found that an eight-inch crescent wrench is the one I pick up most often. I've found that a six-inch is also pretty useful. The main reason you want an adjustable wrench is because whenever you have two motorcycle parts held together by a nut-and-bolt combination (as opposed to a bolt threaded into some part of the motorcycle), you need a second wrench to hold the bolt while you loosen the nut. A single crescent wrench can take the place of a whole second combination wrench set.

Allen Wrenches

These are also known as "hex keys." Your basic Allen wrench is an L-shaped thing made out of precision hexagonal tool-steel stock. The size of the key is determined by the distance between opposite flats on the hexagon. Thus, a 3/8-inch open-end wrench will just fit (and turn) a 3/8-inch Allen wrench. You want a large assortment going up to 3/8-inch size.

You can also get sets that have several Allen wrenches that jackknife into a common handle. These save a lot of futzing around looking for the

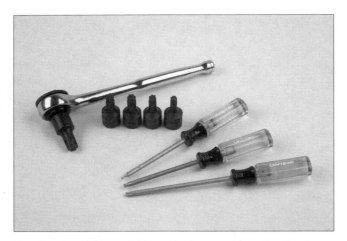

Torx fasteners are used increasingly on motorcycles, in places where high torque must be applied. You'll find a set of drivers and sockets to be very useful.

A socket wrench set includes (at least) a ratchet handle, an extension (to help you reach deeper into the bike and still be able to swing the ratchet), and an assortment of sockets.

right wrench, but they are not as rugged as individual hex keys.

A third variation has what looks like a misshapen ball on one end. Not surprisingly, they are called "ball-end hex keys." The ball end is useful for starting a screw when you can't get a good angle on it because the shafts do not have to line up. To get an ordinary hex key into the screw-head socket, you have to line the axis of the screw and the axis of the key perfectly. That ain't always easy. When the screw is in an awkward position, you'll likely spend more time lining up the wrench and screw than you do turning—very frustrating. Ball-end Allen wrenches make that part of the job a lot easier. You can't, however, sock the screw down tight with a ball-end key, so you have to have some ordinary hex keys available as well.

Slot Screwdrivers

A "driver" is a tool consisting of a "bit" at the business end that is fixed to a shaft with an axially mounted handle at the other end. There are drivers available for every kind of fastener head made: slotted screw, Phillips screw, hex nut, Allen head, and so on 'til morning. There is no better way to drive a screw (which is nothing but a little bolt anyway). The good part about drivers is that they're fast. You can spin those little suck-

ers in place in no time. The bad part is that they're weak. You can't apply much torque with them. That's why we use 'em for little screws rather than big bolts.

A slot screwdriver is used to drive screws that have slots in them. Makes sense, doesn't it? The important dimensions of a slot screwdriver are the width and thickness of the tip (which should roughly match the dimensions of the slot in the screw head), and the overall length of the driver. What you're going to need for a basic screwdriver assortment is a stubby one about two inches long, a larger one with a 1/4-inch wide tip, and a bigger one with a tip about 3/8-inch wide. Almost any assortment you pick up at your local hardware store will have at least these sizes and probably a few more. If you've got choices, the next most useful screwdriver to look for is one with a small tip about 1/8-inch wide. It's great for getting at those few teeny-tiny screws sunk into recesses that your 1/4-inch jobby is too fat to get into.

Torx Drivers

Torx, or star-point, screws are becoming increasingly common on motorcycles. These look a lot like Phillips screws, but instead of a four-armed cross, the "slot" has five or more "points" making it look like an asterisk(*). Star-point drivers are numbered "T9," "T10," etc. and allow you to put a lot more torque on the screw before the driver slips out of the slot.

Phillips Screwdrivers

A Phillips-head screw is one of those ever-popular things with a crossed slot in the head. When you look at the driver, you see that the tip is not flat, the arms come to a point. The important dimensions of a Phillips tip are the thickness of the arms and the angle at which the tip comes to a point. If those two match, you can put a ton of torque on the screw. If they don't the driver will slip and the screw will tear—very badly. Unfortunately, there's no way to tell what the angle is until you shove the driver into the screw and wiggle it around to see how it feels. If it fits, you can feel it lock in. If not, it feels, well, wrong. Phillips screwdrivers are identified by a size number: #0, #1, #2, and so on. You'll need at least a stubby #1 Phillips (its shaft is about 3/16-inch diameter) and a long #3 Phillips (shaft about 5/16-inch diameter). Better yet, since it is so important to match the screwdriver with the screw, get a whole set of them to be sure you have the right sizes.

Pliers

Ah, pliers! You can never have enough pliers. Yet, I also hate the bloody things. They bung up everything. People are always trying to use them as a substitute for the wrench they haven't got. You can't apply any torque worth spit using pliers. Pliers are a substitute for your thumb and forefinger. When what you're trying to pick up is too small for your big fingers to control, use long-nosed pliers. When you need to squeeze or bend something that's just too tough for your poor tortured flesh, use those big fat pliers. You'll also need something to cut wire with. Most pliers have a wire cutter of some sort built into them. It's not a substitute for your fingers, it substitutes for your teeth!

Hammers

"If at first you don't succeed, get a bigger hammer." You can't heed that sage advice if you don't have any hammers in the first place. The most useful hammer is still the carpenter's claw hammer. With it and a block of wood, you can do

The preferred hammer among mechanics is the ball-peen hammer.

The only hammer I've ever seen actually recommended for motorcycle work is a soft-faced (rubber or plastic) hammer.

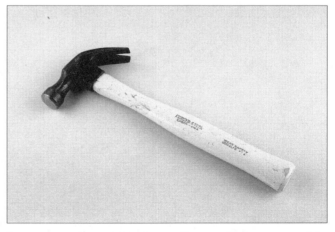

The ever popular carpenter's claw hammer is also very useful in a motorcycle workshop.

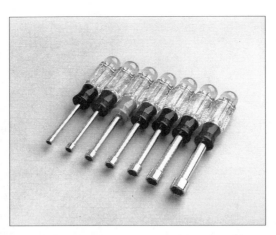

Hex drivers (also known as "nut drivers" and "spin tights") do for hex nuts and hex-head bolts what screwdrivers do for screws. Use a wrench to final tighten any bolt or nut with more than a 3/8-inch hex.

just about anything you'd ever want to do with a hammer.

However, motorcycle mechanics actually try to avoid hammering anything at any time. Except for the odd rivets here and there, motorcycles are bolted together, not pounded. Whenever you have the impulse to pick up a hammer, you should stop, count to ten, and ask "What am I doing wrong?" The only hammer that the bike repair manuals tell you to use is a soft-faced hammer. Once in a while, I'll use the plastic handle of a heavy screwdriver to shock some recalcitrant fittings apart, but that's about it.

Hammer choices include the claw hammer I mentioned above, a plastic or rubber-faced hammer that's softer than the metal you'll be tempted to whack on, and a ball-peen hammer. Ball-peen hammers somehow seem more fitting for mechanical work, but I've always come back to the claw hammer. It just seems to be the best choice for all the things I use a hammer for—mainly putting nails in the wall to use for hooks!

Nut Drivers

This is one kind of tool that is entirely optional in most shops but mighty useful too. If you frequently work with small nuts and bolts, you'll find that a nut driver can make many assembly and disassembly tasks easier.

Chapter 9

The Emergency Tool Kit

An emergency tool kit should be part of the standard operating equipment of every motorcycle. It's a separate set of tools stored on the motorcycle and not mixed with the rest of your tools.

If you have more than one motorcycle, I recommend assembling an emergency tool kit for each bike you own. It sounds like an extravagance, but it isn't. If you have one emergency tool kit and more than one bike, there'll come a day (and it won't be long coming) when you are out on the road with a broken motorcycle and your emergency tool kit will be on another bike that's parked at your shop. Not keeping an emergency tool kit with every bike you own amounts to challenging Mother Nature to a dare. She always accepts—and always wins!

Your shop tools are another story. For 90% of the work you do on your bike, you don't need anything but your emergency tool kit. So, when you're starting out, make up the emergency kit first. As you take over more and more of the wrenching on your bike, you will add to your stock of tools as you go.

Yin vs. Yang

Your emergency tool kit is a compromise between two mutually antagonistic goals. You want to have all the tools you'll need to cover every possible roadside emergency. At the same time, you want it to be as compact as possible.

I've ridden with one guy who had enough room for all the necessary tools. Sandy rode a Harley FLHS equipped with a trailer hitch and had an *assortment* of trailers to choose from. He had a little one for short day trips. He had a bigger one for overnighters and weekend trips when

he was planning to motel it. When he went to a rally, he took his really big trailer that opened up into a tent that was nine feet wide and fourteen feet long—not counting the verandah!

Most of us don't haul trailers behind our bikes, so space is at a premium. A fully loaded touring bike has *maybe* ten or twelve cubic feet of storage space on a good day. Most of the bikes I see tooling around would be happy to see two cubic feet! Your tool kit has got to be compact, it's as simple as that.

Table 9.1 lists the tools I carry at all times on my bike. Notice that it's divided into two pouches. Items that can stand a bit of weather go into the main pouch. Electronic-type equipment—which is traditionally not designed for outdoor work—goes into the second pouch, which lives in the right-hand saddle bag.

The author's emergency tool kit (Harley-Davidson Sportster version).

Table 9.1 Author's Emergency Tool Kit

MAIN TOOL POUCH
- Flashlight
- ⅜-inch to ¾-inch assorted open-end wrenches
- 6-inch crescent wrench
- 8-inch crescent wrench
- Spark plug wrench
- 4-inch vise-grips
- 5-inch channel-lock pliers
- 0-50 psi tire-pressure gauge
- 10-mm combination wrench
- 5/64-inch to ⅜-inch Allen wrench assortment
- 8-inch x ⅝-inch extension handle
- Phillips screwdriver
- Slot-head screwdriver
- 5-inch long-nosed pliers
- Wire strippers
- Black electrical tape
- Feeler gauge set
- Teflon thread-seal tape
- 6-foot tape measure
- Scotch-Brite

- Thread locking compound
- 5-inch tie wraps

SECOND POUCH
- Hand-held digital multimeter (DMM)
- DMM test leads
- DMM test probe tips
    2 alligator clips
    2 long probes
    2 needle probes
    2 spade-lug probes
- 6-foot test wire with alligator clip ends
- Spare breaker points
- 3 #1157 brake light bulbs
- 2 #53 instrument light bulbs
- Spare fuses as needed

ADDITIONAL
- Repair manual in plastic bag
- Key-ring flashlight
- Swiss Army knife (8-blade "Fisherman")

Your emergency tool kit should be strapped or mounted somewhere on the outside of the bike.

All of these items are of the minimum size that would be useful. For example, the 3/4-inch open-end wrench is only 7-1/2 inches long.

Tool sets for the emergency tool kit are also designed to stay together. Those assorted open-end wrenches, for example, all nest together and are held by a clamp. That makes it a lot easier to find the odd wrench when stressed out by the

side of the road or when working by flashlight in the middle of the night. I can find the wrench set by feel, then lay it out neatly on a convenient rock or patch of pavement. It also helps me know whether I've collected all my little metal buddies when I go to pack up again.

The tool pouch itself is a cylindrical leather bag ten inches long and four inches in diameter. Leather is perfect because it stretches. If you need just a little more space for that screwdriver, the leather will give a little to provide it. More importantly, you don't have to pack a leather pouch the same way each time. When you're done, you just stuff the tools back in the order you pick them up. If you get tools crisscrossed so badly that you can't get the pouch closed, a few good shakes or a little kneading will rearrange them so that they fit with room to spare.

Another important point about this tool pouch is that it has straps. This pouch has never spent time in a saddle bag. I've hung it on handlebars, suspended it from sissy rails, and strapped it to front forks. Hanging the tool pouch outside makes a big difference to the amount of room inside the ol' saddle bags.

More importantly, though, strapping your emergency tool kit somewhere on the outside of the bike means that in an emergency it's always right there—on the outside of the bike where you can get at it. There's nothing more frustrating when you're broken down beside the road in the rain than having to unpack your saddlebags to get at your tools.

If you carry your tools in your saddlebags, Murphy's Law requires that they be at the bottom, underneath everything else. It will never fail. The reason it will never fail is because, since you wouldn't dare leave home without them, they go in first when you pack your bike. Everything else ends up on top. The things on the very top are the things you almost forgot!

If you decide to be clever when packing your bike, and hold the tools out 'til last, they'll still be on the bottom by the time your bike breaks down. It works like this: You start out with your tools on top. Ten miles down the road, you stop to top off your gas tank. At the gas station, you pull out a sweatshirt to wear under your jacket and, maybe, a heavier pair of gloves because its a bit colder than you expected this morning. You put your lighter gloves in the saddlebag.

A hundred or so miles later, you're low on go-juice, so you pull into a truck stop for a break. It's gotten warm, so the sweatshirt and heavy gloves come off and go back in the bag.

After eating there and getting gas, you travel on down the road about fifty miles when silence happens. You coast to a stop to find that an ignition wire has come loose. It's a simple job, but you need your emergency tool kit. Well, you were sure smart to put it in last, weren't you? It should be right there on the top, right?

Wrong. By now it has slipped down under all the stuff you pulled out and put back along the way. To get at the tool kit, you have to pull out your sweatshirt, heavy gloves, the towels, the spare clothing, and anything else you touched along the way! The emergency tool kit that you put in at the top is now close to the bottom.

The reason the emergency tool kit is always at the bottom is because it's the first thing you think to bring and (hopefully) the last thing you will use.

The sun is much sunnier, the birds chirp more cheerfully, and life is generally a lot more pleasant if your emergency tool kit has a nice, safe home of its own on the outside of the bike.

Emergency Tools

Enough of generalities. It's time to talk about why those particular tools have earned a place in my emergency tool kit.

The flashlight is there for all the reasons I talked about in Chapter 5 regarding lighting. If you've gotta work on a bike, you've gotta see what you're working on. If the sun isn't out, odds are you'll have to provide your own light. Hence, a flashlight.

This particular flashlight is fairly unique. I don't remember where I got it, but it probably came from someplace where they sell stuff to boaters. This thing is completely encased in a rubber sheath and looks like it would be perfectly happy under thirty feet of water. Because it uses two AA-size cells, it's a lot more compact than the D-cell jobbies you use at home. I used to carry spare batteries for it, but I found that the batteries lasted longer in that flashlight (even

The waterproof-type flashlight often sold in marine and outdoor-equipment shops is the best type to keep in your emergency tool kit.

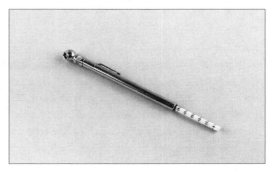

For an emergency tool kit, make sure you use a sliding-scale type tire-pressure gauge. It is more compact than the dial type.

This is the best wrench set I've ever found for an emergency tool kit. Its important features are a clamp system to keep the entire set together and the fact that they are all open-end wrenches.

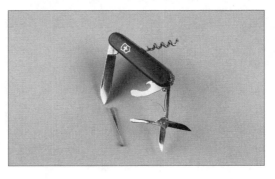

A good-quality Swiss Army knife may be the most useful emergency tool you'll ever have.

when it was being used) than they did laying in a saddlebag in their original packaging!

I've sung the praises of that wrench set already. I did not mention, however, that they are all open-end wrenches. With open-end wrenches you (usually) get two wrenches for the price of one. At least, you get two sizes for the price of one. "Price" here meaning "space taken up." You get the same effect with box-end wrenches, but open-ends are more useful. There are many circumstances when it is difficult or impossible to get a box wrench in there where you need it.

The six-inch crescent wrench is a companion for the open-end wrenches. Whenever I need two wrenches of the same size, one is an open-end and the other is the crescent. The crescent wrench also substitutes for a whole set of metric wrenches and anything smaller than the smallest (5/16-inch) open-end.

The eight-inch crescent wrench is only in there because the six-inch won't open up enough to fit my spark plug wrench. The spark plug wrench was carefully selected out of the used tool bin in a pawn shop. The thing that made it stand out was that it was designed to be turned with an ordinary wrench as well as the usual 3/8-inch ratchet drive. Since I didn't want to carry around a socket set . . .

The four-inch vise grips are about the smallest vise grips I've ever seen. The same goes for the five-inch locking pliers. Yet, they'll do most of the jobs they might be asked to do by the side of the road.

The tire gauge is of the sliding scale rather than the dial type because it is much more compact. The 0-50 psi range is correct for motorcycle tires and air shocks.

I added the 10-mm combination wrench when I got tired of trying to shove that crescent wrench in around battery terminals. The open-end side is much more compact than the crescent wrench's adjustable jaws.

There are only three or four sizes of Allen wrench that you need on any given bike. The problem is knowing which three or four to carry. I've got a whole range dumped into a Ziplock bag. Now, when I need an Allen wrench, I can say, "I know I've got the thing, but which one is it?"

The extension handle is merely an eight-inch section of chromed steel handlebar stock from an old Triumph. It's actually 11/16-inch I.D., but who's checking? I just use it when I need extra leverage on an Allen wrench. It sometimes comes in handy as a light hammer, too.

The Phillips-head and slot-head screwdrivers are medium sized and medium length. I just took the screwdrivers I found myself using the most and stuck them into the emergency tool kit. Then I went out and bought replacements to put in my main toolbox.

The five-inch long-nosed pliers are the smallest I could purchase without giggling. They are for grabbing wires and pulling them out to where I can get at them with my fingers.

The wire strippers are actually on probation. If I don't start using them more, I'm going to

It's a good idea to keep emergency tools for electrical work in a separate, water-tight pouch. Most tools made especially for electrical work do not react well to dampness.

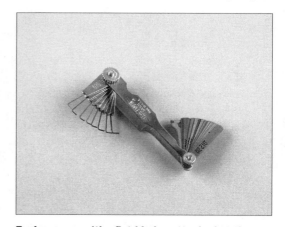

Feeler gauges (the flat blades attached at the lower right) are extremely versatile in experienced hands, but difficult for the uninitiated to use accurately. Wire gauges (the L-shaped wires attached at the upper right) are the simplest to use to accurately set spark-plug gaps.

drop them out of the emergency tool kit. They are only useful when a wire actually breaks, which isn't that common an occurrence. There's nothing you can do with wire strippers that you can't do with a sharp knife. Since I always carry the latter, I'm wondering why I have the former in my emergency tool kit.

Black tape is another story. If anything electrical goes wrong, you'll need black electrical tape to finish the repair. It also has a host of non-electrical uses, from temporarily holding down wires and cables that start flapping in the wind to mending rain gear.

Feeler gauges have only one job to do in an emergency tool kit: resetting breaker-point gaps. If you've got breaker points, some day you'll find yourself resetting the gap by the side of the road.

Keep your feeler gauges greasy! They are made of highly tempered spring steel, chosen for its great dimensional stability, not its lousy corrosion resistance. Keep 'em dirty and greasy and keep 'em in a plastic bag. The day your feeler gauges get degreased is the day they turn to rust. Once they rust, you have to throw them away because their actual thickness no longer bears any relation to what's marked on them. If they're rusty they're thicker. If you then clean them, they'll be too thin.

I keep Teflon thread-seal tape around because I use it for any threaded joint that I expect to hold a liquid—*except motor oil.* So, if I have to play around with, say, a gas-tank petcock or a carburetor drain, I have the Teflon tape to reseal the joint to my satisfaction.

Never, ever, ever use Teflon tape on any threaded joint in your oil system. Unless applied absolutely perfectly, Teflon tape is prone to shedding strings and globs of Teflon into the liquid. You won't know anything went wrong until you discover that what destroyed your motor was a little glob of Teflon plugging up an oil passage.

Scotch-Brite, which is a plastic version of the venerable steel wool, is great stuff for cleaning up corroded terminals and wiring. It's especially good because, being plastic, it doesn't get ruined by moisture. A little patch of Scotch-Brite half an inch wide and an inch long should take care of your emergency sanding needs for years.

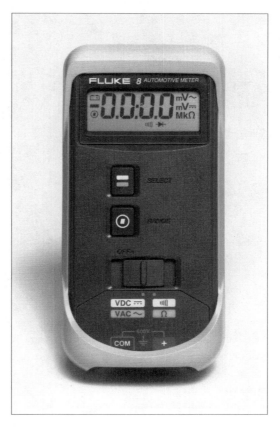

Several companies make compact digital multimeters that fit well into a motorcycle emergency tool kit. *Photo courtesy Fluke Corporation, Everett, Washington*

Be careful of thread-locking compound. There is light duty stuff that barely holds anything, medium strength stuff, and you'll-never-get-it-apart-again stuff. I know bikers who would rather carry around extra hardware to replace the stuff that falls off than use thread-locking compound. I keep some medium-strength stuff in my emergency tool kit so that I can use it if, say, a lock washer rolls into a storm drain. I don't want the fastener shaking loose before I get a replacement.

Tie wraps are to mechanical and electrical work what bungie cords are to packing. You can do without them, but life isn't quite so nice. If you don't keep them in your emergency tool kit, you'll end up with a lot of wires and cables black-taped to your frame.

That second pouch, as I mentioned before, is for stuff that really can't stand moisture. I actually started it when I acquired that really nice little Fluke Model 12 hand-held digital multimeter. (I'll talk more about digital multimeters and test leads and test probe tips later on.) When I got my hands on that neat little unit, it looked at me and

The ultimate in small-sized multimeters is usually called "credit-card size." They are the height and width of a credit card, but much, much thicker. *Photo courtesy Wavetek Corporation, San Diego, California.*

said, "Look how compact and rugged I am! I'd go great in your emergency tool kit!"

If you know how to use a multimeter, get one. Do not, however, carry an *analog* multimeter (see detailed description in a later chapter) in your emergency tool kit. It sure won't make it to Sturgis and back! In fact, I'd be surprised if it worked properly after riding 200 miles. Digital versions are inherently more rugged.

Over the three years I've had that multimeter, it's been the tool I've yanked out most often. That is because the most complicated part of most bikes is the wiring system. It's also the easiest to damage and the part most people (me included) give the least attention to. It will give you absolutely no trouble most of the time, but once it gets funky, you can't find the problem without a multimeter.

The test leads and test probes are necessary to hook the multimeter to the wiring. The six-foot test wire isn't necessary, but it comes in handy once in a while. I use it mainly to repolarize generators in old-style charging systems.

I started this second pouch mainly to carry the digital multimeter. Although the meter is rugged, its plastic face would still get scratched up pretty

badly after a short time crammed into a leather tool pouch with wrenches, screwdrivers, and other sharp, pointy things. It's much better to keep it separate. Of course, you want to keep the test leads and probe tips with the meter.

The spare parts that live in the second pouch are items that aren't too big, and could put you dead in the water if needed and not available.

I always try to keep a repair manual for each bike on the bike. It is usually not the first thing you reach for in an emergency situation, but many times it's the fourth or fifth thing. It can be buried fairly deeply in your saddlebag because if you've dug deeply enough into a problem to need it, you won't mind unpacking to get at it.

The key ring flashlight is just nice to have around. I use it a lot for just checking something quickly without having to dig the regular flashlight out of the tool pouch.

A good quality Swiss Army knife is the most useful single tool you'll ever have. If you've ever carried one, you know what I mean. If not, invest in one, put up the extra bread for its belt holster and wear it around for a while. After about a week, you'll know why you see so many dorks like me walking around with that junk on their belts. Did you think it was, like, a fashion statement?

This, then, is my emergency tool kit (in two pouches). It contains most of the tools that I've needed for most emergency situations. It will take care of just about any minor problem and get you far along in diagnosing major ones. If you duplicate it for your bike, I think you'll find that you don't make any major additions or deletions for quite a while.

You should, however, consider augmenting your emergency tool kit for special trips. For example, if I'm headed off for more than two or three days, I'll typically throw in a 3/8-inch socket set.

Tools for Regular Maintenance

How do you define "regular maintenance?"

Certainly oil changes come under the heading of regular maintenance, and a full-blown major engine overhaul does not. I have a Sportster that went through a period where it needed three top-end jobs in as many thousand miles, so I was beginning to think of removing and replacing heads as regular maintenance. It shouldn't be, however. But, maybe checking valve adjustments should be.

Let's start with what you need to look at often enough to make it a regular thing.

I hope you realize that you have to have a regular Motorcycle Maintenance Day. You should set aside two or three hours on one particular day of the week for a weekly once-over on your bike. If you have more than one bike in service, you should plan more time. But, start at the same time on the same day every week.

You've heard me mention Guy Petagna a few times in this tome. For him, Saturday is Motorcycle Maintenance Day. He goes out first thing every Saturday morning and does his weekly maintenance. If he has a special job to do (such as replacing a drive chain), he segues into it as soon as he's done with the regular motorcycle maintenance chores. And, if he finds a problem while doing the regular maintenance, he still has all day to get up to his armpits in it. Guy says, "Saturday is for working on bikes. Sunday is for riding."

Personally, I prefer to make Wednesday my Motorcycle Maintenance Day. I've found that during riding season, most Saturdays are taken up by one run or another. In fact, there are usually more runs than I can make. Nobody seems to schedule runs on Wednesday, so my maintenance schedule doesn't get disturbed very often.

You have to plan your own Motorcycle Maintenance Day. Try to find a time when you seldom have to do anything else (like work). The trick is to get to it every single week.

Motorcycle Maintenance Day is for all the niddly stuff that takes two seconds, but you never do because you put it off—because it only takes two seconds and you can do it later—and then you forget it. Table 10.1 is a fairly comprehensive list, but it won't exactly fit your bike or your situation.

Table 10.1   Jobs for Motorcycle Maintenance Day

- Check engine oil level and condition
- Check in-line fuel filter for dirt
- Check fuel lines for leaks and seepage
- Inspect engine for oil seepage and leaks
- Check battery liquid level
- Check battery charge condition
- Check lights for proper operation
  Head light(s)
  Directional signals
  Tail light
  Brake light
  Instrument lights
- Check all control cables for condition and lubrication
  Clutch
  Brakes
  Speedometer
  Tachometer
- Check clutch adjustment
- Check mechanical brake adjustments

- Check brake pads and rotors on disk brakes
- Check hydraulic brake lines for seepage
- Check master cylinders for fluid level and condition
- Lubricate kickstand mechanism
- Wiggle all chassis components to check for loose fasteners
  Fenders
  Tanks
  Sissy rails
  Dash panels
  Windshields or fairings
  Anything else you can find to wiggle!
- Check drive chain tightness and condition
- Adjust drive chain
- Lubricate drive chain
- Check tire wear

For example, the drive belt on a brand new Harley shouldn't give you a lick of trouble for a long, long time. So, why should you bother scrunching down to peer at it every week. It's a once-every-5,000-miles kind of thing.

On the other hand, you might want to check valve clearances once a week for the first month after having a valve job. Those clearances change as the valves re-seat. Actually, after a fresh valve job, you should check clearances *every day* until the valves seat. Then make it part of weekly maintenance for the next month or so. Eventually, you'll get bored because they'll stop changing. Then you can go back to the manufacturer's recommended schedule.

OK, I've convinced you to schedule a weekly maintenance day, in case you needed convincing. What tools do you need to do it? Let's go down the list.

REGULAR SERVICE INTERVALS

SUGGESTED OPERATIONS FOLLOWING THE INITIAL BREAK-IN PERIOD

Regular Service Interval	Index No.	Grease	Index No.	Oil	Index No.	Service
300 Miles			7	Rear Chain (Manual) (1977 & later)		
Every 1000 miles	31	Rear brake foot lever shaft	7	Rear chain (with oiler) (1976 & earlier)		Inspect tires
	16	Kick starter shaft	21	Clutch hand lever		Check spokes
	19	Rear brake lever at drum	1	Brake hand lever		Check oil lines and brake system for leaks
	11	Speedometer drive	22	Clutch control cable	4	Air cleaner
	12	Circuit breaker cam-shaft	37	Rear brake cable	25	Battery
			28	Throttle control cable	7	Rear chain adjustment
			17	Rear brake rod clevis	36	Gasoline valve, lines and fittings
						Check fastener tightness
					15	Clutch adjustment
					2,17	Brake adjustment
					30	Front chain adjustment
Every 2000 miles	8	Front brake shaft	9	Front brake cable clevis	13	Tappet adjustment
	31	Rear brake crossover shaft (1974 & earlier)	2	Front brake cable	5	Oil filter
	15	Clutch release worm (1970)	26	Seat post (saddle only)		Check carburetor controls
	14	Foot shift lever			20	Rear chain oiler (1976 & earlier)
	6	Seat bar roller and bolt			12	Circuit breaker points
	32	Rear wheel hub			35	Check brake fluid
	31	Foot shift crossover shaft (1975-76)			24	Inspect, clean and gap spark plugs
						Check fastener tightness
Every 5000 miles or 1 year (whichever comes first)	3	Throttle control spiral			10	Check front and rear fork bearing adjustment
	34	Speedometer and tachometer cables			18	Replace:
					24	Spark plugs
					5	Oil filter element
						Inspect tires
					12	Time ignition
						Clean gas tank strainer
					29	Check generator brushes
					33	Check shock rubber bushings
					23	Change front fork oil (1973 & later)
						Change brake fluid
Every 10,000 miles	18	Repack rear fork pivot bearings				
	27	Repack wheel bearings				
Weekly						Check tires
						Check battery

Scheduled maintenance chart.

Check the Oil Level

Well, you don't need much to check the oil level and condition except your fingers (to pull out the dipstick) and your eyes (to look at it), right? Well, not quite. You see, to get an accurate reading, you need to have the bike standing upright, not leaned over on the kickstand. If your bike doesn't have a center stand, you can pull it upright and lean it against your knee. Or, you can get some poor soul who happens to be standing around to hold it for you.

Or—and this is what I recommend—you can get a big block of wood to put under the sidestand. Every bike I've ever handled for any reason has been stable when propped up to within a few degrees of straight up and down. They're supposed to be! You can use that fact to prop up the sidestand on a big block of wood while you check your oil.

Now, if that block of wood were only useful for checking your oil, I wouldn't even know about it, never mind recommend it. The fact is that almost everything you do on Motorcycle Maintenance Day will go faster and easier if you prop the bike up vertically.

If you don't prop it up, all the stuff you want to look at and do on the left side of the bike will be tucked in under the overhang of the leaned-over bike. You won't see half of what you want to see. The seat will be in your face every time you try to touch something. And, your knees will hate you!

To check your oil, you'll also need a wad of paper towels or a rag to wipe the dipstick with and to clean up the inevitable drip(s). You could wipe it on your jeans, but that's disgusting.

Check the Battery Liquid Level

As you go down the list, you won't need any additional tools until you get to the battery. To do anything to the battery, you have to disconnect it.

Forget that crap about unscrewing the caps on the battery cells and looking in. That may work on a car battery, but it doesn't on a bike. The holes are so small that if you can see the top of the liquid, it just means you're looking at a bubble caught in that cell's filler cap.

To actually determine the fluid level in the battery cells, you have to pull the battery out of

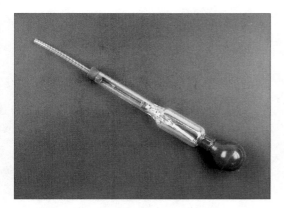

Hydrometers (also known more simply as "battery testers") are fairly easy to come by in a convenient motorcycle size.

SERVICE INTERVAL ENGINE AND TRANSMISSION

	300 Miles	1000 Miles	2000 Miles	5000 Miles or 1 Year	Spring and Fall
Engine Oil	Check	Check	Change		Change
Transmission Oil		Check	Change	Change	

LUBRICANTS TO USE

Use proper grade of oil for the lowest temperature expected before next oil change period as follows:

USE Harley-Davidson Oil	Use Grade	Air Temperature (Cold Engine Starting Conditions)
Medium Heavy	75	Above 40°F
Special Light	58	Below 40°F
Regular Heavy	105	Severe operating condition at high air temperatures above 90°F

HARLEY-DAVIDSON GREASE-ALL GREASE

Use for all bearings on motorcycles.

HARLEY-DAVISON CHAIN GREASE, CHAIN SAVER AND CHAIN SPRAY

Designed especially as chain lubricant. Penetrates inner bearings for long chain life.

GASOLINE

Use a good quality leaded "premium grade" gasoline (94 pump octane or higher). "Pump octane" is the octane number usually shown on the pump.

If leaded premium is not available, unleaded premium grade gasoline (94 pump octane or higher) is satisfactory, provided there is an occasional fill (every 3 or 4 tankfuls) with leaded premium.

Leaded or unleaded regular grade gasoline (lower than 94 pump octane) is not recommended.

BRAKE FLUID

Use D.O.T. 5 brake fluid only.

Engine and transmission oil service requirements chart.

the bike. Bikes vary widely in the way the battery is mounted and how you go about getting it out. You'll just have to dig in and find out what you need to do to remove it.

Once you've got the battery enclosure apart, you need a 10-mm open-end wrench. This is the opposite situation to getting at the battery. Whereas the battery enclosure on just about every model of bike is different, all motorcycle batteries have terminals that you disconnect using a 10-mm open-end wrench. If you don't have a 10-mm open-end, you can usually get the things loose with a small adjustable wrench—but it's awkward at best. Better to get a 10-mm and throw it in your emergency kit, if it doesn't already have one.

By the way, in case nobody ever told you: disconnect the ground terminal first. At some part of the wrench stroke you will touch some part of the wrench to the frame. It happens every time.

When you're disconnecting the ground lead, the business end of the wrench is grounded as well, so there's no problem. You can whack that frame all you want. After the ground terminal is disconnected, you can put that wrench on the hot terminal and whack the other end on the frame all you want, too.

But—if you touch the frame while loosening the hot lead *before* disconnecting the ground, you're gonna get a surprise! At best, you'll get a giant, economy sized *bzzzattt!* At worst, you can weld the ol' wrench between the hot terminal and frame. That leads pretty much instantaneously to

a battery explosion, with ensuing damage from acid pouring down on your expensive battery enclosure and anything else that happens to be located next to or below the battery box. I've seen it happen. It's not a pretty sight. About the only thing left afterwards is the 10-mm wrench that started it all.

OK, now you have the battery loose. Maybe you'll have to unhook a strap to pull the battery out to set it on your workbench.

The next step is to check the liquid level in the cells. Set the battery near the front of the bench and lay the drop light behind it.

Oops! You need to top off at least one of the cells. So, you need some distilled water. Actually, what you need is deionized water. Nowadays they get the minerals out by reverse osmosis rather than distillation. Whatever. You need the stuff and you need to get the stuff out of the bottle and into the battery.

Go get a clean jelly glass. You can use an old peanut butter or mayonnaise jar, but something with, say, Tweety and Sylvester on it has a lot more class. The main thing is that it's gotta be clean, have a capacity of four to eight fluid ounces and be made of clear glass.

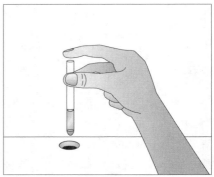

In a pinch, you can refill a battery using a plastic cup and a straw.

What you're going to do with your jelly jar is to decant some deionized water from the gallon jug you bought at the store. For you non-chemists (and non-wine connoisseurs), decanting means you're gonna pour some deionized water into the glass. Then you're going to use some kind of syringe to transfer the water from the glass to the battery.

Why am I putting you through all this? Because you can't just pour from the jug into the battery—even if you use a funnel. You can't control it well enough. If you try it, you're gonna overflow the cell, which will ruin the battery and get acid all over your bench.

You've gotta use a syringe. But, if you dip the syringe into the water, then into the battery, then go back to the container for more water, you're gonna get battery gook into the water. Now, you may not mind battery gook in your cache of deionized water, but I do. Besides, once it's got battery gook in it, it's no longer deionized!

So, you pour deionized water into your jelly glass, then use a syringe to transfer the water into the battery, then flush the excess water down the toilet or into the sink.

Actually, you already have a syringe. It's your battery tester. You need a battery tester for the next step.

Check Battery Charge Condition

To check the battery's level of charge don't use one of those huge automotive battery testers you see in service stations. Go to a hardware store or motorcycle shop and get one of the little itty-bitty ones that hold about a half ounce of fluid and have the four little floating balls. The prob-lem with the big battery testers (they're called "hydrometers," by the way) is that if you can get the inlet tube stuffed down through the battery filler cap, the tester needs so much liquid to make a test that it'll suck your battery dry and still give you a bogus reading.

Besides, the little itty-bitty battery tester is just big enough to use as a syringe to transfer deionized water from your jelly jar into the battery.

Check Lights

The next thing on the Motorcycle Maintenance Day list is "Check the lights for proper operation." You don't need any tools for this, or for the next few items, either.

Check Master Cylinder for Fluid Level and Condition

You'll probably need a screwdriver from your basic tool kit to open the cover(s) on your master cylinder(s).

Lubricate Kickstand

You need two things to lubricate your kickstand mechanism: lubricant and something to apply it with. I've gotten good results using white lith-ium grease from a spray can. The stuff is essen-tially liquid as it squirts out of the tube that comes with the spray can, so it flows right in be-tween the moving parts. Then it thickens up to its proper greasy consistency.

Check for Loose Fasteners on Chassis

You don't need any tools to wiggle all the chassis components. You will, of course, need appropriate tools to tighten any that you find are loose. What you'll need depends on what's loose. All you should need, however, is in your basic tool kit.

Check Drive Chain

Now you get to have a close encounter with your drive chain. It is the ugliest, dirtiest, most disgusting job of the whole lot because you have to get down and dirty with the ugliest, dirtiest, most disgusting part of the bike. If your drive chain isn't ugly, dirty, and disgusting, you haven't lubricated it enough.

The first thing you have to do is reach down to grab your drive chain and wiggle it up and down to see how tight it is. I've found that a half-inch open-end wrench just fits across the chain so you can wiggle it without actually having to put your beloved fingers on it. You metric types can use a 12-mm wrench.

You also have to roll the chain around to try and find the tightest spot. That's where you want to do your adjustment. So, you'll need a long, flat area to roll the bike along.

Alternately, you can jack the rear end up to do the whole job in one spot. Or, put it up on the center stand if you have one. Instead of moving the bike along, you just spin the rear wheel in the air.

If you jack the bike up, be careful not to overtighten the chain. The chains on most bikes tighten as the load (weight) on the bike increases. That's why bike manufacturers recommend sitting on the bike or getting an accomplice to sit on the bike behind you, and rolling the chain around to the tightest spot to adjust the chain. Unfortunately, that's not too practical. I tried it.

Imagine sitting on the bike with the kickstand up (you have to put your weight on it because that's the whole point of the exercise), plus the weight of somebody sitting on the back, the saddlebags filled with junk to add more weight, then reaching down with your half-inch wrench to wiggle the center of the chain—all this without losing your balance and toppling the whole mess. Then you have to roll the bike a couple of inches and try it again. You'll have to roll and check and roll and check eight or ten times to test the whole chain. Then, you have to remember

Table 10.2
Additional Tools for Motorcycle Maintenance Day

OIL CHANGE
- Wooden block for propping up kickstand
- Paper towels

BATTERY CHECK
- 10-mm open-end wrench
- Drop light
- Distilled/deionized water
- Clear glass jar
- Battery tester (hydrometer)

GENERAL EXTERNAL LUBRICATION
- Spray can of white lithium grease

DRIVE CHAIN CARE
- Drive chain lubricant
- Wrenches to loosen rear axle
- Wrench to loosen chain-tensioner locknuts
- Shop rags

Several adjustments require you to have two identical open-ended wrenches.

how tight it was each time to compare the tightness *this* time with the tightness all the other times. I've gotta tell you, it doesn't work for me. I run the chain as loose as I can get away with to give me a big margin for error.

So what if you overtighten the chain? It's just gonna loosen up again, right?

Well, maybe. Or, what could happen to you is what happened to me last summer. I got tired of folks telling me that my chain was loose and tightened it to max specifications. Then I loaded it up and headed down a bumpy section of interstate at 70 mph.

The next day I was replacing a rear wheel bearing.

Adjust Drive Chain

Assuming that your chain is too loose, you need to adjust it. That requires more tools. You're gonna need a huge wrench to loosen the axle nut. Just how big depends on your bike. There's a good chance that you won't have one big enough in your basic tool kit, so go out to your bike on Tuesday to measure the axle nut so you'll know how big a wrench to buy before Wednesday.

You'll also need two identical open-end wrenches to actually do the adjusting. One can come from your basic tool kit, but you have to go out and get a second one from somewhere. In a pinch, you can probably get away with an open-end and the crescent wrench from your basic tool kit, but, like using a crescent wrench to disconnect a battery terminal, it's a pain.

These identical wrenches vary somewhat in size from bike to bike. My old Honda 360 needed two 10-mm wrenches. I sorta remember a Honda 400 needed something bigger (I think it was 11- or 12-mm). Every Harley I've worked on used a pair of 1/2-inch jobbies. Anyway, you need one to loosen, tighten, or hold the locknut while working the adjusting nut with the other.

Lubricate Drive Chain

We're getting down to the end of the Motorcycle Maintenance Day list. It's time to lubricate the drive chain. For that you need a spray can of chain lube and a rag.

Check Tire Wear

You don't need a dang thing to check the tire wear except your eyes and some common sense.

Common sense is a very useful tool, so I'll talk about it a little here.

Common sense with regard to tire wear goes like this:

Think of your tires as your motorcycle's feet.

Think of the tire tread as the shoes on your motorcycle's feet.

Imagine what it would feel like to run at top speed down that superslab in your bare feet. Then, imagine stopping fast 'cause that moron in the Pinto in front of you slammed on his brakes—you don't want to rear end a Pinto! Think about doing it with odd bits of gravel, broken glass, sheet metal screws, and so forth on the pavement.

Makes you want to put on some thick-soled shoes, doesn't it! When your bike has nice, thick tread, it's running on nice, thick-soled shoes. When the tread disappears from the center of the tire, your bike is running barefoot. When cord starts to show, it's like road rash on your feet.

So, what tools have we added to our basic tool kit just to get through Motorcycle Maintenance Day?

Well, we've got a block of wood and some paper towels to make checking the oil a more pleasant experience. You've also got a 10-mm wrench to disconnect the battery terminals and a battery tester that doubles as a syringe to fill dry cells. Don't forget the jelly glass or, of course, the jug of deionized water. I don't know if you want to count the workbench and drop light for viewing the liquid level in the cells, but you'll feel pretty foolish holding the battery up to the sun if you don't have them! Next up is a spray can of white lithium grease for the kickstand and, incidentally, anything else (like, maybe, the throttle return spring on your carburetor) that might need a quick spritz to keep it slick. You'll need a huge wrench to loosen your rear axle nut and a pair of smaller wrenches to adjust the chain tension. Maybe you'll want a jack to lift the rear wheel while playing with your drive chain. You'll definitely need a can of chain lube. Table 10.2 gives a handy list of Motorcycle Maintenance Day tools.

Finally, you'll get to use that most useful of all tools: common sense.

Tools for Scheduled Maintenance

When I planned this book, I intended to have one chapter called "Tools for Regular Maintenance." I figured it would be about six pages long and would start with Motorcycle Maintenance Day, then slide on into oil changes and suchlike scheduled maintenance things. When Motorcycle Maintenance Day alone grew to about ten pages with no sign of stopping, however, I decided we needed a section break. So, I arbitrarily divided between Regular Maintenance (that which you do on Motorcycle Maintenance Day) and Scheduled Maintenance (which is what you do based on mileage per the scheduled maintenance chart in your bike's owner's manual).

This division isn't entirely arbitrary, however. Motorcycle Maintenance Day includes all the stuff that every scooter pilot has to watch constantly just to keep moving down the road. Scheduled maintenance consists of tasks that don't come up that often and which you can, without feeling an ounce of guilt, put in the hands of your local (hopefully reputable) dealer.

To find out what your scoot needs for scheduled maintenance, all you have to do is consult your owner's manual. The tasks are more or less the same from bike to bike, but the intervals can vary widely.

For example, scuttlebutt has it that when Harley-Davidson engineers developed the Evolution engine, they realized that the thing would go quite happily for 10,000 miles before you'd need to change the oil. But, so the story goes, they figured die-hard Harley owners would get nosebleeds just thinking about 10,000 miles between oil changes. So, on the theory that you can never change your oil too much, they recommended replacing it every 5,000 miles.

Well, I always started getting that crawly feeling up and down my spine when the oil in my Evo got up around 2,500 miles old, so I changed it twice as often as recommended. I guess the Harley engineers were right.

On the other hand, my iron-head Sportster (recommended oil change interval of 2,000 miles) got fresh oil every 500 to 1,000 miles. Why? Because I ride every day through 115 degree summertime heat and don't consider anything under 100 miles to be a trip. That's not

To change the oil neatly in most Harleys you need to fabricate a channel to lead the used oil from the drain plug away from the bike and over to the catch pan.

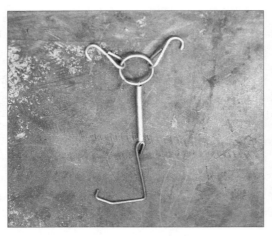

The advanced, high-tech version of a pushrod keeper-upper consists of three pieces of coathanger wire, a couple of old carburetor springs and a key ring.

Specialized equipment can be as simple as four clothespins to hold up external pushrod covers.

what an iron-head Sportster was designed to do. When you beat on a bike, you have to give it a little extra attention.

OK. Let's look at the owner's manual.

What? You don't have an owner's manual? Go to the nearest XYZ Bike Company authorized dealer and get yourself one. Then get a service manual. Then get a repair manual. Get every manual you can and use them as a cross check for each other because *not one of them tells you everything you need to know.*

I've been able to identify three levels of manuals: owner's, repair, and service. The lowest level is the owner's manual. That's the one the dealer hands you when you buy a new bike. It gives you a picture of the bike, and tells you where the controls are and how to operate them. It also includes advice on such things as what oil to use and when to bring it in for scheduled maintenance. I usually find that the most useful thing in the owner's manual is the wiring diagram.

Repair manuals are the next level up. They cover most of the procedures that most amateur mechanics get into. However, they do leave a lot out. At some point (chosen by the author), they decide that some job is just too difficult for poor little you, and tell you to call in a professional. Of course, that's not a bad thing to do. I've done exactly the same thing all through this book. But, different authors may choose different things to leave out. That's why you want more than one

repair manual. One author may cover something another one left out and *vice versa*. If you consult several such sources and they all leave a particular procedure out, maybe you should take that as a hint. Repair manuals may be authored by the bike manufacturer or by independents.

The last line of defense (or offense, depending on your emotional state) is the service manual. They are generally written by the manufacturer and theoretically provide everything a professional bike mechanic needs to know about that model. In reality, they don't answer every question you could possibly ask or cover every situation you could possibly get into. They're just intentionally a whole lot more complete. They especially provide a lot more detailed specifications.

For now, let's drag out the old, venerable, dog-eared, grease-stained "Harley-Davidson Service Manual—Sportster XL/XLH/XLCH/XLT-1000—1970 to 1978," and see what it has for a scheduled maintenance chart. I've reproduced it in the previous chapter, along with its sister chart, which gives the engine and transmission oil service requirements.

Basically, the entries for 300 and 1,000 miles approximate my list for Motorcycle Maintenance Day. There's nothing here that will require any tools beyond what I've talked about already with the possible exception of a grease gun to get grease into some of those fittings.

At 2,000 miles, you get into some things that take some specialized equipment.

"Specialized equipment," he says! The specialized equipment it takes to adjust Harley tappets consists of four clothespins. Harley pushrods run on the outside of the motor through those nice, pretty half-inch chrome tubes. The tubes telescope so you can get in at the pushrods. As soon as you let go of the tube to touch the tappet adjustment (which requires two wrenches and, hence, two hands), the tube falls down to cover the tappet. You clip a clothespin onto the pushrod to hold the tube up while you adjust the tappet. Can you do it without the clothespin? Yes. Is it a pain in the butt? Definitely!

Shown in the photo is a high-tech pushrod tube keeper-upper. You make it yourself from three pieces of coathanger wire, a couple of old carburetor springs, and a key ring. Make two of them and you can just hang all four pushrod tubes at once and forget about them until the job is done.

The other day, I had a pushrod loosen up on me. I had just adjusted the valves on this motor (yes, another iron-head Sportster motor; I just can't seem to stop building those things!) and apparently didn't tighten the locknut on one tappet properly.

Oh, no! I feel another digression coming on!

The moral of this digression is: Don't screw around with anything you don't have to. If it's ok, leave it alone.

I had messed around with the valves on that motor because the heads had been completely rebuilt with new valves. New valves "seat" themselves. Basically, they nestle down into their new valve seats, changing the valve clearances. No, to be more accurate, they *pound* their way into the valve seats! Anyway, the net effect is that the pushrods get tighter. The plan is to leave 'em a touch loose at first. Slightly loose may make them a little noisy, but won't hurt anything. If they get over tight while seating, however, you can burn one of those nice new valves and have to start all over again. After a hundred miles or so, you go in and recheck the adjustment. Rather than just rechecking, I had *assumed* (there's that bad word again) that the valves would need adjustment and loosened the locknuts. About fif-

teen miles later, the motor started making a gawdawful racket. Happily, it happened just as I got to the Western Wear store I was stopping at anyway, so I just pulled in and let the motor cool off for a while. When my wife was shopped out I checked the tappet adjustments. That's when I found that I'd failed to properly tighten one of the locknuts. If I'd just checked the adjustment (which doesn't require loosening locknuts), I would have saved myself:

1. A good scare;

2. An hour or so of sitting around; and

3. The danger of bending a pushrod because, when a valve works loose like that, it *really* works loose—to the point where the pushrod can slip out of place.

Don't screw around with something thinking "Well, it can't hurt." It can hurt. The reason it can hurt is because *everybody makes mistakes.* Furthermore, you never know when you're going to make a mistake. Finally, the only way to avoid making a mistake is *don't screw around with it.*

That's the reason for the "Used Car Rule": If it works, don't fix it.

The good part of this little adventure, and the reason I'm bringing this up at this particular time, is that I found another quick-and-dirty pushrod tube keeper-upper. Actually, I didn't come up with it, a cowboy who was loading hay out back came up with the idea.

While I was busy waiting for the motor to cool, I got into a conversation with this cowboy. During that conversation, I mentioned the problem of holding up the pushrod tubes while adjusting the valves. It was kind of on my mind because I don't keep clothespins in my emergency tool kit.

When I started fiddling with the pushrods, the cowboy saw what a pain (literally, because the motor wasn't all that cool) it was to do without them. He wandered off and came back a few minutes later carrying a piece of rawhide about eight inches long with a bent up paper clip tied to the end.

"Will this work?" he asked.

"You bet," I said.

I hooked the paper clip on the bottom end of the pushrod tube. The rawhide strip was long enough so it would reach any one of several convenient places to tie off the top end. The rig worked perfectly to hold the tube up while I readjusted the valve (remembering to tighten the locknut). If you're in a similar fix, you could use a piece of wire or string to do the same job. The six-foot test wire with alligator-clip ends in your emergency tool kit would probably work, too.

That's for adjusting tappets on a Harley. You folks who have overhead cams do the valve adjustment with a set of feeler gauges.

Feeler gauges are strips of tool steel whose (extremely accurate) thicknesses vary from a couple of thousandths to, say, 25 thousandths of an inch (or roughly equivalent metric dimensions). You can't get much under two thousandths because the metal would be so thin it would crumple in use. If you get much thicker than a few tens of thousandths, you're getting into the world of gauge blocks. You wouldn't need 'em around a motorcycle anyway. By combining strips (each one is individually called a "feeler gauge"), you can accurately measure clearances up to about 45 thousandths. The valve clearance on that Honda 360 I mentioned earlier, for example, was 0.003 inch.

You Harley people won't get away without feeler gauges, though. That's what you use to gap the spark plugs unless you run out and get a

spark plug gap gauge designed specifically for the job.

Actually, the recommended tool for checking spark plug gaps is a round-wire gauge, not a feeler gauge. The reason is that it's a lot harder to screw up the measurement when using a wire gauge. Feeler gauges have to go in *exactly* flat and *exactly* straight or you'll measure nothing remotely like the gap that's actually there. There's also an art to stacking the feeler gauges to get an accurate reading as well.

You can do a lot more with feeler gauges if you really know how to use them, but they're a lot harder to use. If you're an experienced machinist, go ahead and use 'em. If not, get the wire kind at the auto parts store.

At 2,000 miles you have to change the engine oil, too. That takes more specialized equipment. Specifically, you need a pan to catch the oil. Again, you have choices. At your local auto parts store, you'll find those neat little jobbies that look like a plastic jerry can that was run over by a truck. They lay over on one side and the top "side" is dish-shaped with a plug hole in the middle. You unplug the hole and shove the thing under the bike's drain plug. Then, when you open the drain plug, the used oil pours down into the dish-shape and runs down through the plug hole. When all the oil has drained out of the bike and into the "jerry can," you plug the plug hole and stand the container in a corner until the next time you need it. The system combines an oil pan, a funnel, and a used-oil storage tank into one container. Very neat!

Guess what? I don't use anything that fancy. By now, you shouldn't be surprised.

I like to drain oil into a pan that is actually a vegetable crisper tray scrounged from a '50s era refrigerator. It's low enough to fit under most bikes and has enough capacity to hold all the oil from a big-block V8. That nice, smooth, easy-to-clean porcelain surface is, well, easy to clean. For bikes that are too low and for draining Harley primary chain cases, I have a second one that came from the meat-keeper drawer in an apartment-sized refrigerator.

If your bike has an external oil tank, you'll have a problem getting the oil from the oil-tank drain plug into the drip pan without its taking a

Temporarily store your used oil in a closed container with a wide opening. The wide opening makes it a lot easier to pour oil from the pan into the container.

little side excursion all over the frame, kickstarter, and exhaust pipes.

My friend Fred Hutt showed me the answer to that little problem. Take a piece of aluminum flashing material a foot and a half or so long and about six inches wide. Fold it along the middle to make a V-shaped channel. Nestle one end up under the oil-tank drain plug. Set the other end over the lip of the drip pan. When you uncork the drain plug, the oil will pour right down the channel into the pan.

Make sure you hold the channel securely!

Oil is heavy. If you don't hold the channel, the upper end will slip down, fall under the bike, and pour the oil exactly where you don't want it to go—onto the floor under the bike. It's not a bad idea to invest in some wire that you hook over the oil tank to hold the channel in place. Unfortunately, the exact details of how to hang the channel depend on the bike. You'll have to go over to your toolbox and get out your common sense to work them out for yourself.

OK. Now you have a drip pan full of oil. Waddayadowithit?

Temporarily, you can pour it into any closed container. That requires a closed container and a funnel. I use an old 2.5 gallon metal gas can. Don't go for anything much bigger than that because oil is much denser than gasoline and it'll get heavy very fast. You want to be able to carry this dirty, greasy, oily thing easily. Anything you use in the process of changing oil will get dirty, greasy, and oily, no matter how hard you try to keep it clean. If it turns out to be heavy to boot, you'll regret it.

If you get lucky, you'll find a container with a wide enough opening that you can pour the oil directly from the pan into the container without resorting to a funnel. Funnels tend to be top heavy when full of motor oil, and then they try to turn over, spilling the oil. There's also a problem using a funnel when your oil-storage can is nearly full. How do you know when to quit pouring? If you don't stop soon enough, you'll have a funnelful on your floor! So, try to get lucky and find a wide-mouthed container.

If you don't have a temporary used-oil storage container, you can set the drip pan aside until after you've put fresh oil into the bike. Then,

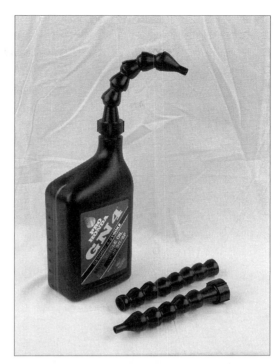

Some flexible funnels are very handy to have when trying to fill the oil in a tight spot on your bike.

pour the used oil into the containers that the fresh oil came in. That absolutely requires a funnel.

This leads us to the next bit of specialized equipment you'll need for changing oil: kitty litter. No matter how well organized, how well set up, and how careful you are while handling that oil, you'll get at least a small spill at least every other oil change. You never know when it'll happen, so be prepared every time. Soak it up with the kitty litter.

Next come shop rags. You may not get an oil spill every time, but you will get drips. I usually at least tear off a couple of paper towels and stuff 'em in some handy corner on the bike before even getting out my oil pan. I know I'll have to wipe down the drain plug, my handy-dandy oil-draining channel, and so forth by the time I'm done. It's part of the job.

Now you have two and a half gallons of oil stored up in your temporary storage container. You're going to have to do another oil change really soon. Where are you going to put the used oil from that next change? Well, you could go out and get another temporary oil-storage container,

Put the right socket in your emergency tool kit for each and every bike you own. It takes the guesswork out of being broken down.

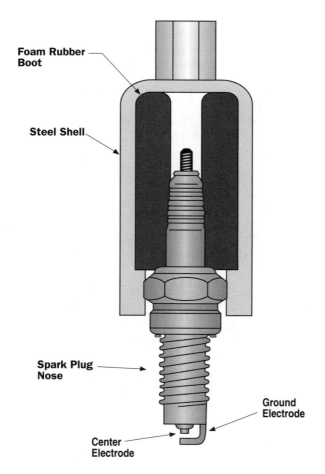

Foam Rubber Boot

Steel Shell

Spark Plug Nose

Ground Electrode

Center Electrode

A spark plug wrench has a rubber insert to cushion and hold the spark plug.

but that can't go on forever. Eventually, your motorcycle workshop will qualify under the Superfund Law as a toxic waste dump! You have to do something with that oil.

Recycle it. Check around with all the auto parts places in town. Odds are that one of them will take your used oil off your hands for a modest fee. Some will even let you dump it on them for free. If you find such a store, go out of your way to patronize them for all your parts needs! That's the kind of thing we want to encourage. In some locations, the town transfer station (what used to be called a "dump") is set up to accept and recycle used oil just as they do aluminum cans. And, there are lots of other options. Just don't drag it out into the boonies and dump it into a hole.

The other items on the 2,000-mile list that take special tools are gapping the points and cleaning and gapping the plugs. Gapping the points calls for your wire gauge or feeler gauges again. Cleaning the plugs calls for a small wire brush.

Frankly, I don't clean plugs anymore. Back in the '70s when that iron-head Sportster manual was written, everybody ran around cleaning plugs. I stopped doing it for a couple of reasons.

For one thing, plugs shouldn't get "dirty." If your engine is properly tuned (not running too lean or too rich), and it's not burning oil, your plugs should pick up a nice amber or dark brown deposit that won't short out the plug. That deposit builds up in about the first mile and reaches equilibrium. It burns off at the same rate it builds up, so the thickness stays pretty much constant mile after mile. If you're fouling plugs, you have a problem and you should fix it.

Once a plug is fouled enough to affect engine performance, there isn't a heck of a lot that you can do about it. Sometimes you can save the plug by cleaning it and sometimes you can't. Why waste your time messing around trying to save a part that costs a couple of bucks? Throw 'em out and put in a new set. Then you know what you've got.

To remove the spark plugs, you will need a spark plug wrench. A suitable spark plug wrench should have come with your socket wrench set. I say "should have come" advisedly. No doubt *a*

Ouch! Playing Hot Potato with Your Plugs

I don't care how tough you are or how long you've studied martial arts, you'll drop a hot spark plug if you pick it up with your fingers. The ol' "drop the hot spark plug" reaction is not under conscious control. It's hardwired into your arm.

The pain nerves from your fingers go up about as far as your shoulder to a little switching center. A sharp pain impulse triggers the switching center, which sends a set of signals back down your arm to contract the muscles that open your hand and pull your arm back—hard!

Milliseconds later, the switching center sends the pain signal up to your brain almost as an afterthought. It's a report that pretty much says, "By the way, this is why I made you drop the plug. Why don't you take a look and see if you've got any fingers left."

The switching center doesn't ask permission, it just drops the plug. Even if you know it's going to happen, you can't stop it. The idea that someone can, through extreme self control or in time of great stress, grab onto something dangerously hot and hold it long enough to do anything useful is pure Hollywood. ∎

---

spark plug wrench came with it, but will it fit. In the past few years (since, say, the early 1980s), manufacturers have managed to come up with a slew of "standard" spark plug sizes. Make sure the one you've got fits the bike(s) you own long before you find yourself needing it.

The diagram on the left shows the important parts of a plug wrench. It is essentially a deep socket with a soft rubber or foam insert to hold the top of the plug.

The insert has two functions. Its most critical function is to keep the plug wrench centered on the plug during that critical first quarter turn when you apply maximum torque to break the plug free. If the wrench contacts the top of the plug while you're yanking on that wrench, you're almost sure to break the plug's ceramic insulator. Insulators are hard, but brittle. They can't take any kind of shear or bending stress. They'll crack like nothing! Then, the plug is trash.

In a pinch, when you don't have a proper plug wrench, you can remove a plug with an ordinary deep socket, a box-end wrench of the proper size, or even a crescent wrench. But, you have to be extremely careful not to break that insulator.

The plug wrench's rubber insert also holds the plug as you ease it out of the cylinder head by hand. This is especially important when the engine is hot. If you try to touch a hot plug with your bare hand, you're going to burn yourself and drop the plug.

The proper procedure for pulling a plug, whether it's hot or not, is to first put the plug wrench onto the plug, then make sure it's all the way down so that the insert is holding the plug top. Then, fit a ratchet or socket handle onto the plug wrench and break the plug free. Unless the plug threads are really screwed up, the plug will then be finger tight. Remove the handle and turn the plug-wrench-and-plug out by hand. If quarters are really tight, you might need to use a socket extension to give your fingers a little more room. Then, it's just like backing a screw out with a screwdriver.

When you get the plug out, *leave it in the plug wrench!*

Don't try to take it out until you're sure it's cool. You can hold it in the plug wrench to inspect it, clean it, gap it, or anything else you want to do.

If, after fiddling with the plug, you aren't going to immediately put it back in the cylinder head, use a shop rag to pull it out of the plug wrench and lay it on the bench out of harm's way. Even if you're sure it's cool, always try to handle spark plugs with a clean rag. Dirty finger prints on the insulator can also short out a plug.

Amateur mechanics ruin more plugs through mishandling than any other cause. Carbon fouling from too rich a mixture runs a close second. If everything is right, you'll just watch the electrodes erode away—after many thousands of miles.

Thousands of miles later, at 5,000 miles to be exact, the manual recommends that you toss the plugs out anyway. At that point, they're nearing the end of their useful life (at least in an iron-head Sportster motor). The electrodes probably aren't eroded so much that you can't re-gap them, but they're probably looking pretty dowdy.

Also at 5,000 miles, the manual recommends that you start fooling around with your front and rear forks. Specifically, it tells you to check the bearing adjustment and change the front-fork oil.

Adjusting the bearings really doesn't take much equipment. Mainly, you want to make sure the forks aren't wobbling around.

Loose fork bearings make for surprise steering adjustments! I always hate it when the direction I go in becomes a matter of negotiation between me and the bike. When I turn the han-

dlebars, I want to know how much the bike will turn. I don't want the bike to say, "How about if we turn *this* much. If you don't like it, don't worry. I'll try something else in a second or so!" Then, there's always the syndrome of going down the street straight, and having the bike suddenly veer a bit to the left (or right) for no apparent reason. Very disconcerting.

On the other hand, you don't want to make the bearings too tight, either. There should be just a little bit of drag.

For example, Harley recommends one to two pounds of drag on the rear swingarm bearing. The manual gives directions on how to set up the adjustment with spring scales and so forth. Guess what? I'm not about to do that. You can if you want to. As far as I'm concerned, if it doesn't wobble and it doesn't bind, it can't be too far off.

Similarly, the manual gives detailed instructions for making a magic front-fork-tube filler-upper. It involves punching holes in the bottom of a coffee can to which you solder a funnel that fits into a piece of transparent flexible tubing two feet long, with this complex dealie at the other end that screws into the top of the fork.

Or, you can just pop the fork caps off, drain the old fork oil (if there's any left), replace the drain plugs, and pour so many ounces (or cubic centimeters, if you're a metric biker) of fork oil in through the top. Then replace the fork caps and pump the front end up and down a few times. You'll need some sort of measuring cup to get the right number of ounces out of the fork-oil container and into the bike. You may be able to successfully pour the fork oil from the measuring cup directly into the fork tube, but I recommend investing in a small funnel to reduce spillage.

Either way, you'll have to jack up the bike. Jack up the front end to take off the weight when working on the front forks. Jack up the back end when working on the back.

Remember when I told you about ruining my rear bearings by making my chain too tight? At first I couldn't figure out what the problem was because I couldn't make the rear wheel wobble by pulling back and forth on it. The situation became crystal clear when I jacked up the bike, however. The same goes for wobbly fork bear-

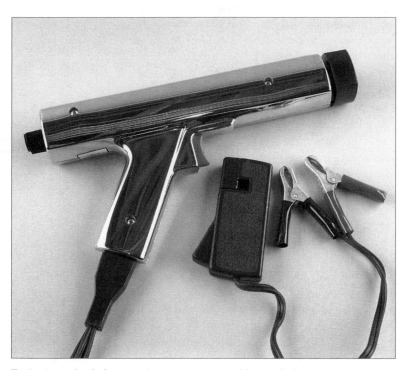

To do dynamic timing, you have to go out and buy a timing light.

ings. In fact, to really see what's going on, you really oughta pull off the rear shocks, too.

I'm not going to go into lifts and jacks at this point. I have a whole chapter on them later. Suffice it to say, there are a kazillion ways to get the weight off one end or the other (or both) of a bike, and any way you can think of to do it is fine. Heck, I once changed the front end of a 1965 BSA while it was suspended by a block and tackle from the rafters in a barn! There are, however, more elegant solutions.

The only other 5,000-mile item recommended by Harley-Davidson that will add to your toolbox is timing the ignition. There are three methods of timing a bike's ignition: static timing, dynamic timing with a timing light, and "Let's see how she runs!" timing.

Static timing is by far the easiest. To make it work right, the manufacturer really had to have designed the bike for it. In the old days of manual spark advance, you just turned the motor around to line up the timing mark on the flywheel, advanced the spark all the way, and set the points so they just opened at that point.

With automatic spark advance, the timing is always retarded when the motor isn't running. Some manufacturers have at some times marked the flywheel with *two* sets of timing marks. One set shows just when the points should open and the other—for static timing—is offset to correct for the automatic spark advance.

If you're going to get involved with static timing, you have to know just when the breaker points lose electrical contact. You can't just look in there and *see* when they first break contact, you have to sense it electrically.

The way the old-time mechanics used to do it was to rig up an instrument lightbulb (12 volt or 6 volt, whatever was right) with two wire leads ending in alligator clips as shown in the figure. You clipped one lead to the "hot" side of the points and the other lead to ground. With the ignition and kill switches on, the bulb would be off when the points were closed and would come on just when they broke electrical contact. Since there's a good chance you'll fire a spark plug while doing all this, it's wise to disconnect the plug wires before fooling around with it.

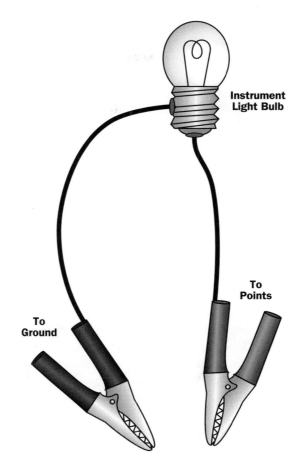

A simple static timing light consists of two leads soldered to an instrument light bulb.

In these days of inexpensive electronic multimeters, it's both easier and better to leave the ignition off and use a meter. If what you have is an analog multimeter (it's got a pointer that swings across a dial), set it on the lowest "ohms" scale, and hook the test leads up just like the old-fashioned lightbulb dealie. When the points are closed, the meter will read zero ohms. When they open the pointer will suddenly swing all the way to the other (infinity) end of the scale. The current the meter puts out won't be enough to trigger a spark.

If you're using a digital multimeter (DMM), the ohms scale display probably won't react fast enough for you. Most of the DMMs I know of have a continuity setting that gives you a quick, and usually audible, signal when the contact is broken. Both of the DMMs I use make an audible tone when the contact is there. The tone shuts off when the contact breaks. It's really neat because

Table 11.1
Additional Tools for Scheduled Maintenance

- Pushrod-tube keeper-uppers (Harley's, Indians and other relics with external pushrods)
- Feeler-gauges and/or wire gauges
- Used-oil catch pan
- Oil-draining channel
- Used-oil temporary storage container
- Big funnel (for pouring oil)
- Small wire brush
- Spark plug wrench
- Fork tuner (front fork oil)
- Measuring cup graduated in ounces or cubic centimeters (cc)
- Small funnel (for pouring oil)
- Continuity tester (static timing) or timing light (dynamic timing)

you can listen for the tone with your ears while your eyes are busy helping your fingers move the breaker-point backing plate or rotate the distributor (on a *really* old bike).

That's all in the happy world of static timing. In the troublesome world of dynamic timing you've gotta go out and buy a timing light. You dynamic time a bike with the engine running at some specified rpm, which means you need a tachometer. If your bike *doesn't* have a tach, you need to invest in a separate one for your toolbox. Some DMMs have a built in tach as well. Mainly, it's got to be turning fast enough to make sure the spark-advance mechanism has the timing fully advanced.

You have to dynamic time any bike with an electronic sensor instead of breaker points. If the engine isn't turning, there just isn't a signal to tell you when the points open. So much for static timing! Get the timing light and read the directions in your shop manual.

The third method of timing is the easiest to do and the hardest to get right: Take it out on the road and see how it acts. If the timing is too far advanced, the motor will kick back on starting and will tend to diesel (keep running) after the ignition is shut off. If the timing is too retarded, the motor won't make horsepower at high rpms.

Of course, having it kick back on starting is a good way to break your electric starter! Also, a good preignition pop when you're kick-starting is a rude shock as well. I believe that one of the main motivations for inventing the automatic spark advance was that everyone used to occasionally forget to retard the manual advance before kicking over their motors. I've done it a few times. Tries to kick you over the handlebars, it does!

It's better to start with the spark too retarded and creep up on the advanced condition. That means a few high speed runs up a hill, which is a good way to get a ticket in the era of 65 mph speed limits. It's also pretty hard to judge unless you are really familiar with the motorcycle and how it should act when it's running just right.

That's pretty much it for the additional tools you need for scheduled maintenance. Table 11.1 lists the tools we've added.

"There's no blueprint for building a shop," according to Jim Hamilton, an amateur motorcycle restorer. "It's kind of whatever fits naturally into the space."

Jim's introduction to motorcycling was similar to what many, if not most of us, experienced. "When I was a kid everyone had bikes, and we all used to hang around, drink beer, smoke cigarettes, and work on our bikes. We'd always learn from each other. There was one guy in particular: he was always into speed. He used to build dragsters and stuff, and he really knew a lot about engine building. I really learned a lot from him about valve grinding, clearances on pistons, and engine internals."

Jim's motivation for restoring motorcycles is purely personal. He has restored motorcycles for others, but mainly works on his own bikes for his own pleasure. "I don't want to do it so much that I ruin my own hobby," he says. "I wouldn't want to get sick of it."

That hasn't stopped him from keeping his shop busy. Over the years, he has restored over twenty motorcycles, ranging from antiques, like the three Triumphs he is working on now, to his present ride, a 1978 BMW R100/7. He spends four hours every weeknight, from 7:00 to 11:00, working in his shop. Why so much time? Motorcycle restoration involves a lot more than unbolting a few parts and swapping in replacements. A proper restoration begins with completely disassembling the bike, then refinishing every piece, repairing all the repairable items, and hunting up just the right replacements for missing or unsalvageable parts. "If you're really going to do res-

torations, you've got to plan on spending a lot of time."

Being an amateur with an amateur's motivation doesn't stop him from having a very professional attitude about his restoration work, either. His shop is immaculate. He believes in having "a place for everything and everything in its place." Sound familiar? It's Ben Franklin's basic dictum.

The diagram shows the layout of Jim's current workshop, which is set up in the basement of his New England home. It is a walk-in basement, so getting bikes in and out is not a problem.

Setting a 3/4-inch aluminum plate into the workbench top provides a great hard point for mounting all sorts of fixtures.

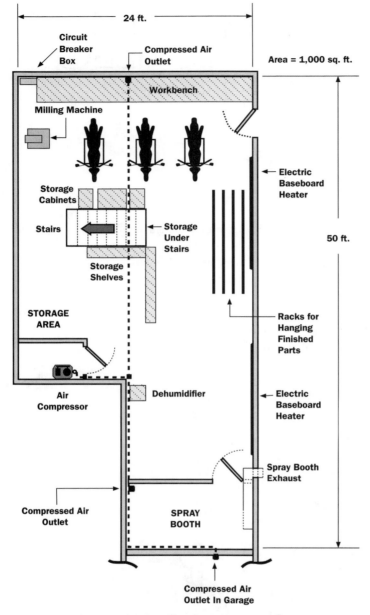

24 ft.

Circuit
Breaker
Box

Compressed Air
Outlet

Area = 1,000 sq. ft.

Workbench

Milling Machine

Storage
Cabinets

Stairs

Storage
Under
Stairs

Storage
Shelves

STORAGE
AREA

Air
Compressor

Dehumidifier

Compressed Air
Outlet

SPRAY
BOOTH

Electric
Baseboard
Heater

50 ft.

Racks for
Hanging
Finished
Parts

Electric
Baseboard
Heater

Spray Booth
Exhaust

Compressed Air
Outlet In Garage

Layout of Jim Hamilton's motorcycle-restoration shop.

bench area, storage, a paint-spray booth, and lots and lots of work space.

While many mechanics go in for roll-around tool chests, veterans like Jim often prefer their tools set in a fixed location as close as possible to their workbenches. The bottom unit of his old rollaway tool chest is shoved in under the workbench. It's not just shoved in there—it's boarded up so it ain't-a-gonna roll away again. The top unit now sits on his workbench right in the middle. A second similar unit sits right next to it, with a wooden toolbox for precision machinist's tools nearby.

Jim's workbench sports an interesting innovation. He took a 3/4-inch aluminum plate 24 inches wide by 18 inches deep, and set it into the top of the workbench and bolted it down. By drilling and tapping holes in this plate, he is able to create solid fastening points to temporarily mount fixtures, such as the homemade truing stand in the photo. When he is done, he simply plugs the holes with set screws. Then he has a flat work surface again—until the next time he needs those tapped holes.

Another innovation that's great for long-term restoration projects is his motorcycle-stand design. Made of lightweight structural aluminum, these stands are easy to slide around—even while carrying a bike—and extremely rugged and stable. They also hold the bike at just the right working height during the months he spends restoring it.

Getting the bike down once it's completed has to be a bit tricky, though. He says it's simply a question of using jacks to lift the bike off the stand, sliding the stand out from under the bike, and lowering it to the ground.

Jim tends to work by himself in the evening when his wife is at work and their two children are asleep, so safety is a big concern. If anything happens, there's nobody around to help him. Aside from keeping a fire extinguisher handy and always wearing safety glasses around machinery, Jim feels that the most important safety tip is to "work cleanly."

"I often see people trying to work in a mess," he recounts, "and they end up tripping over stuff. Try to work cleanly. It's a lot safer!"

"My first house had no bulkhead or anything," he recalls. "When I built a bike I would have to get it to the stage where it didn't have wheels, exhaust pipes, or tank, and we'd have to carry it up the stairs. And, it was a real pain in the butt! You've *gotta* have a walk-in cellar."

He has organized his shop into five discrete areas: a machine shop area (dominated by the Bridgeport milling machine), a very large work-

Pivotal moments, over the span of a lifetime, can sometimes be hard to pinpoint. Not this story. Dave Percival saw his first BMW motorcycle in 1958 when he was stationed in Germany with the U.S. Army Corps of Engineers. Impressed with its clean, unusual design, he bought it for $150— and the rest, they say, is history.

Today, Percival's collection of air-cooled BMWs includes about one hundred machines, one of nearly every model the company produced until 1976, as well as numerous rare factory specials. So, when he decided to build a new home and bike showroom on a nearby piece of property in Andover, Maine, plans necessarily included a new 24 x 40-foot workshop. The original blueprint was sketched out on a napkin, using dimensions he knew would be easy on the carpenters and leave little wasted building material. But, Dave relied on a contractor buddy to refine his plans and put his ideas into action.

Percival wanted a very clean, "functionally efficient" space to work on a few near-term projects. Dave sends most of his painting out, and decided to leave his lathe and sandblasting equipment at his old shop, so he could work on the dirtiest projects there. For small jobs, the new shop has a small grinding wheel that he could roll outside. The eight-foot overhang around the sides of the building provides a semi-sheltered space for things like this, and it makes a great place for visiting friends to park their bikes.

Knowing that Murphy's Law causes things to grind to a halt for a while, Percival wanted to be able to keep a few jobs going at once. But, on the other hand, he was determined not to allow himself so much space that he might be tempted to fill it with the things that always seem to encroach workspaces. He planned for two lifts for long-term projects and room for two more "rollaways." An engine shipping crate outfitted

Dave Percival's workshop has room for two longer-term projects and two "rollaways." The 1950 R51/2 on the right needed some transmission attention after its recent vintage racing debut. On the left, his wife Kathy's 1981 R45 is getting some minor end-of-the-season maintenance and repair.

Countertops extending around the perimeter of the shop provide plenty of room for laying out parts for assembly. Rubber mats make standing a little nicer. For longer jobs, you can pull a stool up to the counter.

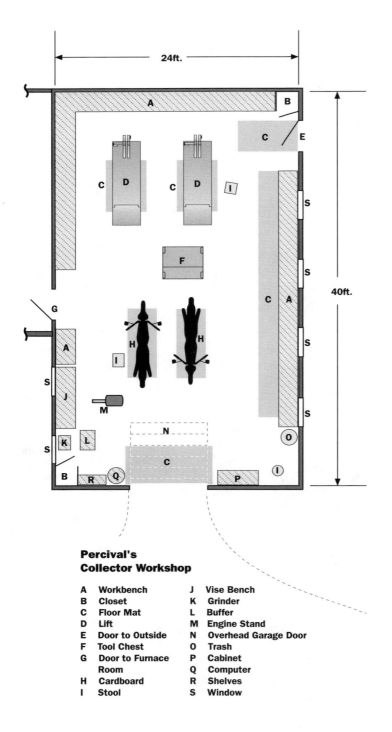

**Percival's
Collector Workshop**

A	Workbench	J	Vise Bench
B	Closet	K	Grinder
C	Floor Mat	L	Buffer
D	Lift	M	Engine Stand
E	Door to Outside	N	Overhead Garage Door
F	Tool Chest	O	Trash
G	Door to Furnace Room	P	Cabinet
		Q	Computer
H	Cardboard	R	Shelves
I	Stool	S	Window

24ft.

40ft.

stranger to the idea of heating with wood. The 20 x 20-foot room next to his shop houses a radial hot-water furnace that puts out 550,000 BTUs to heat the 11,000-plus square feet that make up his home, showroom, and workshop. Six inches of insulation in the walls and ten inches in the cap do a good job of conserving every bit of warmth.

During construction, the crew laid down three inches of styrofoam insulation and floated a continuous length of pipe in the wet cement of the flooring to form a grid 16–18 inches apart. The result is a very evenly-heated shop that begs you to work in it. As Percival says, "When you have a warm workshop, you have a lot more time."

Countertops extending around the perimeter provide plenty of room for laying out parts for assembly, and outlets are available at regular intervals. Rubber mats keep your knees healthy, though for extended, finicky jobs, such as taking carburetors apart, Percival prefers to pull up a stool. As you might expect, the countertop is set at exactly the right height for that sort of thing. Extra-wide cabinet doors mean you can really put the space below to good use for storing everything from shop vacs to spare engines.

With such a big stash of projects as well as inventory, organization is key. Almost everything in the shop is sorted and labeled with Teutonic enthusiasm, and humor. A Yankee to the core, Percival makes good use of practical, everyday items like Rubbermaid boxes and coffee cans (repainted and labeled, of course). Prefabricated sheet-metal cabinets store any remaining details.

Natural sunlight lights the shop for most of the day, even in the wintertime. The windows themselves were "leftover from another job," according to Dave. Two 32-foot rows of flourescent bulbs run over the work stations to smooth out any shadows. A third 24-foot strip in the middle leaves room for the overhead garage door at the far end of the building. At the suggestion of his wife and daughters, Percival painted the interior a lighter variation of the BMW blue-and-black he had originally planned on using. Looking at the result, he's happy with the decision. "It just makes the place that much brighter."

with wheels and a countertop would serve as a sturdy mobile platform for the toolbox.

Heat was a priority in planning the shop. As a retired logging contractor, Percival was no

12

Tools for Electrical Work

Not everyone knows how to do electrical/electronic work. If you're going to do any motorcycle maintenance or repair, you'll end up learning some basic electricity. Most mechanically adept people already know these basics, so I'll assume you either know them already, or will learn them before you go mucking around with your wiring.

Where do people go to learn these basics? Unfortunately, most repair manuals, although they'll give you detailed instructions on how to, say, rebuild an engine, don't tell you anything about electronics. Unless you already know one heck of a lot about electronics as applied to motor vehicles, go out and get a book that explains it all.

The 1980s saw a revolution in motorcycle electrics. It actually started in the 1970s when solid-state electronic components started appearing in motorcycle electrical systems. I believe the first solid-state components were regulators.

Charging circuits in general changed drastically when the old style generators were replaced by alternators. A generator puts out direct current. The regulator's job, in most generator applications, is to control the voltage the generator puts out. In other words, the regulator senses the generator's output and feeds back a signal to keep it more or less constant regardless of engine speed.

Alternators, on the other hand, put out alternating current that must be converted (rectified) to the direct current that the electrical system uses. The alternator gets to put out pretty much whatever it feels like putting out at whatever the engine speed happens to be. The faster the engine turns, the higher the alternator's output voltage.

Most (if not all) motorcycle alternators use a permanent magnet rotating within a set of wire coils (the stator) to generate alternating electric current. Basic physics requires that the alternator's output voltage be directly proportional to the engine speed. Assuming the alternator has to put out at least 12 volts at idle, the voltage will be much higher at operating speeds.

Let's say that idle speed is 1,000 rpm. That's fairly typical for a modern engine that might redline at 10,000 rpm and cruise at about 5,000 rpm. If the alternator puts out 12 volts at idle, it will put out five times that (60 volts) at cruising speed and peak up to 120 volts at the top end! In such an alternator-powered charging system, the regulator's job changes to one of reducing that output voltage from whatever it happens to be at the moment to whatever voltage the electrical system needs. Some regulators also include the diode bridge needed to rectify the AC to DC, but

---

Table 12.1
Tools for Electrical Work

- Wire cutters
- Wire strippers
- Soldering iron
- Electronic solder
- Needle-nosed pliers
- Heat-shrinkable tubing
- Cigarette lighter
- Crimping tool
- Assorted crimp connectors
- Multimeter
- Test probe set

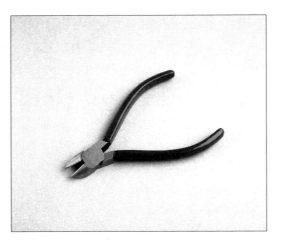

Wire cutters (also known as diagonal cutters or "dikes") are absolutely necessary for electrical work.

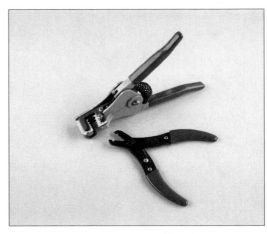

Fixed-type wire strippers (top) and adjustable-type wire strippers (bottom).

some systems include the diodes in the alternator housing. Others even put the diodes in a separate module by themselves.

Thus, when motorcycle manufacturers started using alternators, the job each component had to do was radically altered. That's why they made a big deal about renaming the thing that produces electricity. What mechanics call an alternator is really just an AC generator. To prevent confusion, however, the folks who decide such stuff (the guys at Lucas, for example) insisted that their AC generators be called "alternators," and reserved the older term "generators" for those things that put out DC at a controlled voltage.

Later, things really changed for motorcycle electrics when manufacturers started using breakerless electronic ignitions. Since then, motorcycle electronics has followed automotive electronics very closely. There have been three basic trends: greater functionality, greater reliability, and increasing unrepairability.

Greater functionality comes from doing certain necessary functions electronically, such as spark advance, that used to be done some other way. Other functions, such as electronic rev limiting, that were hardly ever done at all, have become routine.

Greater reliability comes from the fact that these solid-state electronic systems simply don't wear out.

That's not to say that solid-state electronic systems don't fail. They do. But, their failures are not due to wear. You cannot assume, as you used to with electromechanical technology, that an electronic ignition module is good for, say, 20,000 miles and then it should be replaced. It just doesn't work that way. With good luck, the thing'll outlast the rest of the bike. With poor luck, it can fail at any time.

To give you an example, I bought a brand new Harley-Davidson Heritage Softail in 1988. In 1989, after almost exactly one year of use, the ignition module went "pfft." The warranty replacement unit lasted all of an eighth of a mile! The replacement for *that* one was still ticking along five years later when I sold the bike, despite having been hammered by a power surge that fried just about everything else in the electrical system.

With the older electrical systems, you could pretty much bet that component X would fail after so much use. With the new electronic systems, you know that any component could fail at any time—but may last forever.

I don't know which I like better: to *know* that something is going to fail predictably (and thereby have some hope of heading off the problem by replacing it before it fails), or to know that the electronics will almost never fail, but have a small chance of going out at any time.

After years of experience with both types of electrical systems, I've grudgingly come to trust the newer systems a lot more.

After you've outfitted yourself with a couple of books on motorcycle electrics (and read them, by the way), you're ready to dig into your bike's electrical system. The first thing to understand is that you aren't going to fix any parts or modules.

There are two rules. First is the ol' Used Car Rule: "If it works, don't fix it." The second rule applies to modular components: "If it doesn't work, rip it out and throw it away."

These rules apply both to the older electro-mechanical modules, such as regulators and relays, and the new solid-state modules. The older equipment is repairable, but very few people have the skills needed to repair them. The people who actually do have those skills have learned that their time costs more than the replacement unit.

The new electronic modules are unrepairable even by the people who designed and made them! There's no way to get at their guts without completely destroying them. That's the third major trend in motorcycle electrics technology.

So, your motorcycle electrical work is limited to replacing modules and repairing the wiring that hooks them together. You'll be cutting and splicing wires, and maybe attaching some connectors.

Solder Connections

There are two ways of making electrical connections in motorcycles: solder splicing and solderless connectors.

As you read the following explanation, it may seem that I'm giving step-by-step instructions on how to make a good solder joint. I'm not. I'm not even hitting the high points. This part of the book focuses on stocking a tool kit, so all I'm going to do is mention those steps that directly affect tools and tool choices. If you want to learn to solder, you'll need to get your instruction somewhere else. The best thing to do is get some friendly electronics technician to show you how.

To make a solder splice, you need to cut the wire to length, strip off some of the insulation to expose the wire, melt solder into the splice, and finally replace the insulation. That means you

need wire cutters, wire strippers, a soldering iron, electronic solder, and something to replace the insulation.

Wire Cutters

Don't try to use the wire-cutter part of the jaws on your general-purpose pliers. Get yourself a small pair of cutters designed specifically for the job. They are typically about four inches long overall with cutting edges about 3/8-inch long that meet (not scissor). They're called "diagonal cutters" or "dikes."

In a pinch, and if the wire is smaller than 16 gauge, you can use the scissors on your Swiss Army knife, but they have to be extremely sharp. Misusing them that way can damage them. Get a set of wire cutters and put 'em in your toolbox.

Wire Strippers

There are two types of wire strippers. One type is adjustable and the other fixed.

The adjustable type looks like a clunky pair of scissors with V-shaped notches in the cutting blades. A moveable stop in the handle limits how far the blades close. What you do is adjust the stop so that when you hold the blades closed, the notches leave a gap just large enough for the wire itself to slip through. You fit the wire in between the notches, close the blades, and rotate the tool around the wire to slice through the insulation all around the wire, then pull the tool off the end of the wire, pushing the insulation away. I've found these to be a pain in the butt to adjust, especially if you get involved with several wire sizes.

The fixed type is based on the wire cutters (the cutting blades meet rather than sliding past each other). There are several round notches in these blades, each fitting around the wire core of a different gauge wire. Instead of adjusting the stripper, you just pick the proper sized notch. From there, you use the tool the same way you would the adjustable type. These are a lot quicker and easier to use than the adjustable type. They are however, bigger (thus taking up more room in your saddlebags) and clumsier to use in tight places.

You can, of course, use a knife blade to strip wires. Just cut around the wire to detach the portion of insulation you want to remove, and pull it off with your fingers. It sounds simple, but it takes longer, can take a lot more physical force if the wire is not in good condition, and dulls your knife blade. If you're not careful, having your fingers in such close proximity to a (hopefully) razor-sharp knife blade can lead to blood loss!

At this point, you want to look at the color of the wire. In most cases, the metal will look bright yellow, silver, or reddish yellow. That's clean copper (yellow or reddish yellow) or clean tinned copper (silver). If that's what you have, you're ready to make the joint.

If, on the other hand, the metal is dark red, brown, or (omigod!) green, you have an oxide

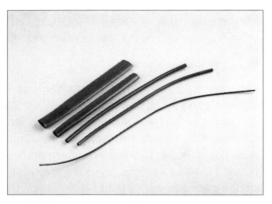

Heat-shrinkable tubing is available from most hardware, electronic-hobbyist, and automotive parts stores.

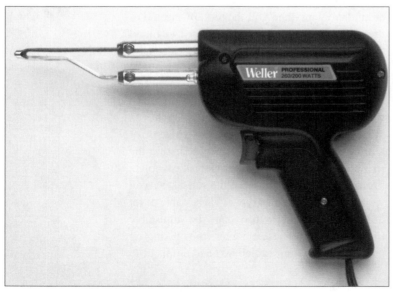

Soldering guns heat rapidly when their trigger is depressed (poor thing) and stay hot as long as the trigger is held.

problem. Copper oxide is a non-conductor. Even worse, solder won't stick to copper oxide. Red or brown indicates surface oxide that can be cleaned. The best way to do it is to use a sharp knife blade (from your Swiss Army knife) to scrape the oxide away. Red oxide comes off pretty easily. The brown stuff takes a while. When the wire has turned green, it means the oxide has eaten into the wire. Rip out any green wire and replace it. Often, you'll see green oxide on wires in the charging system near old solder joints. You can sometimes clip off the corroded portion of the wire. If too much of the wire has gone bad, replace the whole thing.

Making Connections

Now that you have the wire cut to length and the end stripped and clean, you have to make the connection. You have to start with a mechanical connection. There are two situations (notice how this stuff is all coming in twos?): soldering on a connector, or splicing two wires. If you're fitting a connector on, simply slide the connector over the bare wire end. If you're joining two wires, you need to twist the wires together.

Stop right there! How are you going to cover the bare wire? We'll talk about this later, but you have to consider it now. If you're going to use heat-shrink tubing, slip the piece you're going to use over the wire and slide it as far as you can away from the joint. If you don't, you'll have to take the whole joint apart again to fit the tubing on. Then, you'll have to remake the joint. So, think about it now.

Soldering Irons

OK? Ready to make the joint? Pull out your soldering iron. Again, there are two basic types of soldering iron: soldering guns and soldering pencils. The main difference is in how fast they heat up.

A soldering gun has a trigger that you pull (and hold) to heat up the tip. The tip takes three to fifteen seconds to heat up to soldering temperature. It cools almost immediately when you let off the trigger. Soldering guns are great if you have just one or two joints to make.

Soldering pencils have no trigger. You plug them in when you sit down to start your wiring job. By the time you're ready to heat your first joint, the iron will be hot. If, on the other hand, you forget to plug it in ahead of time, it'll take a minute or two to heat up.

"A minute or two" may not seem long when you're sitting here reading this book, but when you're twiddling your thumbs waiting to fix your wiring, it is an *awfully* long time.

Of course, while you're cutting and stripping and scraping and twisting, there's this 600-degree soldering tip sitting next to you, waiting for your next wrong move. If you need a reminder of what that can do, refer to the section on workbench space in Chapter 7. My layers of soldering-iron scars are now so thick that I barely feel burns on my hands.

You want to use a soldering gun when making one or two joints or when you are moving around a lot next to the bike. You want to use a soldering pencil when making a lot of joints at your workbench.

Solder

You can't solder a joint without solder. Use electronic solder from Radio Shack, or some such electronics do-it-yourself outlet. Hardware stores also stock electronic solder, but make sure it *says* "Electronic Solder" on the package. Don't use plumber's solder.

Electronic solder may look like just a soft, skinny wire, but it's not. If you take your wire cutters and nip off the end, you'll see that it is actually a hollow metal tube (made of a lead/tin amalgam) filled with brown rosin. In more expensive grades of solder, there are sometimes several rosin cores rather than just one.

The rosin is an organic material that "burns" when it comes into contact with metal oxide. All copper exposed to air has a thin film of oxide. Remember that reddish-yellow wire you didn't have to clean? The reddish-yellow color came from a layer of oxide that was thick enough so you can see it. The oxide layer on a bright yellow wire is so thin that it is completely transparent, not even affecting the wire's color. The rosin core in the solder melts under the soldering iron's heat and flows over that oxide layer. The rosin burns by stealing oxygen atoms from the copper oxide, leaving pure copper behind. The

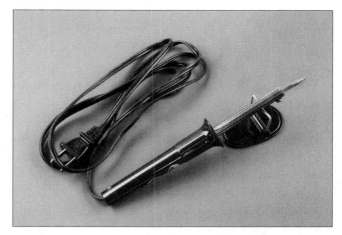

Soldering pencils take a couple of minutes to reach operating temperature and stay on until unplugged.

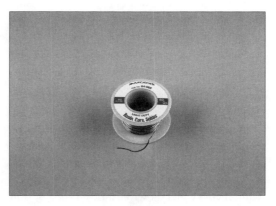

Always use rosin-core electronic solder for wiring.

lead/tin amalgam then can bind to that pure copper surface. I told you to clean the more heavily oxidized wires because their oxide coats are too thick for the rosin to deal with.

What diameter solder should you use? You have a lot of leeway there. The best diameter is probably about half the thickness of the wires you are joining. But, you can get good results with solder that is anywhere from a quarter of the wire diameter to double the wire diameter. Thicker solder wire fills up the joints faster, but is much clumsier. Thinner solder wire takes more time to do the job, but gives you much better control of the result.

Having melted the right amount of solder into the joint, you now have to cool off the joint. You could just patiently wait until the joint cools naturally.

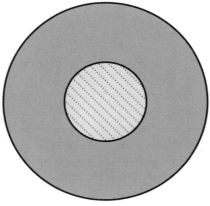

Single Core Solder

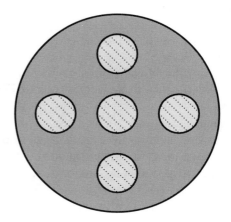

Five Core Solder

Electronic solder consists of a lead/tin alloy sheath with one or more cores of organic rosin. These cross-sections show both types.

This, however, is one time when patience is not a virtue. Heat leaves the joint mainly by soaking its way down the wire. At the other end of the wire there is likely to be some electronic component, such as a transistor at the input of your $100 electronic ignition module.

Heat is the great enemy of all electronic equipment (which is why Harley's idea of bolting electronic modules right under oil tanks on some models earned them a dummy slap in the late '80s). Whenever you heat up any piece of electronics over its normal operating temperature, you damage it. You might damage it a little or you might damage it a lot, depending on how much you overheat it. But, you damage it.

So, simply waiting for the metal-melting heat of a soldering iron to gently waft away to wherever it wants to go is not a good idea. Grab the joint with a pair of needle-nosed pliers and squeeze hard until the heat soaks away from the joint and into the pliers. After twenty or thirty seconds, the joint will be cool to the touch. If it hurts to touch the wire, the wire is still way too hot.

This is one application for needle-nosed pliers. Needle-nosed pliers are holding tools. You use them to grab stuff that your big, stubby fingers can't get a grip on. (You may think that your

fingers aren't big and stubby, but compared to needle-nosed pliers, they are!) Needle-nosed pliers are not a substitute for a wrench. They can't apply enough force to compress anything. They can't even hold on really tightly. Use them only for poking and grabbing things in places that are simply too tight for you to get your fingers into. You also use them to bend wires into shapes that are too small for your fingers to do the job.

Once the joint is cool, you have to cover it with insulation to prevent accidental short circuits. Guess how many choices you have. That's right, two: shrink tubing and black vinyl tape.

Most of the time, people (even experienced professional mechanics) slap a wad of tape over the joint and walk away. It's quick and easy, and most of the time you can get away with it perfectly well. If something goes wrong, you can just yank the tape off and replace it when you've fixed the problem.

Make sure you get *black vinyl* tape, though. The good stuff retains a stretch after you pull on it. So, if you're going to cover a length of bare wire that is, say, one inch long, pull off a piece of tape that is *two* inches long. Start one end of the tape an inch below the bare spot, then stretch the heck out of the tape as you spiral it along the wire. By the time you run out of tape, you'll have

Needle-nosed pliers are an absolute necessity if you are going to do electrical work on a motorcycle.

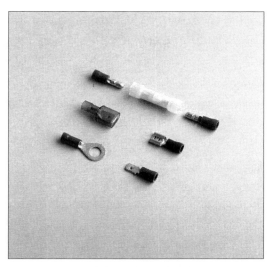

Crimped connections are standard for automotive applications. They cannot, however, be made watertight. For that reason, some mechanics don't like them for motorcycle applications.

gone an inch or more beyond the bare spot because you will have stretched the tape by over 50% while wrapping it around the wire. The reason I keep talking about stretching the tape is that's how you make it conform to the shape of the wire. Stretching makes the tape hug lumps, irregularities, and changes in diameter. It also squeezes out air between the tape and the wire.

A tightly stretched taped joint can last for years, even when repeatedly driven through pouring rain. If you don't stretch the tape, the covering will fall off in minutes even if you don't do anything to it.

Vinyl tape can't stand up to oil. Put a drop of oil on a taped joint and the tape will fall off the next day (latest). Oil is what vinyl-makers call a "plasticizer." It softens the vinyl. Unplasticized polyvinyl chloride is hard as rock. As you add more and more plasticizer (in other words, oil), the stuff gets softer and softer. Instead of holding its nice, stretched shape, hugging and protecting your solder joint, it simply lets go. It won't even hold onto its own adhesive, which ends up as a gummy residue on your now completely exposed wiring.

Vinyl tape is neither air tight nor watertight. If wrapped tightly enough, it can be water *resistant*. But, if you get it wet enough for long

enough, water will soak in along the edges of the tape and between layers. Then, of course, it won't let the water out! So, you end up with water trapped in next to your wiring. That leads to electric-current leakage (chronic partial short circuits) and corrosion. What is even worse, the wiring looks perfectly fine, because it's dry on the outside. You never find the problem until, in your frustration, you rip all the tape off all the wiring just to find this short. Then you see the water and swear you'll never put tape on again. Until the next time.

Don't go ape wrapping layer after layer of tape on the joint. You only need one layer. Black vinyl electrical tape is made to stand off 600 volts—even after being stretched. Your piddling little 12-volt electrical system isn't going to short through the stuff, so wrapping extra layers isn't going to do you any good.

Wrapping multiple layers of tape will, however, do you harm. It'll do harm by trapping moisture between the layers. That moisture then, instead of evaporating away before it gets to do any harm, gets to hang around waiting for an opportunity to corrode your wiring or cause a short.

Finally, vinyl-tape adhesive gets heat stroke. It forgets whether it's attached to the tape or the wire. There's no problem until you have to strip off the tape to work on the wiring. Then you have a gummy mess. It's not really a problem, just icky.

Your other choice, heat-shrinkable tubing, is really nice stuff. It's hard to find fault with it. Except, of course, that it's *too* good. More about that later.

Heat-shrinkable tubing, or shrink-tube for short, is made of a plastic material that permanently contracts by up to 50% when heated to over something like 150 degrees Fahrenheit. I'm kind of guessing at that temperature. It can't be much lower than that because I've never heard of the stuff shrinking just by being left out in the sun on a hot day. It can't be too much higher, because boiling water will do it.

All you have to do is slip a length of shrink tube over the solder joint (obviously after waiting for it to get cool), and waving the flame from your handy-dandy Bic lighter under it for a few seconds. The shrink tubing goes "thubb" around the wire, locking out air and water, and locking in electricity.

The only down side I can think of to using shrink tubing is that, once it's on, it's *on!* The stuff gets denser and tougher as it shrinks. In the end, it's much more rugged than the insulation the wire came with. If you ever have to remove it, plan on a dicey session with your Swiss Army

knife set for "killer-sharp blade." Often it's easier to just cut the section with the shrink tubing on it right out, and splice in some new wire.

Crimp Connections

The alternative to soldering connections is to use any of the kazillion types of crimp fittings. Crimp fittings are standard in automotive aftermarket applications, where they seem to last for years.

I know people, however, who swear that crimp connections are death in motorcycle applications. I've never had much trouble with them myself. If improperly made, they can work loose or pull off. Also, they are not something that you can make moisture tight. If you're going to use crimp connections, make sure they are done right, leave plenty of slack in the wires so they don't get pulled accidentally, and tuck them in places where they have some protection from the weather.

I like crimping for attaching lugs to the ends of wires. For example, key switches almost universally use screw-on terminal connections. I use crimp-on lugs at the ends of the wires that attach to those terminals.

Obviously, it's better to have your wire end in a substantial lug made for that screw to clamp down on than to wrap the wire around the screw's shank and hope that the head clamps down on it when you tighten the screw. I've been known to make my own terminal lugs by forming the wire into a loop of the proper size and tinning it with solder. That's a little better than just wrapping the wire around the screw, but is only marginally reliable.

Another place I like to use crimp connections is on push-on connectors. For example, say you're installing a handlebar-mounted aftermarket speedometer. You need an electrical connection to its light for night riding.

You know from the nature of the Universe that you'll want to disconnect that speedo at some time in the future for some reason. Who knows why, but it's a solid bet that it'll happen. Maybe you'll want to change the handlebars. Maybe you'll want to change the speedo's position. Whatever the reason, you'll be glad all you have to do to break the electrical connection is

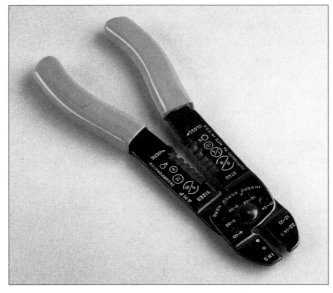

A crimp connector tool looks like an odd pair of pliers with cutouts in the jaws.

pull that connector apart. Then, when you want to put it back, all you have to do is push the connector back together. Without the connector, you'd either have to leave the speedo hanging by its wire, or cut the wire and splice it back later.

By the way, you can add solder to a crimp connection to make sure the electrical connection is good and remains good. To do so, however, you have to sacrifice any insulation that came with the connector because the heat from soldering will ruin the insulation.

To make a crimp connection, you still have to cut the wire to length and strip an appropriate amount of insulation from the end(s). Instead of pulling out a soldering iron and solder, you pull out a crimping tool. The crimping tool you need for most connectors associated with motorcycle wiring looks much like a pair of pliers except that the jaws are shaped differently.

To make the connection, hold the crimp fitting loosely in the jaws, stick the wire into the fitting, and (without letting the wire slip out) squeeze the crimping tool handles together until the jaws close completely. When you set the connector up in the crimping tool, pay particular attention to where the split in the crimp connection goes. It has to face the tool exactly as shown in the figure.

If you do everything right, you'll get a nice, tight symmetrical crimp that will last for years. If you don't, you'll get a sloppy mess that won't last a week. When that happens, cut the connector off and do it over. There's no way to fix it.

To make crimp connections, you need to add a crimping tool and an assortment of crimp connectors to your list of electrical tools.

Electronic Multimeters

The last item you need for doing electrical work on a bike is a multimeter. I say it's the last item not because you pull it out last. Actually, it is usually the first item you pull out. It is, however, the last item you should get because it takes the most knowledge to use.

Multimeters come in analog and digital varieties. An analog meter has a big dial with a needle that swings across its face. Analog meters also all have a big rotary switch with which you can select different ranges and functions. Digital

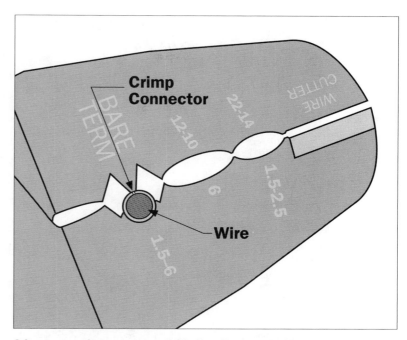

Crimp connections are only reliable if made properly. Make sure the point of the crimping tool lines up perfectly with the split in the uninsulated crimped ring as shown.

multimeters (also known as DMMs) have a window that will (when the unit is turned on) display numbers.

I don't think there is any point to my delving into how these beasties actually work. If you're really interested, you should run down to your local library and take out a couple of books on electronics. Every one will have a section on how meters work. If they're written before the middle 1970s, they'll probably only cover analog multimeters. If they were written after the late seventies, they'll cover both.

Analog multimeters have been around for about a hundred years, are relatively inexpensive, and do basic functions. These days, the really nice meters with all the bells and whistles (literally!) are digital.

Multimeters perform three basic functions: they measure voltage (volts), current (amps), and resistance (ohms). In fact, we used to call them Volt-Ohm-Milliamp meters (VOMs). Whether the meter measures milliamps (thousandths of an amp) or amps depends on the meter. You tell the meter whether you want it to be a voltmeter, an ammeter, or an ohmmeter by setting a switch. Most multimeters use a rotary switch.

 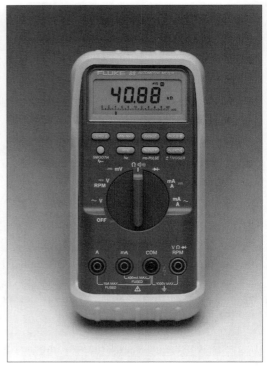

After telling the meter what function (volts, amps, or ohms) you want, you have to tell it how sensitive to be. That is called the *range*. If you were going to measure the voltage of your house current, for example, you would probably want to use a 200-volt range. That is, the maximum reading on that range is 200 volts.

You wouldn't want to use the 200-volt range to check your charging voltage, however, because the 200-volt range on, say, an analog multimeter is only accurate to within about four volts. You would rather step down to a 30-volt range, where you could trust it to within about half a volt.

The rotary switch on most analog multimeters has extra positions that allow you to select the range at the same time you select the function. For example, a multimeter with four voltage ranges would have four of its rotary-switch positions allocated to voltage ranges. You'd see a 1 V range, then the next switch position might be a 3 V range, then 10 V, and finally 30 V. The next few positions might be allocated to resistance scales. Of course, there have been as many switching arrangements as multimeter models because each one is a little different.

Digital multimeters have a lot of advantages over analog units. Probably the most important for motorcyclists is the fact that DMMs are far more rugged. Not only are they entirely solid-state, with no delicate mechanical movements, but many are available with a foam "holster" that surrounds the sides and back. Such a unit can survive a fall from a pretty respectable height without damage.

Digital multimeters tend to be rugged electrically as well as physically. The magic of semiconductor engineering makes it possible to cram hugely complicated circuits into extremely small spaces and do it inexpensively (when produced in large quantities). That means DMM makers can add all sorts of gimcracks and whizzers into their products to idiot proof their equipment.

"Idiot proof" is a well-defined technical term. Multimeters, like any precision measuring instrument, mainly tend to die from misuse.

My favorite way of killing multimeters has always been to set them on the most sensitive ohms range and connect them across a source of 150 volts. I don't do it intentionally (meters usually last me several years and I have one that was made during World War II), but once in a while I

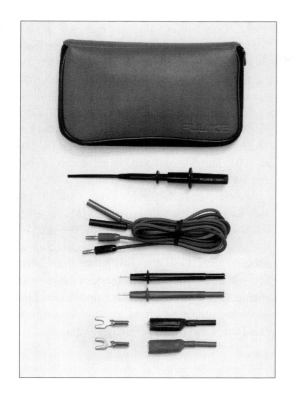

forget to switch scales before connecting to an unknown voltage. The technical term for doing that is "smoking the meter."

The two features I like the most about good DMMs are *autoranging* and the fact that you can hook them up backwards. An autoranging meter (not all DMMs have autoranging, by the way) will set itself for whatever range will best display the measurement result without your having to fiddle with a range switch. If you hook the meter up backwards (black to positive instead of negative), the display reads perfectly accurately. It simply displays a minus sign to show that *something* is reversed. When hooked up backwards, an analog meter, by contrast, simply bangs its needle on its stop, often bending it in the process.

You also need a set of test probes. Test probes, or test leads as they are sometimes called, consist of a pair of long, flexible wires that are color coded: one is red, the other black. At one end of each wire is a connector that plugs into its appropriate (also color coded) socket on the multimeter body. At the other end, the wire ends in a long plastic handle with a metal contact at the tip. The less expensive probe sets have a fixed tip. That is, the business end of the tip is

fixed on permanently. Other types have demountable tips, so you can fit, say, an alligator-clip tip on at one time, then later change it to a sharp needle tip that you can push through plastic insulation to contact the circuitry underneath.

There are a kazillion different tip styles. The probe set I use most has four tip styles: alligator, straight, needle, and spade. The alligator tip has spring-loaded jaws that grab onto whatever it is you want to connect to. The straight tip looks a lot like a not-very-sharp nail that you simply touch onto whatever you want to contact. The needle tip is a shorter, sharper version of the straight tip. The spade tip has two flat "toes" that you can tighten a terminal screw down onto to make a solid connection. The whole kit, including DMM, wires, and probe tips, fits into a package just a bit larger than my fist.

I like to keep two DMMs in service. One, which I selected especially for compactness, goes into my emergency tool kit along with its test leads. The other is larger and has more features. It, along with its test probes, lives in my toolbox.

The last electrical item, which I carry in my emergency tool kit, is a length of test-probe wire with alligator clips on the ends. I use it to temporarily connect whatever I want to temporarily connect while my test probes are busy being connected to the meter. You never know when you'll need a length of wire!

As far as I know, there aren't any DMMs made specifically for motorcycle applications. There are, however, models designed for automotive technicians whose special features help with motorcycle work as well.

For example, you can get DMMs with an inductive pickup that senses the spark traveling through your spark plug wires. Such an inductive pickup will give you accurate rpm indications no matter how many cylinders your bike has.

Harley mechanics beware, however. Harley-Davidsons use a so-called "dual-fire" ignition system, where both plugs fire at the same time even though only one of them is on the power stroke. Dual-fire ignition systems will give a false tachometer reading. That is because each plug fires twice as often as on the more usual single-fire ignition system. To get the correct rpm, simply divide what the meter tells you by two.

Another mechanic-friendly feature of automotive DMMs is the Lo-Ohms display. On Lo-Ohms, the meter can measure resistance as low as 0.01 ohms—low enough to detect a bad ground or a marginal connection.

Various manufacturers have worked out various goodies to add to their DMMs for automotive (and by extension, motorcycle) mechanics. As motorcycle electronics become more complex, electronic measuring instruments will become more important to the motorcycle mechanic. If you value your ability to diagnose bike problems, make an effort to learn motorcycle electronics and keep up with developments.

Chapter 13

Tools for Motor Work

I have a rule for this book. I can get away with issuing this particular rule because this is primarily a book for amateur motorcycle mechanics, and there are things that amateurs just shouldn't screw around with. The rule I'm talking about is one of setting limits. It's important to set some realistic limits. It comes down to my setting a limit on what I advise you to do. This rule is: I won't tell you how to set up your shop to do something that I avoid doing.

We can go wrong in one of two ways with this rule. It could be like the guy who says: "Don't do anything I wouldn't do." Then you realize that he makes a living by, say, hijacking airliners and making his getaway by parachuting into the Amazon rain forest, but he doesn't worry about getting hurt because he's always stoked on PCP! Not doing anything he wouldn't do gives you a lot of latitude.

On the other hand, the guy could be such a milquetoast, whose most critical concern when comparison shopping for a car is how well it rates in crash-test reports. Not doing anything that guy wouldn't do means that you pretty much won't do anything worth doing. You can't grow unless you take some risks. You can't learn without making mistakes.

The rule that I use to separate what I'm willing to try (as an amateur) and what I leave to the professionals involves a nice calculation of margin for error. If you can do it right the first time by carefully following the directions, it's a job an amateur can legitimately attempt. If it involves a skill that can only be learned through training and practice, or if it requires expensive special-

ized tools, it's probably better to leave it to the professionals.

Ninety percent of what you need to do on most motorcycles (especially older motorcycles) fits into the you-can-do-it-the-first-time-if-you-follow-the-directions category. Also, very little motorcycle work requires specialized tools that are terribly expensive or that you can't fabricate pretty easily.

For example, in order to assemble a Harley-Davidson clutch, you need a specialized tool to compress the springs. But, you can fabricate the needed tool out of a harmonic balancer puller that you can buy in any auto parts store, plus a few bolts and some mild steel flat stock. It takes less than an hour with ordinary hand tools to

Some specialized operations require relatively expensive specialized machine tools, such as this boring bar for reconditioning cylinders, as well as the training to operate it skillfully. *Photo courtesy of KW Products, Marion, Iowa.*

Table 13.1   Tools for Motor Work

- Motorcycle trailer (optional)
- Compression tester
- Borescope (optional)
- Deep socket set
- Impact driver set
- Bits or sockets for unusual drive patterns
- Compressed air
- Inside dial caliper (optional)
- Cylinder hone
- Variable speed electric drill
- Retaining ring pliers
- Scratch awl
- Machinist's scale
- ½-inch-drive socket set including:
    - Assorted sockets ($\frac{7}{16}$-inch to $1\frac{1}{4}$-inch)
    - Ratchet
    - Two-foot breaker bar
    - Short (2-inch) drive extension
    - Long (6-inch) drive extension
    - Torque wrench
    - Assorted drive adapters
    - Universal joints for each drive size
- Clutch-spring compressor

make one of these rigs. I consider it something an amateur can jump into with every expectation of success.

Boring out a cylinder, on the other hand, requires a milling machine and boring bar, plus training in how to use it. Measurements should be made to sub-thousandths-of-an-inch precision. It's not a job for an amateur—unless his day job happens to be master machinist!

You don't need much more than your basic tool kit to take a motorcycle engine apart. Repairing it and putting it back together is another matter, however. That's how people get into trouble. It is possible to blissfully start unbolting things only to get yourself into a position where you got it apart, but you can't get it back together. The reason you can't get it back together is often that you simply don't have the tools you need.

Clutches are an example. You can take most any clutch apart just by loosening the nuts that compress the springs that hold the clutch plates together, and letting them pop off.

It is also possible, on small clutches, to push *really* hard and get those springs compressed enough to put those nuts back on. That's on a small clutch. By the time you get to clutches for

motors as big as 500ccs, however, there just ain't enough force in your puny little fingers to compress those springs. Unless you have a tool designed to evenly compress all the springs at the same time, you ain't-a-gonna get that clutch back together!

Diagnosis on the Road

Let's start from the beginning. You're tooling down the highway and your scooter stops scooting. You check to make sure you've got fuel in the tank and that the fuel is getting to the carburetor.

Maybe you pull off the air cleaner to make sure fuel is getting through the carburetor and into the manifold. All you have to do is look into the carburetor and twist the throttle. As you open the throttle, you should get a nice squirt of fuel into the carburetor throat. You'll probably have to pull off your air cleaner to look into the carburetor, but that's still a job for the tools in your emergency tool kit.

Next, you pull a plug to make sure you have spark. Ground a plug against a bolt or any unpainted spot on the engine or frame and, with the ignition on, turn over the engine. You see a nice blue spark, so you reluctantly admit that your motor is lunched. Deep in the bowels of that infernal combustion engine, somethin' just ain't right.

Having exhausted your roadside options, you call some Good Samaritan who eventually hauls your untrusty steed back to your shop. Now you really have to find out what's going on in that motor.

Motorcycle Trailers

By the way, hauling crippled scooters brings up our first piece of motor-repair equipment. This item is entirely optional. There are a host of ways to get around not having it, and sometimes having one at your workshop is totally useless. This piece of equipment is a motorcycle trailer.

Having a motorcycle trailer at your workshop is great when your buddies break down while you're at home. Then you can proudly go bail them out of motor trouble with a self-satisfied smirk. It gets you a small pile of chips you can cash in when it's your turn to stand fuming in the weeds, looking daggers at your broken down bike. It is also useful for avoiding having to cash in those chips the next time you get to kick weeds.

If you can't walk it back, you've gotta find a ride. My experimentally determined maximum pushing-a-bike-out-of-the-desert distance somewhat exceeds two miles. If it had been any farther out, I'd have left it in a ditch!

Diagnosis in the Shop

Anyway, you've managed, by hook or by crook, to get the distempered pile of rubbish that not long ago was your favorite object in the Universe back to the barn. It's time to make it whole again.

Being the smart little mechanic that you are, you don't just start ripping things apart. There are tests that you can do with the motor together that you can't do with the motor apart. So, you don't take the motor apart 'til you've done those tests. Sneaky, huh?

Actually, I'm assuming that what is wrong with your motor is that generally everything is worn out and you'll end up doing a major rebuild. But, you don't know that yet.

Will the Motor Turn?

The first test is to find out if the motor will turn. If it's a kick-start bike, simply put the transmission in neutral and push the kick-starter around by hand. Be gentle, because if there's something actually broken and flapping around in there, a good boot on the kick-starter can do more damage.

I once had a little Honda that suddenly began refusing to shift. Eventually (after opening up the transmission case to find that there wasn't anything at all mechanically wrong with anything) I found the reason for my problems: the engine oil, which the transmission shared, had gotten so dirty that the straight-cut gears weren't lining up to mesh. Hence, the shift linkage jammed rather than shifting. All I had to do was change the oil!

While trying to force it into gear, however, I'd managed to damage the splines on the shifter shaft. The shift lever wouldn't hold well. As time went on, the problem got worse and worse because each time it slipped during a shift, it did a

Most of the time, a motorcycle trailer is an unused space waster. But, when you gotta have it, you've gotta have it!

Some specialized tools you can fabricate for yourself, such as this clutch-spring compressor, made from an inexpensive harmonic balancer puller, a couple of pieces of 1/8 by 1-1/2-inch steel, and assorted hardware.

little more damage. Eventually, I had to replace the whole shift mechanism. All because I got too brutal while trying to diagnose a problem!

That was then and this is now. Because I was a bozo then, you can avoid being one now. Be gentle with that kick-starter.

If you don't have a kick-starter, I recommend avoiding the temptation to hit the electric start button. Electric starters are not gentle. They are both strong and stupid. If the motor doesn't turn over, they simply and stupidly apply more

The thumb-over-the-sparkplug-hole test is a quick-and-dirty compression test. It will find gross problems like holed pistons.

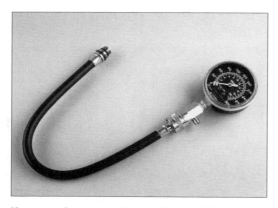

If your engine passes that test, you still need to use a compression tester to make sure that the compression is the same in both cylinders.

torque. And, they aren't gentle about it. When you hit that button, that starter bangs on the engine with all the torque it can muster.

Much better to pull the plugs (to let out the engine compression), slip the motor in gear, and roll it gently to determine if the motor is seized. If it doesn't turn easily, don't force it. You can break something that wasn't broken before.

Compression Test

Let's say that the motor turns all right. (Whew!) While the plugs are out, you should check the compression and inspect the cylinder walls.

The quick-and-dirty compression test is to hold your thumb over the spark plug hole (forming an airtight seal) and crank the engine. If you have good compression in that cylinder, you

won't be able to hold it. On the compression stroke, the air will escape from under your thumb with a loud pop.

The quick-and-dirty compression test isn't really good enough, though. Not only do you need compression in both cylinders, but it should be even. That is, you should get nearly the same compression in both cylinders. To find that out you need a compression tester.

I'm not going to teach you how to use a compression tester. Get one and read the directions. To find out what the compression should be, read the repair manual for your bike. That's what it's for.

OK, you've done your compression test and it stinks. There are lots of reasons why it might stink. Your rings could be gone. Your valves could be gone. Your head gasket could be gone. You could have a hole in your piston (ugh!).

Inspect Cylinders

Now is a good time to take a look at your cylinder walls. You can get a fair idea of their condition by shoving a flashlight beam in through the spark plug hole and looking around.

If your cylinder walls are in good condition, you should see fine cross-hatched scratches from the cylinder hone. A shiny mirror finish indicates that the cylinder is worn and needs honing. If you see vertical scratches, that means the piston has gotten so loose that it scraped the side of the cylinder. That means boring out the cylinder and putting in oversized pistons and rings.

You can't see much through that little spark plug hole, though. You might want to use a borescope.

Borescopes come in all sorts of sizes and shapes. Basically, a borescope is a periscope that you shove in through the plug hole. It has a built-in light to illuminate what you are looking at, and a lens system that carries an image back up to an eyepiece. You turn on the light and look through the eyepiece. By twisting and turning the borescope around, you are able to inspect the whole inside of the cylinder, the top of the piston and the inside of the cylinder head.

Most mechanics don't use borescopes. Almost any problem the borescope reveals will require you to take the cylinder head off to fix.

The Magical Impact Driver

Another little item you're likely to want while pulling apart a motor is an impact driver. Actually, I find impact drivers to have an affinity for primary chain covers. You may want an impact driver almost any time you have something held together with screws. Especially screws that are really tight and get corroded. Most especially screws that are really tight, get corroded and then have the screwdriver slots mashed.

I got my first impact driver when dealing with a small Honda that had Phillips-head screws holding the points cover on. The little "X"s that you fit the Phillips-head screwdriver into had gotten so bunged up that there was hardly any trace of X left. It looked like an irregular cone in there! There was no way I, or anybody else, was ever gonna get those screws out with a screw driver.

A few taps with an impact driver, however, and the screws were out.

The photo shows an impact driver. It looks like a beefy screwdriver with no neck. The shaft, which helps provide leverage in a normal screwdriver, has been shortened and thickened until it merges with the socket at the end. That socket at the end is to hold one of a small assortment of bits. Any impact driver will come with, at least, a couple of Phillips bits and a couple of slot bits.

At the other end of the impact driver, opposite where the bits fit in, is a big, solid, knob-like metal end. What you do is fit the bit into the screw, twist it in the direction you want it to turn, and wham the knob-end with a hammer. Wham it really hard.

The mechanism inside the impact driver converts the linear force of the hammer trying to mash the impact driver into the screw head into a torque in the direction you twisted the driver by hand. The compressive force is many times more than you could ever hope to exert by

Impact drivers have an affinity for primary chain covers, but are necessary whenever you have screws that are overtightened, corroded or have their heads damaged.

pushing on a screwdriver with your hands. Similarly, the torque produced makes the biggest ham-fisted biker look puny by comparison.

If you can't get the screw loose with an impact driver, you can't get the screw loose. It's time to drill out the screw.

Impact screwdrivers are made to take out screws. They're practically useless for nuts. The reason is that they work when you need to push and twist. If all you need to do is twist—which is the case when wrenching on, say, a hex-head bolt—the compression shock from the hammer blow is just going to break something. You'd be better off with a really long wrench.

By the way, the impact driver is not to be confused with an *air impact* tool. Mechanics often omit the word "air" when talking about the latter. They aren't the same and they don't do the same job. ∎

Once the head is off, you can see everything without the borescope.

Thus, a borescope is optional. I don't have one and I have no plans to get one, even though there have been many times I've thought having one would be really keen. I've never actually *had* to have one, though.

Check Valve Adjustments

Finally, before you take the cylinder head off, you want to check the valve adjustment. As I mentioned before, valves do "seat" themselves over time, thereby reducing valve "lash" (valve lash is the total clearance in the valve train when the lifter is on the base of the cam and the valve is

Deep sockets help you reach over fancy acorn nuts and the ends of overly long bolts.

A well set up toolbox should include an assortment of 12-point sockets.

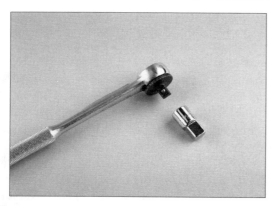

Socket drive adapters let you turn a socket with, say, a 1/2-inch drive with a 3/8-inch drive ratchet.

In cramped spaces where you can't get your socket wrench to fit squarely onto the nut or bolt, you have to use a universal joint.

fully closed). If the lash has been reduced to zero by the seating process the valve train will prevent the valve from closing completely and the valve will leak. You'll have the same symptoms—loss of compression—you would have with bad valves.

Valves do most of their seating during the first few hundred miles after you do a valve job. But, you never know. If you don't check them now, you really will never know, because you can't check them after pulling the head.

We've talked about the tools needed for checking valve adjustment. For external pushrod motors (specifically, Harleys and Indians) you need the super-duper pushrod-cover keeper-uppers I told you about earlier and a couple of wrenches. For overhead-cam motors, you need feeler gauges and wrenches.

Remove the Heads

Well, now it's time to pop the heads off. Depending on the bike, you might need to remove some sheet metal or plastic body parts. You probably will need to pull off the fuel tank or tanks. You definitely will have to remove the carburetor, manifold, and the upper motor mount. All of that you should be able to do with your basic tool kit.

Somewhere along in there, you may need a deep socket or two. Deep sockets are just like the rest of the sockets in your socket wrench set, except that they are longer. Because there is more room between the drive end and the wrench end, you can, for example, reach over one of those stylized tall decorative acorn nuts that defy socket wrenches. A more common situation is one where a nut and an overly long bolt have been used to fasten something together. You may see over an inch of threads sticking out through the nut. No normal wrench socket is going to reach down to that nut, but a deep socket will.

Anyway, somewhere at some time, you will run across a situation where a normal socket just isn't deep enough to do the job. That is when you want to see a set of deep sockets in your toolbox. I'm bringing them up now because practically the only time I feel the need for a deep socket is when I'm working on a motor. I don't know what it is about motors that seems to need deep sockets, but that's the way it seems to be. Maybe they get kinky for each other.

Before you really get into pulling the heads off, look at all the bolts you'll have to remove, especially the head bolts. Motor manufacturers often use unusual drive patterns on head bolts and other high-tightening-torque applications. For example, Harley-Davidson uses 12-point bolts for cylinder heads.

Although you can use a 12-point wrench on a 6-point (hex) bolt head, you can't use a 6-point wrench on a 12-point head. Make sure you have the wrenches you need for the bolts you have.

Inspect the Valves

Well, by now you've got the cylinder heads off. Before you take them apart, you should check to see if the valves are leaking.

You don't need fancy tools, but compressed air helps. To leak check a valve, say an intake valve, put the head upside down on your workbench. You may want to prop it up on something like a wooden block so that you have easy access to the intake port for that valve.

You will now be looking at the inside of the combustion chamber top—the underneath side of the head. Since it's upside down, it will look like a shallow bowl. Fill the bowl with a thin liquid. Motor oil is too thick. Almost any degreasing solvent will do. You can even use water if you remember to dry the head out thoroughly afterwards. Don't use gasoline; there's no point in creating a fire hazard.

Now, take a shop rag, wrap it around the nozzle of your compressed-air hose, and shove it up into the intake port and squirt in a shot of compressed air. The rag is there to plug most of the port, so you can get a little air pressure (you don't need much) in behind the intake valve you're testing. If the valve seals, you won't see a thing. If it leaks, you'll see air bubbling up from the intake valve through the pool of liquid. You repeat the process for each valve in each head.

If you don't have compressed air available in your shop, you can probably get enough air pressure by just blowing through a fairly large diameter tube. Anything from a 5/16-inch gas line on up to about a half-inch or more will work. When you start getting up to 3/4-inch diameter, you'll

Complete inspection of a cylinder wall requires the use of an inside dial micrometer. *Photo courtesy of Fred V. Fowler Co., Newton, Massachusetts.*

use up most of your lung power just filling up the tube and have nothing left for the test.

Remove the Cylinders and Inspect the Bores

Next after removing the head comes the cylinder or "jug." Again, you just need ordinary wrenches to unbolt it and pull it off. You can do a cursory inspection of the jug by eyeball. Look for longitudinal grooves parallel to the cylinder's long axis (bad) and cross-hatched scratching (good). For this discussion, we'll assume that you see generally a mirror finish (indicating that the finish is worn off the cylinder wall) and some deep, nasty longitudinal gouges.

Complete inspection of the cylinders includes carefully measuring the diameter and roundness of the cylinder at several points along its length. Machinists tend to call making these measurements *mic-ing* (pronounced "mike-ing") the cylinders. There are two types of instruments you can use to do this job: inside calipers and telescoping gauges.

Inside calipers look like outside calipers at the handle end, but their business ends—the points that actually contact the places you're measuring—point the other way. Outside calipers reach

Chords

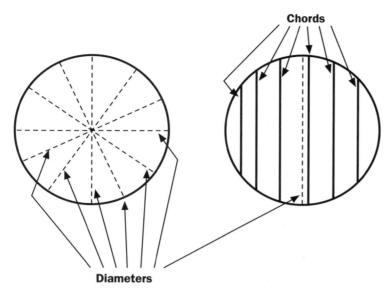

Diameters

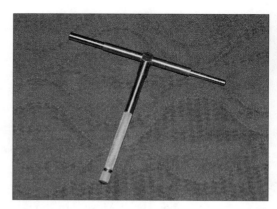

It is much easier to take cylinder measurements with a telescoping gauge.

"Diameters" are lines that cross a circle, always passing through the center. "Chords" are lines that cross the circle without passing through the center.

around to touch the outside of whatever you are measuring, while inside calipers squeeze down into whatever you're measuring.

These are *transfer* type calipers. They don't have built in measuring scales. What you do to use transfer calipers to measure your cylinder's inside diameter is to fit the calipers to the inside diameter, then remove them and measure the distance between the points using the outside-measuring jaws of a combination dial caliper.

Why would you use a transfer caliper when you have a perfectly good combination caliper? Because the combination caliper can't reach way down inside the cylinder where you want to make at least some of the measurements in order to measure necking of the cylinder.

Cylinders tend to wear unevenly along their lengths. The middle wears slightly faster than the ends because the piston moves faster in the middle than at the ends. It slows and stops at top dead center and bottom dead center, and really books through the middle. Cylinders can also turn out to be necked if the last person to hone the cylinders did a sloppy job.

To make sure the dimensions are good all the way along the cylinder, you have to mic it at one or more places near the middle as well as at the top and bottom. You can get the top and bottom

with the combination caliper, but there's no way that it will reach the middle.

There are, of course, inside dial calipers, but they are relatively expensive and not needed very often. The combination calipers cost about the same, but you'll use them a lot. The transfer calipers are relatively inexpensive, so buying one combination caliper along with transfer calipers in the appropriate sizes can save you a lot of money.

Telescoping gauges are an alternative to the inside caliper. They are a little easier to use.

To use the inside transfer caliper, you first turn the knurled thumbscrew between the caliper's legs until the points fit into the cylinder with room to spare. You then slowly turn the thumbscrew to open the points until they just contact the cylinder walls. It is very important to make sure the points are both exactly the same distance from the cylinder's top (or bottom) edge. Otherwise, the measurement will come out too large. It doesn't take much to make an error of a thousandth of an inch or so, which is the kind of tolerance you have to hold.

Basically, you contact the cylinder walls lightly, then try to rock the points back and forth to make sure they're square in the cylinder bore. If they're not, you won't be able to rock the calipers without ripping a great ugly scratch in the cylinder wall, which you do *not* want to do. When you have the calipers set correctly, the points will just lightly brush the cylinder walls when you rock them.

At the same time you are trying to make sure that the points are square in the bore, you also have to make sure they line up across a diameter. There are an infinite number of diameters you can use, as well as an infinite number of *chords,* which are not diameters. The diameters are (ideally) all the same length. The chords, however, are all different lengths. Luckily, all of the chords are also shorter than the diameters, so all you have to do is find the longest distance across (while keeping the points square to the bore), and you can be sure it's a diameter.

As you can see, measuring the diameter can be a ticklish prospect with transfer calipers. Telescoping gauges make it all oh-so-much simpler. A telescoping gauge is a T-shaped affair with spring loaded "points" (really rounded ends) at the ends of the top bar, and the upright being a handle.

To use the telescoping gauge, you start by compressing the points on the top bar to slightly less than the cylinder diameter and twisting the handle to lock them in place. Then insert the gauge into the cylinder. Next, twist the handle to unlock the points.

The springs push the points out to the cylinder walls. Because the points are really just rounded ends, they don't dig into the walls the way real points would, but try not to let them bang on the walls too hard, anyway.

There's enough pressure from the springs so that the bar naturally seeks a diameter. Then, you rock the handle back and forth until you've got the bar square to the bore. Now, you twist the handle again to lock the points.

Remove the gauge (all you have to do is rock the handle so the bar is no longer square in the bore, and the points immediately disengage from the walls), and measure the top bar's length with the dial caliper. It's really very easy to do and surprisingly hard to mess up.

Hone the Cylinders

If the cylinder's finish is a little shiny, but the cross hatching is still there, you might want to just touch it up a bit with a cylinder hone. A cylinder hone consists of (typically) three whetstones mounted in a spring contraption that holds them out against the inside of the cylinder wall.

The stones are relatively long so they lie parallel to the cylinder's axis. The spring contraption holds them equally spaced around the cylinder wall and holds them with equal force. In the middle of the contraption is a flexible shaft that you attach to an electric drill. To operate the thing,

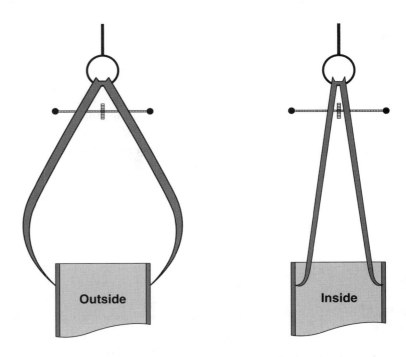

Inside and outside calipers look the same at the handle, but the measuring ends—the part that actually contact the places you're measuring—point in opposite directions. Outside calipers reach around to touch the outside of whatever you are measuring, while inside calipers squeeze down into whatever you're measuring.

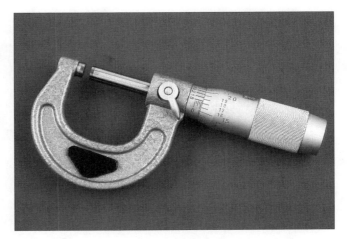

You'll find lots of uses for an outside micrometer when working on engines. Buy a quality instrument that won't rust.

you fit it into the cylinder, start the drill rotating relatively slowly, and slide the contraption in and out along the entire length of the cylinder.

Don't hold the hones still!

Remember that they are grinding off metal on the inside of your cylinder wall. If you don't move them evenly through the whole length of the cylinder, you'll "neck" the cylinder. That means you'll make the cylinder diameter slightly wider in some places than in other places along the cylinder's length. That, of course, is BAD. Also, don't overdo the honing process. If you have to do more than a few passes just to break the glaze, you'll oversize the cylinder. Then your rings won't seal and you'll have to pull the engine down again to bore the cylinder oversize.

The cylinder we have in hand is worn out to the point where it needs to be rebored for oversize pistons. It's a good bet that they're out of round and necked as well.

You could mic them to find out how many sizes over you need to make them, but, at this point who cares? You know you're going to rebore them, so take 'em to a professional. He's going to mic them anyway because if he's truly professional, he won't believe *your* measurements. He'll tell you what's needed and, if you've got a brain in your head, you'll trust him.

Inspect and Remove Pistons

So much for cylinders and inside dial calipers. Look at your pistons. Look for places where

Retaining-ring pliers are specially made for removing C-shaped retaining rings

metal has been broken off or burned away. If you see any, you can bet you've got debris in your bottom end and that will have to come apart, too. Look for cracked or broken rings, too. There's a fair chance that the piston skirts (the thin metal below the rings) will show longitudinal scuffing. That's not as important as scuffing on the cylinder walls because the aluminum of the pistons is so much softer than the steel in the cylinder wall.

Now, the pistons have to come out. The tool you need will depend on the type of wrist-pin retaining clips you have. If you have the little C-shaped retaining rings, you're best off using retaining-ring pliers. If, however, you've got those little round circlips, you can get them out using a scratch awl.

A scratch awl is an extremely useful tool for many applications. It's basically a sharp nail on a handle. It looks like a little ice pick. Use a scratch awl any time you need to shove a sharp, pointed thing in under something else (such as a circlip) and lever it out. It is also useful for scraping crud out of interior cavities. Unfortunately, scratch awls are also useful for gouging deep scratches in things that you don't want deep scratches in, such as aluminum surfaces and finger tips.

Now you have the pistons out. The next question is: "Are your wrist pins worn out?" The only way to be really sure is to mic them with an outside micrometer or caliper. But, I usually just figure that if I've got the motor apart this far anyway, I might as well replace the wrist pins. That way, there's no question.

Inspect Bottom End

Now, we're down to the motor's bottom end. Don't mess with it unless you have to. But, there's a fair chance you'll have to. The first test is to look at the play in the connecting rod bearings. Depending on the motor you have, you judge bearing slop by measuring the side-to-side motion at the top of the connecting rod, or the up and down play. Check your repair manual to find out.

Don't imagine, by the way, that you know more than the manual. You don't. What you don't know will come back to bite you.

I learned this one the hard way when rebuilding a BSA motor.

As I've said before, I claim to be a fairly competent BSA mechanic. I've done a ton of chassis work on them and have a fair handle on their oddities, so I had no compunction about digging into that worn-out, won't-make-power-for-anything motor with the blown head gasket and no compression.

Where I made my mistake was listening to my buddy (name withheld to protect the guilty) whom I imagined—no, I *knew*—was generally a lot better at wrenching scooters than I was. I still think he knew more about wrenching bikes than I did, and possibly more than I do now, some fifteen years later. He just thought he knew something that he didn't.

According to the repair manual, the test for bottom-end condition was to feel for up-and-down play in the main bearings. The manual specifically said that side-to-side slop was unimportant.

I checked for up-and-down play and found none. So, according to the manual the bottom-end was golden.

My friend, however, who came by later to help figure out what needed to be rebuilt, had different ideas. He was used to working on Harley motors, where the test for main-bearing condition is measuring side-to-side play. So, he just walked up to the half-stripped motor sitting on the engine stand, and waggled the connecting rods from side to side.

Being a BSA motor, the thing had *huge* side-to-side slop on the connecting rods. My friend promptly went ballistic about rebuilding the bottom end. He was so sure that he wouldn't listen to a thing I said.

The upshot was that we started tearing down the bottom end, got into trouble with a jammed Woodruff key, and ruined the crankshaft. Months later, the guy I'd bought the BSA from told me that he'd redone the bottom end just a few thousand miles before selling it to me. He hadn't done the top end (which I knew was bad when I bought it) because he couldn't find oversize pistons. Instead, since it was still serviceable, he just buttoned it up with what he could get. I'd started in on the motor after locating a source for the top-end parts.

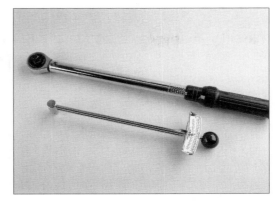

Don't try to put a motor together without a torque wrench. Shown here are two types: the "click" type and the deflecting beam type.

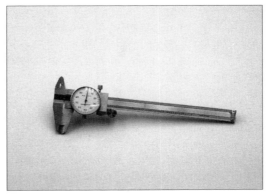

Use vernier calipers to get linear measurements accurate to thousandths of an inch or tenths of millimeters. This set has jaws for measuring outside dimensions (at bottom) and blades for measuring inside dimensions (top).

By not believing what I'd read in the manual, I'd turned a simple top-end job into a disaster.

Measuring the side-to-side play simply requires a machinist's scale. To the untutored, that's a fancy metal ruler. The difference between a machinist's scale and a carpenter's ruler is that the machinist's scale has its graduations etched on, rather than painted on, and those graduations are accurate to well under a thousandth of an inch. Carpenter's rulers are accurate to one thirty-second of an inch, so the carpenter's ruler won't cut it.

No matter what kind of motor you have, if there is any up and down slop at all, you have to replace the connecting rod bearings. That means taking the motor completely out of the frame and splitting the crank case open.

Remove Engine From Frame

Pull off the primary cover. You're going to have to take the primary chain off. If your bike has a separate transmission case, you'll need to take off the chain to get the motor out. If not, you'll need to take the chain off to split the case anyway, and it's easier to do it now.

When You Really Have to Get It Off

A breaker bar is a big, though very simple, tool. It looks like a really long ratchet handle, but instead of a big knobby ratchet mechanism at the business end, it just has a simple one-axis joint. What makes a breaker bar useful is the fact that the one-axis joint is much stronger than a ratchet mechanism. When you've got a big nut or bolt that's frozen on really tight, you need something that can apply humongous torque, just to get it started. Once you've got the thing broken free (hence the name "breaker bar"), you can switch over to a ratchet handle.

Breaker bars are strong. I once took my two-foot breaker bar, applied it to the frozen right CV joint on a Volkswagen Rabbit, oriented it so that the handle was horizontal, then jumped up and down on it to break the joint free. The CV joint came loose with a bang, scared Hell out of the four guys keeping the Rabbit from moving (in gear with the brakes on), but didn't bother the breaker bar one bit! ∎

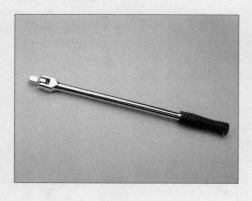

You need a breaker bar to initially loosen any large (over one inch or 25 mm) nut or bolt.

Start by removing the compensating sprocket (the big nut on the motor shaft). The compensating sprocket nut is usually well over an inch in diameter, so your little 3/8-inch-drive socket set won't do the job. The day I did my first Harley compensating sprocket was the day I went out and bought a 1/2-inch-drive socket-wrench set.

There are four elements you want in your 1/2-inch-drive set. You want, of course, sockets, a ratchet, at least one extension, a two-foot breaker bar, and a torque wrench. Actually, my torque wrench also ratchets, so I've never invested in an actual 1/2-inch-drive ratchet.

While you're out buying big wrenches, you should pick up two extensions: a long one (say,

about six inches) and a short one- or two-inch one. You should also consider getting adapters to match different sockets to different drives. Generally, you will find adapters to let you use one size drive (female side of the adapter) to the next size up socket (male side of the adapter). Less easy to find are adapters that go the other way: large drive for small socket. That is because handles made, say, for 1/2-inch drive can generate enough torque to literally explode a socket made for 3/8-inch drive.

Finally, you should consider picking up a universal joint for each size drive that you have. A universal joint is a hinged dweedlie that allows you to use a socket wrench when you can't quite get a straight shot in to the bolt head or nut that is the object of your attention.

Now you've got the compensating sprocket off. The next step is to dismantle the clutch. As I mentioned before, you can take the clutch apart without any special tools. It's a bit easier on the threads, however, if you use a clutch-spring compressor to take the tension off the adjusting nuts as you back them off. And, you *will* need it to put the clutch back together.

Earlier in this chapter is a photo of a clutch-spring compressor I cobbled together from an automotive harmonic balancer puller, some mild steel flat stock, and assorted hardware to hold it all together. That harmonic balancer puller has turned out to be an extremely useful multi-purpose tool. Not only does it form the heart of this clutch-spring compressor, it doubles as a gear puller, steering wheel puller, and a few other jobs. It just takes the harmonic balancer puller, some hardware, and a little imagination.

If you look inside the primary cover, you'll probably (depending on the motor you're dealing with) see a needle bearing pressed into it. That bearing supports one end of the starter shaft. Whether you have electric start, kick only, or a combination, that bearing is probably there.

That is a blind bearing. Replacing it is not normally part of an engine rebuild, but now's the time you'll see if it's worn out.

While you can get away with not having the right tool for most amateur-friendly jobs around a motorcycle, replacing blind bearings is not one of them. I've seen people try to remove them with pliers, vice grips, and other implements of destruction, and it's not a pretty sight. There is no part to grab that will support the forces needed to extract them.

Blind bearings consist of a thin-walled, stainless-steel cup with a lip and needle-shaped rollers that ride around the cup's inside wall. You can't press the thing out, since you can't get at it from the back side because it's in a blind hole. That's why they call it a "blind bearing."

All you grab with ordinary hand tools is the lip. When you start hauling away on that lip, you can't get a straight pull on it. You end up pulling to one side or the other. It won't slide straight out, but jams inside the hole.

Of course, you keep applying more and more pressure, and soon rip the lip off. The needles all fall out and you're left with an empty cup pressed into the hole. Now there's nothing to grab, period. It's all smooth stainless steel walls.

Eventually, everyone who sees this job through to the end uses a die grinder to remove the stainless-steel cup. If they're very, very careful, it is possible to remove the stainless steel cup without grinding into the aluminum wall of the hole it's pressed into.

Finally, I got tired of going through this miserable ordeal and bought the blind-bearing puller. To be honest, it wasn't a motorcycle engine that pushed me over the edge. Motorcycle primary covers cost a couple hundred dollars at worst. If you ruin one, you can throw it away and replace it with an even shinier one. No, I sprang for the puller when facing a blind bearing (also to support the starter shaft) let into the block of an antique aircraft engine worth $30,000 (if you can get one—only 800 were ever made). That bearing was so loose that it's amazing the starter ever engaged, so I couldn't ignore it. The block was so valuable, however, that I didn't want any damage at all. I also had an FAA inspector looking over my shoulder as well!

Anyway, I got the thing, and it worked so well that I'll never try to dig out a blind bearing with the wrong tools again.

The blind-bearing puller's business end is simply called the puller. It's got a set of jaws that point outward to grab inside the cup's lip. You insert this puller with the jaws behind the lip and

screw it down tight. There's actually a center piece called the "puller screw" that pushes down into the puller, spreading the jaws.

Tighten it down good and hard with a wrench so that it really locks in solidly. It'll jam in between the rollers and the lip, ruining the bearing, but you wouldn't be doing this if the bearing weren't already junk, right?

Next, you attach the pulling bar (the long shaft), slide on the slide hammer, and screw on the handle. You only have to hand tighten the pulling bar and handle. The handle has two purposes. First, you hold it to support the puller's free end, so everything stays in line. Second, it serves as a stop for the slide hammer.

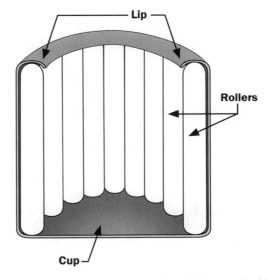

Blind bearings consist of a set of rollers rolling around inside a steel cup. A lip around the cup's open end holds the rollers in place

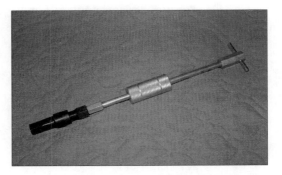

When you need to remove a blind bearing, there's no easier way than with a blind bearing puller!

Slide the hammer all the way down to the puller's business end. Then slam it back against the handle. While you're pulling the hammer back, it gains momentum and energy. When it hits the stop, it stops *real fast!*

It uses the same principle as an ordinary hammer. Stopping a heavy thing that fast requires a humongous force. By Newton's Third Law, that humongous force acts on the bearing as well. Since everything stays in line, that humongous force acts in just the right direction to slide the bearing neatly out of the hole in one piece.

The bearing doesn't come out all at once, though. The force multiplier is the distance the hammer moves divided by the distance the bearing moves.

On the first try, the bearing probably won't move at all because you were too tentative. You've gotta try harder.

When you gain confidence and really start slamming the hammer back, the bearing will suddenly move a little bit. Next time, it'll move a little more. Then it'll really move as the steel stretches out. Finally, it'll come flying out.

Now you have all the tools needed to take apart the clutch and remove the clutch hub nut. At this point you're left with the clutch shell (also called the clutch basket) sitting loose on the transmission shaft with the primary chain still wrapped around it. Before you can slide the clutch shell, primary chain, and engine sprocket off as a unit, you have to loosen the engine sprocket, which is a tight fit on the crankshaft splines.

No, no! Don't bother trying to use your handy-dandy gear puller. There isn't enough room behind the sprocket for the gear puller to get a grip. Use the harmonic balancer puller again. See those threaded holes in the side of the engine sprocket? They're there to give you a way to get a good grip on the sprocket. Find a couple of appropriate-sized bolts that will thread into those holes and hold the harmonic balancer puller on the sprocket. A few turns of the lead screw in the center of the puller and the sprocket will slip right off.

You have to slip the engine sprocket, primary chain, and clutch basket off as a unit because, as you found out when you tried to take only one

end off (I knew you were going to do it. You couldn't just follow the directions. You had to try a short cut, didn't you?), that wide primary chain won't twist enough to let you do it.

The rest of the process of stripping the motorcycle and removing the engine will be eventful, but won't require any additional tools. So, for the purposes of this book, we'll skip over it.

Repair the Bottom End?

Now, you have the bottom end of your motorcycle sitting on your workbench ready to be rebuilt. If you've done this job before, you don't need my help figuring out what tools you'll need.

If you've never done it before, load it up in your truck, car, little red wagon, or whatever and take it to a professional. Yes, you *can* rebuild the bottom end just from the directions. And, you might even get everything right. I don't recommend it, though.

The bottom end of a motorcycle engine is where all the force happens. The only big stresses in the top end are the gas pressure in the cylinder during the compression stroke. That's all held together by the head bolts. The rest of those parts rock, spin, bounce, and otherwise gyrate all over the place. But, they don't carry really big forces.

All the action, forcewise, happens in the bottom end. It's not a place for novices to be fiddling around. If you want to get into motorcycle bottom ends, find somebody who knows what they're doing and is willing to teach you.

A similar caution goes for rebuilding your cylinder heads. If you haven't done it before, get somebody with experience to show you how it's done. Having the tools in hand won't guarantee success. With so many things moving around with such tight tolerances, there is a lot that can go wrong. And, the penalty for failure can be a completely destroyed engine.

Well, maybe not *completely* destroyed. It's hard to see how a top-end failure can destroy a crankcase and is unlikely to ruin the crank. The connecting rods are likely to survive as well. But, I've got a motorcycle sitting out back waiting for a top-to-bottom rebuild because it swallowed a valve.

Don't take a chance, take a lesson!

Chapter 14

Tools for Chassis Work

I'm calling the chassis everything that isn't part of the engine. That really covers a lot of territory, and goes far beyond the Standard English definition of the word "chassis." But, we've covered just about all the tools you need, so there isn't much point in breaking the bike down in gory detail.

I will, however, organize this chapter a little bit into drivetrain, wheels and suspension, and frame. These are the main systems that are left.

Drivetrain

The drivetrain consists of the primary chain (or belt) and clutch, the transmission, and the rear chain (or belt or driveshaft). About all you can do in the primary case is dismantle the compensating sprocket and clutch, and yank the primary chain. I snuck in all the special tools you need for that when I was talking about the engine. (So, sue me!)

By the way, for those with primary belts, rather than chains, the procedure is about the same, as are the tools. Primary belts are just as wide as primary chains, and you can't get them off any more easily.

You don't need any fancy tools to yank the transmission. Nor do you really need anything fancy to see if the gears are badly worn. My personal philosophy on transmissions is that if nothing is chipped or broken, and the gears all turn, mesh, and shift smoothly, it isn't broken and you ought not fix it.

When you do need to fix it, tolerances can be in the 0.0001-inch range. Novices shouldn't mess with anything whose tolerances are less than a few thousandths. That makes transmission

rebuilding verboten. Yes, amateurs can do it. No, novices can't.

Secondary Drive Chain

The secondary, or drive, chain looks darn simple. But, believe me, it can be a royal pain.

To get control of the situation, start by jacking the bike up. For that you need a lift or jack. That will likely lead to the need for assorted wooden blocks. If your bike has a center stand, by all means use it!

After loosening the chain to get some slack (which just takes your assortment of wrenches—including the half-inch-drive socket set), you need to take apart the master link to get the thing

If your bike has a center stand, it makes an ideal built-in jack for many routine service operations.

off. That takes the short blade on your Swiss Army knife and a pair of needle-nosed pliers.

The only thing you can do with a drive chain is replace it. When you replace it, you have to cut the new one to length.

No, don't lay the old chain out on the shop floor and measure it with a tape measure. The whole point of the exercise is that the old chain has "stretched" so that now it's too long. If it's too long, you don't want to make the new chain the same length, now do you?

Don't measure the old chain's length; count the links. In fact, what you count is the rollers. The number of rollers doesn't change when your chain stretches. So, if you make your new chain have the same number of rollers that your old chain had, your new chain will be just as long as the old one was when *it* was new.

By the way, the chain doesn't actually stretch. What happens is all the little bearings on the rollers wear. Each one gains a few thousandths of extra clearance (which the chain tension promptly takes up). Multiply, say, twenty thousandths of an inch of extra slop by one hundred bearings and you've got an extra two inches of chain!

Well, now that you know how long your new chain has to be (in rollers, not inches), you've got to cut the new chain to length. Don't use a hacksaw! The metal in the chain is *way* too hard for that. I tried it once. I went through two carbide hacksaw blades before I got through the bluing on the chain. Even if you did cut the chain, you'd have a couple of sawed off link ends with nowhere to put the master link. You've got two choices: use a link cutter or use a grinder. I've never owned a link cutter. My friend Loyd down at H&H Cycle Works has a link cutter. Basically, what it does is press the pin out of the roller on the first link you want to remove.

Say that your old chain has 104 rollers. The end of the new chain starts with a roller. Count 104 rollers and mark the 104th. I don't care how you mark it. Once you've got the 104th roller identified, Count them again! That's the old carpenter's rule: measure twice and cut once. If you make a mistake on the long side, you can cut again. But, if you err on the short side, the chain becomes a souvenir.

The chain cutter is a little doohickey with a thumbscrew. You apply it to the target roller, twist the thumbscrew in and pretty soon the pin pops out and the link falls apart.

OK, you don't have the torture-chamber gizmo for drive chains. You'll have to use a grinding wheel. See those little nubs on the sides of the links? That's where the chain maker peened the ends of the pins over to hold the links

Table 14.1
Tools for Chassis Work

DRIVETRAIN
- Lift or jack
- Assorted wooden blocks
- Knife
- Needle-nosed pliers
- Bench grinder or vise and sharp file
- Hand drill
- Grinder
- Cold chisel

WHEELS AND SUSPENSION
- Lift or jack
- Tire irons (2)
- Wheel support frame
- Compressed air
- Truing stand
- Wheel balancing weights
- Long straightedge for aligning wheels
- Grease gun
- Shock absorber wrench

FRAME
- Portable grinder
- Welding jig
- Welding outfit

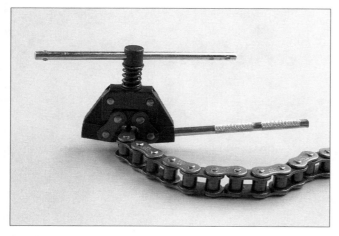

Special chain cutters are available to remove links from drive chains.

together. If you grind the peened-over part off flush with the side of the link, the link will fall apart. Well, you might have to coax it a little with a big screwdriver, but it'll come apart.

Make sure you grind off the right two nubs! There's a nub for each roller. You need to grind off the nub for your target roller (in this case the 104th) and the nub for the first roller you are going to throw away (in this case the 105th).

When I say "use a grinder," what I mean is that you have to grind away the metal rather than cut it. You can use a bench grinder. You can clamp the chain in a bench vise and attack it with a sharp file. I've successfully used both tactics. There are surely others that will work, too.

Sprockets

The only other thing you can do to the rear drive is change the sprockets. You should change the front sprocket (which is simple—it comes off the same way the compensating sprocket comes off, except more easily) and rear sprocket (which is a whole 'nother story) at the same time.

I know of three ways to hold a rear sprocket on: bolt it, rivet it, or weld it. If the last guy bolted it on, you just have to unbolt it. If he riveted it on, you'll have to drill out the rivets with a hand drill. If it was welded on (not too common), you'll either have to go at it with a portable grinder and cold chisel, or throw the brake drum away.

Wheels and Suspension

Of course, to remove a wheel you need a jack or lift. Unbolting the wheels typically takes just the tools from your standard tool kit. There are three basic wheel operations: spoking, truing, and tire replacement.

Frankly, I don't screw around with wheels anymore. Once a year I drag my scoot into a professional shop and say, "Baby needs new shoes."

At the same time they replace the rubber and inner tube, they check the spokes, true the wheels, and so forth. Maybe I'm just lazy, but it just seems easier to earn the money to pay them to do the job than to do it myself.

But, maybe you don't feel that way. Since fiddling with wheels is certainly something within the purview of an amateur, I'll go into what you'll need.

Bench grinders are excellent general-purpose shop equipment useful for everything from sharpening drills to cutting drive chains.

Before you start jacking up a bike, make sure you have a handy supply of assorted wooden blocks to make the job go smoothly and more safely.

Changing Tires

To remove and replace a tire, all you really need is a pair of tire irons. You can do the job with one tire iron, but I've found that having a second one makes it easier.

If you change tires often, you can make the job easier by building a frame to support the tire

Use a truing stand to check wheel-rim alignment and for static balancing wheels once the tires are on and inflated.

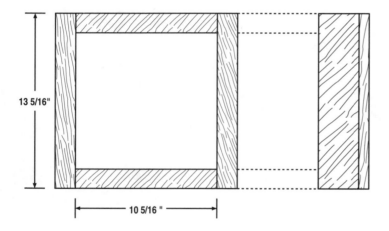

Building a wooden frame makes working on tires and rims easier. This plan is dimensioned for a 19-inch spoked wheel.

rim from the underside. Shown here is a simple frame you can make out of two-by-four inch lumber and a sheet of plywood. The dimensions are not critical, but remember that the wheel diameter should just fit over the frame's *diagonal.*

Since the frame is square, each side (measured on the outside) should be 70% of the rim diameter. If you have a 19-inch rim, multiply 19 by 0.7 to get 13.3. That is just about 13-5/16

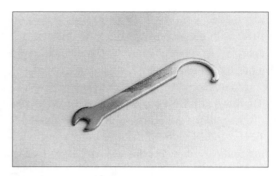

The only specialized suspension tool is a shock-absorber adjusting wrench.

inches. The two side pieces (in the picture) are just that long.

The top and bottom pieces have to be cut shorter by twice the thickness of each of the side pieces. The standard thickness of a two-by-four is 1.5 inches (don't make a funny face at me, I don't mill the lumber, I just use it!), so the top and bottom pieces should probably be 3 inches shorter, or 10-5/16 inches long. That's what to expect, but measure your wood before starting to cut it, just to be sure.

The plywood is a square, 13-5/16 inches on a side. The thickness isn't critical. Quarter-inch plywood is a little on the flimsy side and I can't guarantee how long it will last. Three-quarter is overkill and will make the thing awfully heavy. Half-inch is a good compromise.

The purpose of the frame is to support the rim evenly from underneath while you wrestle the tire off it. Without some kind of support, the wheel ends up resting on the hub. It is then unstable and the job is at least twice as hard. You also stand a greater risk of bending spokes or the rim itself.

Of course, to reinflate the new tire, you'll need compressed air. If you have a compressor in your shop, you're all set. If not, you'll either have to do it the old-fashioned way with a tire pump, or load the reassembled but uninflated wheel in your pickup truck and trundle on down to the nearest automotive service station to use their air pump.

Balancing

Harley-Davidson recommends balancing tires with these words: "Wheel balancing is recommended to improve handling and reduce vibration, especially at high road speeds." Sounds like understatement to me!

For a number of reasons, balancing motorcycle tires is not as fussy as it is for car tires. You can get away with static balancing on a truing stand. The photo shows a homemade model. Of course, to adjust the balance, you need appropriate weights.

You need the truing stand to align spoked wheels. You can use a truing stand to check a solid (mag type) wheel, but I don't know how you could fix one that was bent.

Spoked wheels are adjusted by tightening spokes to pull the rim one way or another. There are such beasties as spoke-nipple wrenches, but you can usually get by with a crescent wrench, or even vise grips.

Greasing Bearings

Before you put the wheel back on the bike, you should make sure the bearings are loaded with grease. If your bike has grease fittings for this purpose (some do, some don't—look for the little nipples), you'll need a grease gun.

I suppose I should tell you how to use a grease gun. OK, slip the "muzzle" end of the gun (the place where the grease comes out) over the grease fitting until you feel it pop into place, then squeeze the handle, which pushes grease out through the muzzle and into the grease fitting. The grease gun muzzle snaps onto the grease fitting so you can use both hands to operate the grease gun.

If your bike doesn't have grease fittings on the wheel hubs, don't despair. You'll need a grease gun *somewhere* on the bike.

Before greasing the bearings, of course, you should check to make sure they're in good condition. Consult the repair manual to find out how to inspect the wheel bearings on your particular bike.

If they need replacing (wheel bearings are, like most bearings, a non-repairable item), you may find the old ones simply slip out easily, or you may need to use a pilot bearing puller.

To use a pilot bearing puller, start by winding the extracting nut at the middle of the threaded shaft all the way up to the T-handle. Then, back

the pointy-ended tapered screw all the way out so the three jaws fold down together.

Now, position the stand legs on the cross bar so that they are just wide enough to stand on the bearing seat straddling the bearing. Make sure that the legs are evenly spaced so that the threaded shaft runs down exactly through the middle of the bearing's opening.

Put the jaws through the bearing so that they can grab the back side. Then, run the threaded

Pilot bearing pullers are a little tricky to use, but still useful for an ordinary workshop to have.

Most motorcycles have grease fittings on the wheel axles (as well as several other places) that allow you to pack grease into the hubs using a grease gun.

shaft down in between the jaws, pushing them out against the bearing's inside diameter. Tighten it by hand until the puller stands solidly erect.

Position the stand legs so that they press against the bearing seat, then run the extracting nut down against the cross bar. Use a wrench to tighten the extracting nut, drawing the bearing out of its seat.

This procedure goes more smoothly if you happen to be one of those rare individuals with three hands. We benighted souls with only the usual complement of two tend to be clumsy with it, but it'll work out in the end. Once everything's all set up square and hand tightened, turning the extracting nut (you'll have to hold the cross bar to keep the puller from trying to twist off its legs) will neatly draw the bearing out in no time flat.

Of course, if you don't have everything squared up, the puller will get all out of kilter and you'll get nowhere fast.

Also, make sure the legs are pressing against the bearing seat that you're trying to pull the bearing out of. If you stand them against any part of the bearing, it won't work, either.

Wheel Alignment

Once your wheels are back on the bike, you'll have to check them for alignment. That is, make sure the front wheel lines up with the back wheel. For that you need a straight board or aluminum angle—anything light enough to hold up with one hand and stiff enough to remain perfectly straight—that is long enough to reach from the back of the back wheel to the front of the front one.

To make the test, hold the straightedge alongside the rear wheel so that it contacts the tire in two places: in front of and behind the hub. Adjust the position of the front forks (i.e., turn the handlebars) until you can also touch the two corresponding positions on the front tire as well. If the wheels are aligned, the straightedge will touch all four places. If you can't touch all four, the wheels aren't aligned.

Re-aligning the wheels is a matter of loosening the rear axle, just as you would when tightening your chain, and separately adjusting the chain tensioners on the left and right sides to square up the axle. You use exactly the same tools as you use to adjust the chain tension.

Shock Absorber Adjustment

About the only specialized suspension tool I know of is a shock-absorber adjusting wrench. If your bike has adjustable shocks, either as original equipment or aftermarket replacements, you'll want to have a shock-absorber wrench like the one in the photo. You *can* change the adjustment by jacking the rear end up to unload the suspension, then go at the shocks with big vise grips, locking pliers, or even a strong pair of hands, but I definitely don't recommend it. You'll likely gouge the heck out of your pretty chrome shocks. Get the right wrench.

Although I just got through saying there were no more tools you particularly need for suspensions, there is a caveat: Before you dig into your

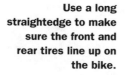

Use a long straightedge to make sure the front and rear tires line up on the bike.

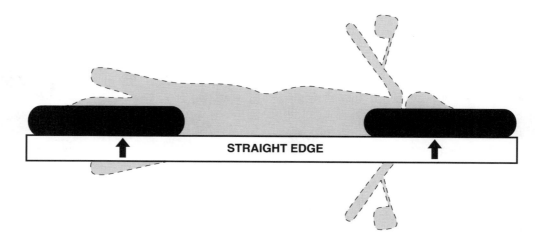

STRAIGHT EDGE

**Critical dimensions of
a typical motorcycle
frame.**

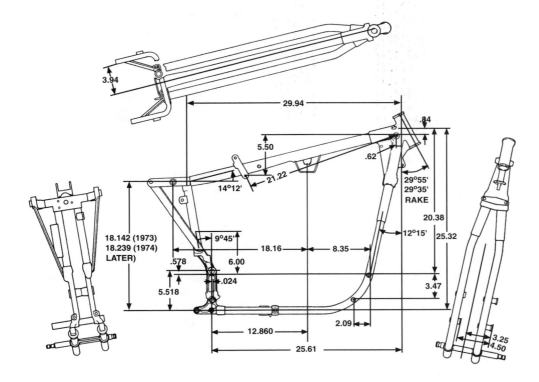

suspension, check to make sure you don't need an odd-size wrench or other tool particular to your bike.

Suspension fasteners (bolts and nuts) tend to be larger than most other fasteners on your bike because they have to stand up to all the stupid things you drive your bike into. Make sure you have the right tools for *your* bike.

Frame

In a word (or five), Don't mess with your frame! No matter what you do to it, you'll be worse off than when you started.

Having warned you in no uncertain terms, I now feel free to tell you what you'll need when you succumb to temptation.

There are three things you can do to your frame: cut, weld, and bend. All three can hurt your frame, and you can't do them as well as a professional.

Cutting a frame is not a case of yanking out a hacksaw and having at it. Motorcycle frames are made of specially tempered alloys that are hard to cut. In addition, the places you would want to do your cutting are at the existing welds, not in the middle of a frame member. Because of the

conditions under which welds are made, they're even harder to hacksaw.

If you want to make the mistake of cutting your frame, use a portable grinder with a cutoff wheel. A cutoff wheel is a thin, large-diameter carbide disk that mounts in the portable grinder.

When you use the thing, you *must* use goggles. Not just safety glasses; use full goggles. This isn't just an OSHA bureaucrat talking! What cutoff wheels do for a living is turn pieces of steel into a shower of flaming metal particles. They will get into your eyes, and they will injure your eyes.

Now that you've sliced through your perfectly good frame, you'll have to build a jig to hold it straight while you reweld it. I can't give you a set of plans for such a jig because what you need depends on where you're trying to weld.

The diagram, however, at least shows the most critical things to worry about. Of course, you need to make sure the engine mounts line up. A lot of people ensure this by the simple expedient of having the motor bolted in place when they work on the frame. The second critical area is to make sure that the axis of the front-fork bearing is in a plane that is accurately perpendic-

Biker Rags

What? You don't know about biker newspapers? There's at least one (usually monthly) newsprint publication covering motorcycling news in just about every part of the United States, and probably most of the world. In the Northeast, it's called *The Motorcyclist's Post*. In the West, look for *Thunder Press*.

The best way to get hold of a copy, since you're laid up in a hospital bed, is to send your ol' lady, ol' man—whatever, down to the nearest motorcycle shop. Even better, don't wait until you're laid up in the hospital with a bent scooter. Go out *right now* and scout up a copy. You'll find out that it's the best way to keep up with what your fellow bikers are doing. ■

The best tool for cutting frame members is a portable grinder or hand drill with a cutoff wheel. Whenever you use a cutoff tool, be sure to wear full goggles, not just safety glasses.

ular to the rear swingarm bearing, and is centered. Finally, make sure that the rear shock absorber mounts are accurately parallel to the rear swingarm bearing.

Welding is an art. You need three things to make an acceptable weld: a generous supply of electricity, a welding outfit, and lots and lots of practice. You can get the first two by throwing a few bucks around. You get the latter by buying a load of scrap steel and spending many hours welding it together. Even better, take a night course where they'll also teach you how to prepare the edges to be joined.

Finally, we come to bending. I'm not talking about bending individual pieces of frame tube (which you shouldn't be doing at all), I'm talking about bending the entire frame.

You can't do it.

If your frame is so out of whack that you have to straighten it, take it to a professional.

Having a bent frame is unusual. To bend a frame, you just about have to drive a car over it. Now, that does happen. And, whenever you go to buy a used bike, check carefully to make sure it hasn't happened. Sometimes it happens to your bike.

If it happens to your bike, the best thing to do is to pick up the telephone next to your hospital bed and call around looking for a motorcycle frame straightening specialist. That means checking the Yellow Pages of the phone book, asking at all the local scooter shops, and finally finding an advertisement in the biker newspaper that covers your area.

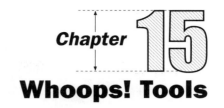

You just dropped a screw into your oil tank! Now, what're ya gonna do? You can't reach in there to retrieve it. Your fingers won't fit. You can't just leave it there. It might get sucked down into your oil pump (or worse) when you're doing 70 mph on a dark desert highway at 2:00 a.m.

"Whoops! tools" are odd little items that you need when things go very seriously wrong. Either you make a mistake, or it's just your turn to have bad luck.

For example, bolts usually break off because they were over-torqued. Nuts rust solidly over studs because they weren't properly weather treated. Maybe it's not your mistake, but bad things usually happen because somebody did something wrong.

Pick-Up Tools

The simplest pick-up tool is a magnetic pick-up tool—a magnet on the end of a stick. There are also mechanical jobbies with three or four wire jaws at the end of a long flexible tube. You open the jaws by depressing a plunger at the other end of the tube. These items are not tremendously strong, but are capable of picking up small parts dropped into small places.

Nut Buster

A nut buster removes nuts that are seized onto a stud or bolt and have been so badly damaged that there's no way to unscrew them. The nut buster consists of a C-shaped frame with a chisel-point blade at one end of the C. You fit the frame around the nut and use a wrench to tighten a screw that drives the chisel point into the side of the nut. In theory, the chisel splits the nut so that

it breaks free of the thread and comes off in one or two pieces.

Impact Screwdriver

I went into great detail about impact screwdrivers earlier in this chapter. I bring them up again here because they are the port of last resort for those screws with bunged slots.

Easy-Out

When a screw or bolt breaks off in a cast part, such as a crankcase, you need to use an Easy-Out. An Easy-Out is about the size and shape of a tap, and you use a tap handle to turn it. The difference between an Easy-Out and a tap is that the

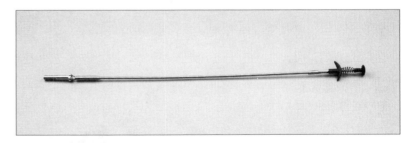

Mechanical pickup tools are useful for picking up non-magnetic parts.

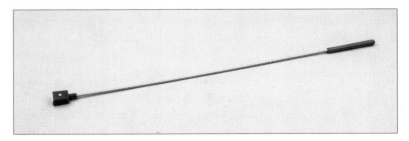

Magnetic pickup tools have saved many a motorcycle teardown by retrieving small parts dropped into unreachable places.

A "nut buster" removes a frozen or damaged nut by literally slicing it open.

Easy-Outs are often the only hope when you break a bolt off inside a cast part (such as an engine block).

Impact drivers are the port of last resort for screws with bunged slots.

Heli-Coils replace stripped threads in cast parts (especially aluminum castings).

Easy-Out doesn't really have threads, it has spiral flutes that have a *left-handed* twist. In other words, when you turn them counterclockwise, they drive into the part instead of pulling out.

You start the procedure by drilling an appropriate sized hole down through the center of the broken bolt. Then you take the appropriate sized Easy-Out and tap it snugly into the hole with a light hammer. Then you apply the tap handle and turn counterclockwise. The Easy-Out drives into the hole. The flutes dig into the sides of the hole, transferring the torque from the tap handle to what's left of the bolt. In theory, that torque backs the broken bolt out of the threaded hole.

Heli-Coil

A Heli-Coil technically isn't really a tool. It looks for all the world like an automotive throttle-return spring. It is made of spring-steel wire, but the wire cross-section is square rather than round. You use it to replace threads that have been stripped out of a threaded hole. The Heli-Coil kit consists of a tap, an installation tool, and some coils.

Say that you've stripped one of the tapped holes in your Harley's front fork slider. You need those threads to screw in one of the bolts that hold your front fender on. Start by drilling out the remaining threads with a 1/4-inch drill. Then use the correct tap that comes with the Heli-Coil kit to form a new set of threads. These new threads have the same 20-thread-per-inch pitch as your bolt, but are necessarily of larger diameter. Next, you take your Heli-Coil installation tool and use it to screw one of the coils into the new threads. The coil's outside diameter is larger than the diameter of those new threads, so the coil is squeezed into the hole. That's important because it is that compression that holds the coil in place. When you remove the installation tool, you'll find that the inside of the coil forms a beautiful set of threads!

Heli-Coils are especially useful around aluminum cast cases and parts. Aluminum is soft, and even a little over-torquing can strip the threads. I once worked at a company where they had so much trouble with threads in aluminum castings that they didn't even bother threading aluminum. They started installing Heli-Coils in all aluminum threaded holes. They never had trouble with stripped threads again.

Frank's Brit Bike Barn, owned and operated by Frank Holmes, is housed in a small converted 40 x 22-foot horse barn conveniently located a short distance from the inn where Frank and his wife live in New England. While the space isn't Frank's ultimate dream shop, it's been a compact and comfortable shop that has allowed his business to grow.

Frank outfitted the space for his small motorcycle restoration business in the late 1990s, adding insulation and a poured concrete floor. The main shop is 25 x 22 feet, with an insulated overhead garage door providing easy access to roll in the latest project or ride out a newly-restored Triumph. Windows in the garage door and in the back wall provide some natural light. Next to the workshop is a 15 x 22-foot showroom where a black and white tile floor helps feature bikes Frank has for sale and store restored machines waiting to be picked up, and where he plans to add toilet facilities in the future. A second floor is used primarily for storage, but also houses an air compressor and blasting cabinet.

The floor of the main shop is concrete with a sheet of chemically resistant landfill liner over it, which not only helps manage moisture and heat loss, but makes inadvertent spills easy to clean up. To further insulate and provide comfort while working, Frank also put down sections of 3/4-inch thick horse stall mats. Heat comes from an Empire through-the-wall propane heater with electronic ignition (no open-flame pilot light). General lighting comes from the ubiquitous overhead fluorescent shop lights, with additional task lighting positioned to brighten up key work

areas, and electrical outlets are generously placed as well.

The shop is compact, and storage space is at a premium with $40,000 in supplies and parts inventory on hand at any given time, plus parts such as fuel tanks, fenders, or wheels from ongo-

Frank uses a combination of home-built work benches and a commercial Air Lift, giving his shop a homey, semi-professional feel. Horse stall mats make long days working at the bench or lift easier on the feet and help insulate the concrete floor during the long New England winter.

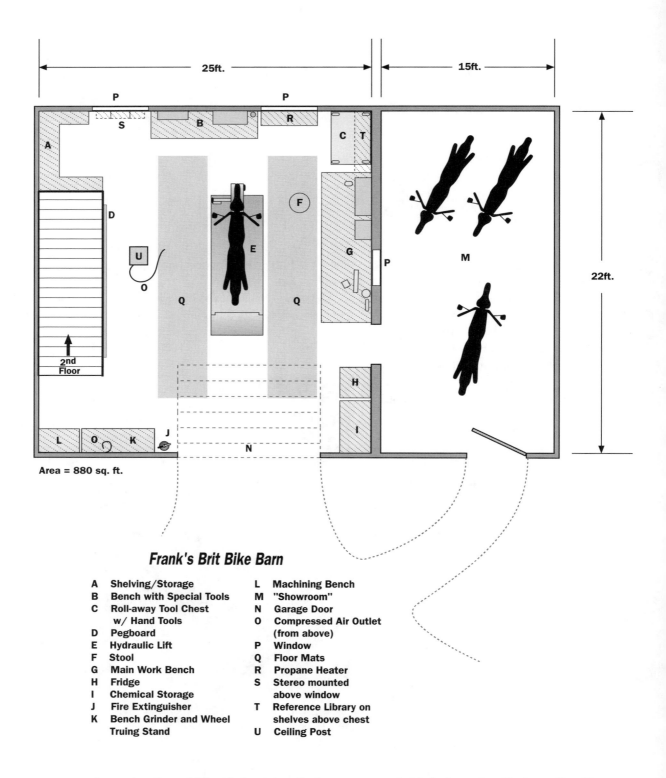

25ft. **15ft.**

P P R

S B

A

C T

D

F

U

O E

G

P

Q Q

M

H

I

J

L O K

N

2nd Floor

Area = 880 sq. ft.

22ft.

Frank's Brit Bike Barn

A	Shelving/Storage	L	Machining Bench
B	Bench with Special Tools	M	"Showroom"
C	Roll-away Tool Chest	N	Garage Door
	w/ Hand Tools	O	Compressed Air Outlet
D	Pegboard		(from above)
E	Hydraulic Lift	P	Window
F	Stool	Q	Floor Mats
G	Main Work Bench	R	Propane Heater
H	Fridge	S	Stereo mounted
I	Chemical Storage		above window
J	Fire Extinguisher	T	Reference Library on
K	Bench Grinder and Wheel		shelves above chest
	Truing Stand	U	Ceiling Post

ing restorations. Although the stairwell takes up valuable room in the main shop, Frank has lined the walls up to second floor with pegboard to make use of the otherwise wasted space. Additional shelving for storage is tucked into the cor-

ner behind the stairwell. A small refrigerator keeps cold ones close at hand.

One shelf at nearly ceiling height holds the library of books and restoration manuals for reference, while another shelf above one back window houses a stereo. Between the windows on the back wall, Frank has spared some rare wall space for a classic bike calendar and other wall art, which is nearly the only wall space not used to hang parts or tools. On the interior wall between the garage door and door to the showroom is a freestanding shelf dedicated to chemical storage.

Air tools operate from the Craftsman compressor located out of the way upstairs. Frank used 1/2-inch PVC pipe to run air outlets to all the key work areas, including the air-powered motorcycle lift. The PVC pipe works fine, he says, and can be easily installed with only a handsaw and PVC cement—no soldering required. All the fittings for his air supply system were purchased at Home Depot.

An air lift dominates the center of the main shop, surrounded by workbenches and tool storage along the walls. To lift a front end of a bike, Frank uses tie downs to either suspend the frame from the floor joists above, or puts the bike on its center stand or other support and holds down the rear.

In addition to the commercial grade lift, Frank uses a small 1,500-pound capacity motorcycle jack with locking wheels. The small jack allows him to roll bikes in various states of disassembly around the shop while he works on other projects.

The main workbench is directly opposite the motorcycle lift, with small parts storage above the bench. In addition to the main workbench, Frank has set up a specialty tool workbench along the back wall of the shop, and a "machine shop" in a work area at the foot of the stairwell that includes a drill press, small metal lathe (used primarily for truing and cleaning), grinders, benchtop wire wheel brush and polisher, and a whetstone machine used for sharpening drill bits. A portable wheel-truing stand can be used on any of the workbenches.

Since Frank runs a one-man shop, he often must do two things at once. He uses a cordless phone with a headset so that he can keep working while he talks to customers on the phone. Always safety conscious, Frank has easily accessible fire extinguishers, safety glasses and goggles, ear plugs, and even a respirator for use

Rolling open the overhead garage door reveals the compact and tidy shop known as Frank's Brit Bike Barn, a small restoration shop converted from a horse barn. Owner Frank Holmes dedicated most of the space to a one-bay work area, and finished off a nearby room (to the right) as a showroom.

Through the doorway is Frank's showroom. Though a small shop, Frank's Brit Bike Barn is well organized, maximizing the use of space.

when he's glass beading in the blasting cabinet upstairs. He wears nitrile gloves while wrenching on the bikes to protect his skin and keep his hands clean.

Among the tools Frank keeps handy is a digital camera to document the disassembly of the bike as well as the stages of restoration. Not only do the photos aid him in the restoration and re-building process, but he often emails the photos to his customers so that they can follow the progress of the job, helping them to feel like part of the process.

Frank plans to add a computer to help maintain his inventory, and says that ideally he would include a hydraulic press and a "dirty room" in his ideal setup. But for the average restorer, the setup in Frank's Brit Bike Barn is more than adequate.

Contact **Frank's Brit Bike Barn:**
http://www.franksbritbikes.com
info@franksbritbikes.com

"We specialize in big-inch motors, hot rods, building 'em from the ground up and one-off customs," explains Loyd Hall, proprietor of H&H Cycle Works in Needles, California. "We've been very successful with that and have die-hard customers who keep coming back.

"This is basically an old time 'chopper shop.' A guy can come in here and feel comfortable. He doesn't have to feel he's got to have on a business suit or $1,000 in his pocket. We will answer questions and tell somebody how they can fix it themselves. It's not been a 'let's make lots of money' shop.

"Our mainstay is the service department: We have three service bays. That's what's fun and that's what we like to do. We do oil changes, tune ups, carburetor rebuilds, adjusting valves, changing tires and chains, building motors, balancing, big-inch stuff, and hot-rod stuff."

H&H has been doing business in Needles for 15 years. For most of that time, running the shop has been a part-time thing.

"For me, it's been basically a toy shop. I get to build all the motorcycles I want to build, play with mine and make all kinds of changes, and with the shop I can better afford to do it. And, of course, I put everything I make back into it. I make my living from the railroad."

Loyd is an engineer with the Santa Fe Railroad. He has kept the shop going and growing with the help of partners, first with Larry Hart (who has since left the firm) and now with Tom (TV Tommy) Nelson.

"I've been very lucky that I didn't have to have the shop support me," says Loyd. "But, it's grown to the point now where it's kinda hard to do on just a part-time basis. Now I'm in here five days a week every week. I'm probably going to get early retirement from the railroad, so I'm tied up pretty well here."

The diagram shows the general layout of H&H's facility. The building is a converted warehouse that they moved into five years ago. It took two men two or three weeks (at a cost of $15,000) to construct partitions, install the three lifts, set up wiring, lighting, workbenches, shelves, and so forth. Each workstation has its own air-over-hydraulic lift, generous workbench space, and a full toolbox.

"When we set up a workstation," says Loyd, "we set up a workstation where you don't have to walk around the bike. You don't have to be away

The parts counter provides an easily identified central location to greet customers, an attactive place to display impulse items, and reliable crowd control.

131

from your toolbox. You can stand right on one side where you can reach into your toolbox or reach your workbench, or your vise, and spin the motorcycle around so you don't have to be away from your bench. You can vary the height of the motorcycle according to what part you're working on."

In addition to the three workstations, the shop area includes storage for up to a half-dozen motorcycles waiting for attention, as well as machine tool areas and lots of storage. Machine tools include a lathe, a boring bar, a vertical sander, two bench grinders, a drill press, a band saw, and a radial-arm saw with a cutoff wheel for a blade. The shop also has a complete set of welding equipment.

"A mechanic's most important necessity is tools," Loyd points out. "The more tools you've got, the easier the job is. You'll find out what you need as you go along. You can start out with basic automotive type hand tools and, as you see the need, add more specialized tools. You know you need a specialized tool when you look in the book and it tells you!

"The main drawback of the shade-tree mechanic is that he doesn't have the specialized tools that it takes to work on the bike. Without the right tools, you're hurtin'! You can make do,

As do most professional shops, H&H Cycle Works uses a variation of the common work area floor plan. Up to half a dozen motorcycles can be stored in the motorcycle storage area while waiting their turn in one of the workstations.

as I did for a lot of years, but you'll eventually end up with $20,000 worth of specialized tools just to do certain jobs that would take 4-5 times longer if you didn't have them—that is, if you could do them at all!"

The photo shows a customer's-eye view of H&H's parts department. "When you're setting up shelves," Loyd advises, "leave yourself enough room to keep expanding. You never have enough shelves.

"I organize my shelves by areas of the motorcycle. I've got all my electrical stuff in one section. I've got all the bottom-end stuff in another section: Cases, wheels, sprocket shafts, pinion shafts, and all those bottom-end parts are together. I've got all my carburetion stuff in another section. Speedometers, wheel stuff, transmission stuff, sheet metal, brake parts—all these different categories of parts have their own areas. If somebody comes in and wants a brake part, I go over to where I keep the brake stuff and that's where it's gonna be."

Pictured also is part of the showroom area. "There are a lot of impulse items that you can do really well with according to how much traffic you've got and what your location is," Loyd points out. "If you're in the right place, T-shirts, wallets, glasses, and stuff like that can pay your overhead and then your service department can make your money."

Making the transition from amateur to professional can be difficult. "If it's a business for hire, where you make money," says Loyd, "it's altogether different from working out of your garage.

"You have to keep records of anything you do for money. If you're working for somebody for free, what do you need records for? Everything is done with a handshake and you're doing it for nothing anyway. If you are in the business, however, your reputation is based on the kind of work you do, and the kind of warranty, and the kind of backup you give it.

"I keep all receipts for everything I buy and everything I sell, and records of anything related to taxes, whether it be sales tax or federal tax. Without records you can get yourself in a lot of trouble. If a customer comes in and says, 'you did this,' or 'you did that,' I'll pull out that work

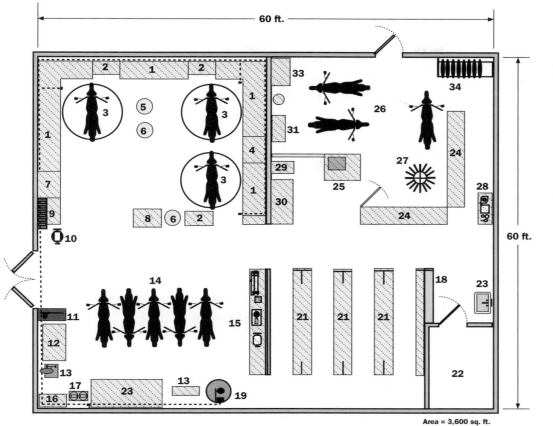

**H & H Cycle Works
Needles, California**

1	Workbench
2	Tools
3	Bike Lift
4	Degreasing Tank
5	Dirty Rag Barrel
6	Trash
7	Hardware Assortment
8	Roll-Away Cart
9	Manuals
10	Pedestal Grinder
11	Radial-Arm Saw
12	Welding Bench
13	Press
14	Bike Storage
15	Machine Tools
16	Storage Cabinet
17	Cutting Torch
18	Misc Storage
19	Air Compressor
20	Hanging Parts
21	Parts Shelves
22	Rest Room
23	Sink
24	Display Case
25	Cash Register
26	Showroom
27	Motorclothes Display
28	Coffee Maker
29	File Cabinet
30	Desk
31	Oil
32	Water Cooler
33	Soda Machine
34	Tire Display

Area = 3,600 sq. ft.

order and know for sure whether we did it. It's protection for us as well as for the customer.

"Get with somebody to get a little shop experience," Loyd advises anyone contemplating opening a shop. "There are some parts that'll sit on the shelf for years, but you've gotta have 'em. Some parts move quickly."

Most distributors require that you have a valid seller's permit and tax number, which means dealing with the state board of equalization and with sales tax. You may have to pay sales taxes yearly, quarterly, or monthly.

Normally, a distributor would want to see a photocopy of your business license and your franchise tax permit. In California (and probably it's going to be this way in all states before too long) you've also got to have EPA permits. After all, you're a hazardous waste generator—you use oil, solvents, battery acid and, even worse, batteries.

"They had me wound up, bound up, and tied up," Loyd recalls, "I was about ready to close the doors! Finally, after my wife wrote our senator, a man came down here from the EPA in San Bernardino County and we finally worked out a compromise that was livable. They were treating me like I was some huge corporation! I had to have everything from disaster plans to maps of where everything was—every fire bottle and every quart of oil—but that's part of doing business and something you've got to put up with."

Distributors will also make sure you have a business residence. They'll often want a picture of it with your business name on a sign outside to prove that you are really doing business with the public. That keeps people who work out of their garages from selling parts for next to nothing to all their buddies and cutting out the guys who are spending $50K to open up a business.

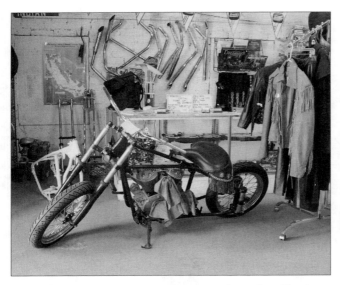

The showroom area puts custom motorcycles—the ultimate biker's impulse item—right where customers can come in and drool over them.

When you first start out, your distributors will want a minimum $500 order. Loyd suggests that the easiest way to get in contact with distributors is to call around to aftermarket shops and ask them for the numbers for reputable distributors, such as Chrome Specialties, Nempco, Custom Chrome (CCI), Gary Bang, and Drag Specialties. "You've got to be really careful because some of the smaller distributors sell aftermarket parts that are mostly seconds," he warns.

With almost all of the distributors, if you order enough parts per year, they'll give you a low free-freight minimum, so you may be getting free freight for orders as small as $50 or $75. You can also get open accounts.

"I don't normally like to run an open account," says Loyd. "Most of my accounts are C.O.D. That keeps me out of trouble. An open account can get you into trouble because you can spend a whole lot of money and at the end of the month when it comes due, you're saying 'whoops!' You have to go out and borrow money to cover it. Then you're playing catch up."

Most distributors also have a "spring dating" program where you can spend whatever they set you up for, and then they give you about six months to pay it off.

Loyd considers spring dating to be a useful financing tool, if used cautiously: "If you're get-

ting set up to expand or something like that, and if you have capital coming in that you can count on, spring dating may be a good way to go. If you're buying all this equipment or all these parts to, say, build a motorcycle for sale or build engines for sale, then you will sell those engines or sell those motorcycles to get the money to pay off the spring dating. But, you've got to have some sort of a plan. You've gotta use your head."

Inventory

Parts are always the most expensive item in a professional motorcycle shop. "With the price of Harley parts now," Loyd says, "you could spend $4,000 and not have anything. You could spend $15,000 and just barely get by."

With UPS and 2nd Day Air, you don't need to carry a large inventory. Minimizing your inventory is important because large inventories tie up too much money. Your best bet is to carry a minimum amount according to your volume, then count on reordering frequently.

The most important items to keep on hand are hardware, electrical items, gaskets, and fluids.

Electronic components die more frequently than anything else on the Harley-Davidsons H&H specializes in. So, Loyd has to make sure he has everything from wire and connectors to ignition modules on hand.

He also keeps a full set of gaskets and seals in stock. "You can't fix something if you don't have a gasket to put it back together!" he points out. Although customers might be willing to have their cycles tied up for a week waiting for a special stroker crankshaft, they'll get pretty upset if you run out of primary cover gaskets.

"A full set" does not mean one set for one type of motor. It means multiple items of every gasket for every motor likely to come through the shop. Most distributors sell complete gasket and seal board kits. They send you a board with all the gaskets relevant to all the different Harleys. And, it's got all the part numbers right there so you can keep a little bit closer track of your inventory— what you've got and what you don't have.

"Finally," says Loyd, "unless you have enough money to live on for a year without drawing a salary from your shop, expect to go under! That's what kills most shops that don't make it."

Parts and Consumables

You're pretty well set up except that, as you look around, you have a lot of empty shelves and cabinets. You know that's not right because as soon as you haul your bike in and take something off because it's worn out or broken, your next task will be to put something else in its place. That brings us to parts and consumables.

Parts

Parts can be specific motorcycle bits and pieces, such as carburetors and primary cases, that you don't plan to replace if you can avoid it, or they can be things like nuts, bolts, screws, and so forth that you need often enough to make it worth keeping some on hand just in case.

Most amateurs don't keep a lot of new parts around. It would be a little strange to walk into the average biker's workshop and see an assortment of brand new S&S carburetors holding down a top shelf. When the average biker drops a few hundred dollars on a counter for a new part, he usually knows exactly where it's going and is planning to spend the next three hours putting it there.

What you see on amateurs' parts shelves are used parts. They are either the parts he or she took off in order to put something better on, or they are glitzy bits saved from a bike he or she parted with.

Hardware is a different story. You have to lay in a stock of nuts, bolts, screws, lock washers, cotter pins, and so forth.

You have choices. The simplest thing to do when you're starting out is to purchase a hardware assortment. Begin by determining whether your bike uses metric or American standard fasteners, or, perhaps, both. Most motorcycle manufacturers have been using metric sizes for decades. The only modern bikes you'll need American standard for are Harleys. Beware, however, because even Harley uses metric fasteners in places where they think you won't notice.

If you're into antiques, you may have problems. Some older English makes (I'm thinking specifically of BSAs and Triumphs) use Whitworth threads, which you ain't-a-gonna find in a hardware store.

When you run low on a particular item, that means you use it a lot. The best way to replace such items is to buy them by the box.

The back of the workbench is a good place to keep consumables handy but out of the way.

Harleys use American standard fine threads as well as coarse threads. You're less likely to find fine-thread fasteners in a hardware store, but you will find them in almost any automotive-supply store.

When you go looking for a hardware assortment, look for metric sizes from 6 mm to 14 mm and American sizes from 1/4-inch to 3/8-inch. Fasteners smaller and larger do appear on bikes—most bikes will have a few—but these are odd items that you should purchase individually when you have the bad luck of damaging or losing the ones already on your bike.

As time goes on, you'll find particular items that you use a lot of. They'll be the ones that disappear first from your assortment. At that point, it's a good idea to replace them by the box.

Most hardware stores and many automotive stores will be happy to sell you hex-head bolts, or nuts, lock washers, and so forth—buy the box of 50 or 100. You can set aside a shelf on which to arrange your little boxes of favorite bits.

Your third choice is to buy loose hardware. Hardware stores sell these things individually for pennies. I swear that the things are a loss

leader. I can't imagine that what a hardware store makes from selling 6-32 machine screws one at a time could possibly pay for the checkout clerk's time, let alone the shelf space. I'll bet the only reason they bother to stock them is that hardware stores are the only place you can buy such small items individually and they want you to be tempted by all the geegaws you have to walk past on the way to the loose-fastener department.

Automotive stores usually stock small packages of fasteners. You'll get, maybe, two 10-mm bolts in a package.

Actually, the only reason I stock a lot of hardware is because I do a lot of serious custom work. If you're just bolting on a luggage rack, the necessary hardware usually comes with the rack. It's a whole 'nother story when you start fitting Fat Bob tanks onto a Sportster. I also recycle a lot of parts from one bike to another. In that case, the hardware seldom travels along with the parts.

What typically happens in the recycled parts game is that you strip perfectly good parts from one bike in order to customize it. The old parts go onto the shelves and the hardware goes into wherever you store used hardware. Later on, you decide to take parts off the shelf and recycle them onto another bike. Then, you have to go hunting up appropriate hardware to hold it on.

One major difference between motorcycles and cars is that while auto manufacturers hold just about everything together with sheet metal screws, those things are pretty rare on bikes. The reason is that motorcycle vibration levels are a whole lot higher. Sheet metal screws would work loose in no time.

Consumables

Consumables include oil, grease, cleaning solvents, brake fluid, and so forth. Table 16.1 gives a list of the consumables I found around my shop this morning.

I keep these things all together in one place, but in no particular order. They are all handy to the workbench, but out of the way. I know where to find what I want, but I don't have to spend a lot of time keeping up a fixed seating plan.

The oil on this consumables list is not the stuff I put in my motor! It consists of open containers of oil that I use to lubricate parts as I put them together. For example, whenever you put a motor together, you *have* to oil up all the moving parts—especially bearing surfaces. Otherwise, when you first start it, your motor will eat itself up before the lubrication system pumps oil into all the nooks and crannies.

Also, you should never thread a bolt into a part (such as an engine block or a frame) dry. Always put a drop of oil on the threads just before you put it in. The oil will spread around the threads in a thin film. The oil film makes torquing much more accurate, prevents galling the threads (where metal is rubbed off one surface and sticks to the other—ruining the threads), and prevents rusting. The squirt can of oil provides for that little operation.

There are also anti-seize compounds that you can get for this purpose. I prefer motor oil out of habit. Professional mechanics seem to prefer the specially formulated stuff. Either way, it's a lot cheaper than replacing an aluminum head.

I buy oil for the motor by the case, and stick the case in a corner or on a bottom shelf. When I get down to the last quart or so, I throw the empty carton away and buy another case.

Other consumables range from chrome polish to deionized water. You'll find out what you need as you go. What is important here is to make sure you have some storage space set aside for the stuff.

So far in this book I've mentioned three separate consumables storage areas you need: at the back of your workbench, non-flammable storage, and flammable storage.

Items you put at the back of your workbench shelf should come in small packages because workbench space is limited. Also, many of those items will vary from flammable (such as denatured alcohol) to little bombs (any spray can) that would go off in a fire. If you minimize the size of these items, you minimize the trouble you'll have when some idiot stubs out a cigarette in the puddle of gasoline that spilled out of the carburetor you placed on your bench.

Flammables include gasoline, paint thinner, and certain (but not all) solvents. Actually, any petroleum product is likely to be flammable, so keep that stuff all together in your flammables storage cabinet.

My contact at the Bullhead City (Arizona) fire department says that motor oil wouldn't be

Table 16.1   Consumables

- Distilled (deionized) water
- Axle grease
- White lithium grease spray
- White lithium grease in bulk form
- Silicone spray lubricant
- Penetrating oil
- Waterless hand cleaner
- Denatured alcohol
- Spray paint (assorted colors)
- Spray metal primer
- Emery paper in assorted grades
- Scotch-Brite
- Medium strength thread lock compound
- Teflon thread-seal tape
- Motor oil
- DOT 3 brake fluid
- RTV sealant
- Permatex gasket compound
- Cyanoacrylate (super glue)
- Two-part epoxy cement
- Primary chain case fluid
- Drive-chain lubricant
- Dual-filament brake light bulbs
- Single-filament turn-signal bulbs
- Miniature instrument-light bulbs
- Squirt-can of motor oil

considered a fire hazard because the ignition temperature is too high. That makes me happy because I've never treated motor oil as a flammable and I don't know anyone else who does, either.

One item that most people don't realize is a fire hazard is anti-freeze for water-cooled engines. I found out the hard way (as usual) by doing some welding near a leaking auto radiator. When sparks hit the floor, it caught fire! I couldn't understand how the cement could be burning. There wasn't even a puddle, just a damp area on the floor. When I traced the damp area to the dripping radiator the light dawned. It turned out that ethylene glycol burns like crazy even when mixed 50/50 with water.

Non-flammables, of course, can go anywhere. You mainly want to keep them together and easy to find. Pick a convenient shelf (or shelves) and put all your non-flammable consumables there. Non-flammable consumables include everything from deionized water to battery acid. You want to keep this stuff low down so that when you drop the bottle, it'll have less far to fall.

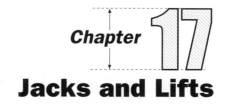
Jacks and Lifts

Let's start by talking about the difference between a jack and a lift. A *jack* is a device for applying a lifting force at a point. The jack will take care of getting the bike up in the air, but questions of balance and stability—actually *keeping* the bike up there so that it doesn't come crashing down—are another matter. Getting it up is the jack's responsibility; keeping it up is yours.

A *lift,* on the other hand, not only picks the bike up, but provides a platform that is wide enough and stable enough to let you work on it without fear that it will topple over.

In general, no matter whether you use a jack or a lift, you should always support a bike by the frame. The frame is the only part of the bike made specifically to be able to carry the bike's weight no matter what.

Oh, yes, the wheels and suspension hold the bike up nearly all of the time. But, even while cornering, the force is almost vertical with respect to the wheel. Give a wheel a good whack from the side and it will crumple pretty fast. Besides, wheels rotate freely, so there's no way you could jack a bike up by the wheels. So, if you're going to raise a bike up in the air, you should pick it up by the frame.

A floor jack is the only type of jack I would recommend you use to raise a motorcycle. I've tried pedestal jacks, scissor jacks, I've even used a two-by-four for a lever and a cement block for a fulcrum. None of 'em worked worth a . . . They're all floppy and generally fall over before you get anywhere. If you've got enough people around to hold the bike up on one of those rigs,

A jack is any device for applying a lifting force at a point.

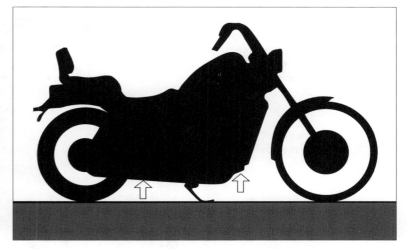

There are two useable points for jacking up a motorcycle that has a kickstand. One is on the frame near where the swing arm pivots, and the other is just behind where the front of the frame starts to curve upward.

it'd be easier to get everyone together and lift the bike up onto a couple of cinder blocks.

Jacking

The reason scissor jacks and such don't work is that they can't move. Why should that be important? The answer starts with geometry: to jack a motorcycle up successfully, you have to make sure it is always supported by exactly three points.

Notice that I said "exactly." If you get it supported at two points, it will fall over. If you support it at four points, you won't be able to move it until one of those points lifts up. Since you're not controlling which of those points lifts up, the bike will become unstable and fall over. Take it from me. You have to stabilize with exactly three points.

It can't be just any three points, either. They have to form a triangle, with the bike's center of gravity somewhere in the middle. That means

you have to know where the center of gravity is. But don't worry about that too much. As soon as you start taking the weight off the suspension, you'll very quickly see where the center of gravity is.

The jacking process works best if two of the three points are pretty well fixed in position. The third point, however, has to move. The diagram shows why. On the left is a solid object resting on fixed pivot points at its left edge. In the second view the right-hand corner of the object has been lifted, pivoting it around the fixed corners. As the corner of the object is lifted, however, it has to move in toward the pivot points. That's why the jack has to roll across the floor as the bike rises.

The diagram on the previous page shows the two usable points for jacking up a motorcycle that has a sidestand. If you want to jack up the front end, catch the frame just at the front motor mounts on the side opposite the sidestand. If you want the back up in the air, put the jack as far

Above:
There are three safe pedestal configurations you can use depending on whether you want the front wheel off the ground, or the back wheel, or both wheels.

Right:
Always pick a bike up by the frame.

back on the frame as you can get it (safely!). Be sure that the jack *hooks* the frame in such a way that the bike can't slide off by rolling forward or backward. If it can, it will.

Working on a bike while it's up in the air on a jack is dumb. It'll wobble around and slip off somehow. Use the jack to get the bike up so that you can prop it up on a stable pedestal. (See the series of diagrams.) To get the bike onto the pedestal, first jack the bike up high enough to slip the pedestal all the way under the frame. Then lower the jack slowly until the low side of the frame contacts the pedestal. Hold it there until you are sure that the center of gravity will be ahead of the pedestal if you're jacking up the rear wheel, or behind it if you're jacking up the front wheel. Then, lower the jack all the way and roll it out of the way. At this point it will be very easy to pull the bike into the vertical position, with both frame rails resting on the pedestal and the sidestand up in the air. The triangle is formed by the points where the two frame rails contact the pedestal and the wheel that is still on the ground.

To get the bike down, start by making sure the sidestand is in the out and locked position. Then you can push the bike over onto the sidestand, jack up the frame, and pull the pedestal out. Then lower the jack and drive away.

To get both wheels up off the ground using two pedestals, first jack the back end up (because it's heavier) and set it on the first pedestal. Then put the jack in the middle of the frame near the front and jack it up using the two frame contact points as your fixed points in the triangle. Then slip the second pedestal under the front of the frame.

Lifts

The simplest kind of motorcycle lift can be used to pick up either the front or the back end of the bike. Essentially, it is a square frame with a long handle that also serves as a stop when the frame is upright.

The frame can lay flat on one side (handle up) but not on the other. With the handle down, the frame stops just a little way past vertical. You can use this lift to pick up either the front end or the back end. Using a pedestal, it is even possible to get both ends up off the ground.

A lift raises the entire bike and ensures that it is stable enough to work on. *Photo courtesy of Western Manufacturing Co., Marshalltown, Iowa.*

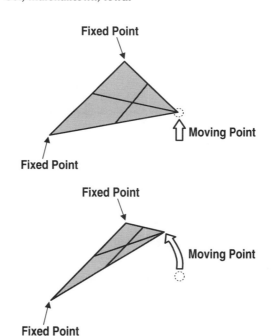

When jacking up a bike, two of the three support points have to stay fixed while the third must move horizontally as well as vertically.

When raising the front end, set the lift up so that you rotate the handle down toward the back. When lifting the back end, set it up so that you rotate the handle toward the front.

This is a great lift if all you really need to do is get the wheel clear of the ground. It will not get the bike up to a comfortable working height, however. To get the bike well up in the air, you need a parallelogram lift. This type of lift has

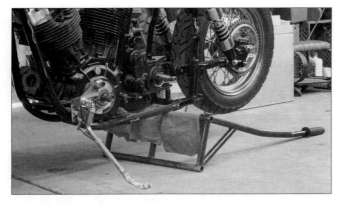

The simple motorcycle lift picks up either the front end or the back end, but not both at the same time.

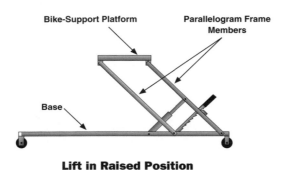

Lift in Raised Position

Lift in Lowered Position

A platform-type lift uses geometry to pick a whole bike up by the frame and hold it level.

four components: a base that stabilizes the whole thing on the ground, a frame consisting of two coupled parallelograms, a platform that actually holds up the bike, and a lifting mechanism that raises the parallelogram.

The frame has to be a parallelogram because, as any high-school geometry whiz kid knows, opposite sides of a parallelogram are always parallel. That's why they call it a "parallelogram!"

Specifically, the base side of the parallelogram stays parallel to the floor, so the platform attached to the opposite side also has to stay par-

allel to the floor. That way your bike stays upright while being lifted, instead of rolling off.

There are many ways to power this type of lift, but most are operated either by pumping up a hydraulic cylinder or by compressed air. In either case, there's always a safety locking mechanism that will hold the bike up if the hydraulic or air cylinder starts to sag. The best plan is to lift the bike up, then lower it onto the locking mechanism. To get it down, lift the bike a tad, unlock the mechanism, and lower the whole thing down to the ground.

Another variation, popular with many small professional and advanced amateur shops, consists of a steel platform a bit wider than the bike that rises on a scissors mechanism. It usually has a clamp arrangement to hold the front fore—and by extension the whole bike—upright.

The fourth style of lift is the motorcycle version of the automotive service station lift. It has a large diameter central pillar that is actually the top of a huge hydraulic cylinder. Compressed air forces hydraulic fluid from a reservoir into the cylinder, pushing the top of the post (with the bike perched on it) up in the air.

Such a center-post lift allows fine control of how high you lift the bike and allows turning the bike around the post to put it in the most convenient position.

Of course, installing a center-post lift is a major construction project. You have to have a high volume of work to justify the trouble and expense. Nearly all amateurs, and quite a few small professional shops, simply don't feel they can justify it.

Important safety tip: When working on a bike on a lift, it's a really good idea to strap the frame to the lift platform. Don't use bungie cords. They aren't strong enough. Use a motorcycle tie-down strap. Wrap the strap over the frame members that sit directly on the lift platform and then under the platform. Pull the strap really, really tight! The idea is to keep the bike from rocking over far enough to topple off the platform. Dropping your bike three or four feet onto the cement floor (you wouldn't operate a lift on any other kind of floor, would you?) would ruin your whole day, even if you aren't under it when it falls.

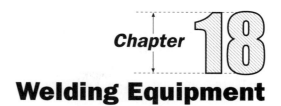

Chapter 18

Welding Equipment

Welding is simply the process of fusing two pieces of metal together. There are a kazillion ways to do it, but only three are of interest to amateur motorcycle mechanics: gas welding, arc welding (sometimes called "stick" welding), and inert-gas welding (usually called MIG welding). To avoid confusion I should first contrast *fusion welding* with *brazing* and *soldering*. As the name implies, fusion welding relies on heating two pieces of metal to the molten state at their junction and allowing the molten puddles to combine (fuse) and then return to the solid state as they cool. Usually, a filler metal is also introduced into the junction to form the weld bead. The heat to melt the metals can come from a gas flame or an electric arc, according to the welding process being used.

Brazing and soldering are two gas welding processes that are used to join two parent metals by melting a metal welding rod to fill the junction between them. In contrast to fusion welding, the brazing and soldering processes do not melt the parent metals, but only the filler metal. In a properly prepared joint each of the parent metals forms a bond to the filler metal as the filler solidifies.

Gas Fusion Welding

The most common welding process uses a gas flame to heat the joint. Several kinds of gas are used for welding, depending on the temperatures needed for the particular process. Gas fusion welding of steel requires high temperatures to melt the parent metals. The most common gasses used for this process are acetylene with oxygen. In this process, a steel filler rod is held in the

flame as the junction between two parent materials is heated and melted. The trick is to control the temperature of the parent metals and the filler rod—simultaneously. The joint formed by gas fusion welding can be very strong but you'll need a lot of experience to make high quality joints.

Brazing

Brazing is another type of gas welding. It is also sometimes called "hard soldering" or "silver soldering." The different names come from the different filler materials used, but the process is pretty much the same for all of them. Brazing and soldering don't need as high temperatures as fusion welding, since only the brazing rod or solder need to be melted and they have a lower

Gas welding uses a mixture of a flammable gas, such as acetylene, and oxygen to produce a highly controllable flame to flow filler metal into a joint.

melting point than steel. The filler metal is chosen to have chemical, mechanical, and thermal expansion properties similar to the materials you are joining. Propane or natural gas can sometimes be used for brazing and soldering.

Uncoated metal in air always has a thin film of oxide, which interferes with bonding of the filler metal. To get rid of this oxide layer, coat the filler rod and the joint with an organic *flux,* which literally pulls oxygen away from the metal surfaces before burning away in the flame.

The torch you use depends on the gas you use, and that in turn depends on the filler metal. For example, the soft solder that plumbers used decades ago was a 50/50 mixture of lead and tin. Plumbers have gone to a much harder solder these days, mainly to reduce the amount of lead introduced into their customers' drinking water. Soft 50/50 solder melts at a low temperature that you can achieve using a propane or butane torch with ordinary air as an oxidizer. When you go to filler materials with a higher melting temperature in an effort to get a stronger, more vibration-resistant joint, you need to use pure oxygen under pressure to achieve the higher temperatures.

If you're going to set up for gas welding, I recommend jumping right into an oxyacetylene cutting torch. Most oxyacetylene rigs consist of two tanks, one of pressurized oxygen and the other of pressurized acetylene. Each tank has a regulator that drops the high (and variable) pressure in the tank to a lower and constant output pressure. You can vary the output pressure by turning a handle on the regulator.

The gasses combine in the torch, where there is a throttle valve for each gas line. You start the torch by opening the acetylene throttle valve (red knob) to start the flow, then light the acetylene flame using a striker that is much like the flint-and-steel striker built into a cigarette lighter.

Once you have an acetylene flame at the tip of the torch, adjust its size, then start the flow of oxygen using the green knob. Adjust the flow until you have just enough oxygen to completely burn all the acetylene. At that point, you will have a dense blue flame surrounded by a thin sheath of paler blue flame. If the pale sheath is very narrow, you have too much oxygen. If the flame has a smoky orange tip, you have too little oxygen. The torch is now ready for gas welding.

The *cutting* torch also has a trigger that looks like a clutch lever. When you squeeze that trigger, the torch dumps extra oxygen into the flame to produce a bright blue-white flame that literally roars out of the torch. It is hot enough to melt steel and has enough oxygen to burn the steel it melts. This puppy is used to cut cars in half!

Table 18.1 lists the bits you'll need to set yourself up for gas welding. You use gas welding for non-structural components, such as gas tanks and fenders. When you get into structural components, such as frames, you have to go to arc welding.

Arc Welding

Straight arc welding is simple in principle. The heat comes from an electric arc that you strike between a welding rod (which provides the material that will fill in the joint) and the metal pieces you are joining.

The first thing to remember is that the arc will go only where there is a good electrical ground.

A so-called "cutting torch" has a trigger to dump extra oxygen into the flame to change a nice, tame welding flame into a roaring beast that will eat its way through the toughest steel. *Photo courtesy of Victor Equipment Co., St. Louis, Missouri*

> **Table 18.1**
> **Gas Welding Equipment**
>
> - Oxygen tank
> - Oxygen regulator
> - Acetylene tank
> - Acetylene regulator
> - Cutting torch
> - Tank cart
> - Goggles
> - Striker
> - Brazing rods
> - Paste flux

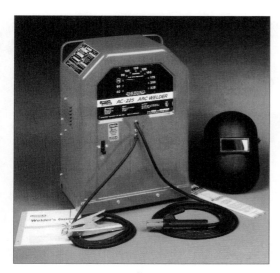

The basic arc welder is a current-limited step-down transformer with some means of adjusting the output current. *Photo courtesy of Lincoln Electric Co., Cleveland, Ohio.*

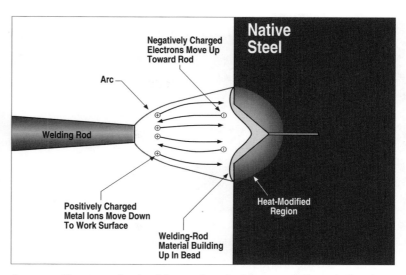

An arc welder generates heat by running electric current through the air. The arc is hot enough to vaporize and ionize metal from the welding rod. Positively charged metal ions then pile up on the negatively charged work surface, lose their charge and form a bead that is usually stronger than the original steel.

In other words, you have to pay attention to the electrical contact between the two pieces you are joining, and from them to the ground side of the welder.

The welder itself is a big box containing a current-limited step-down transformer with some means of adjusting the output current.

There are two basic welder types: AC and DC. Alternating current, or AC, welders are less expensive. They are little more than a big voltage-step-down transformer. The transformer construction serves to limit the current available at the various output taps. Direct current (DC) units also have a rectification circuit that converts AC from the transformer to DC to the taps.

These two types also differ in performance. Welding only occurs when the welding rod or wire is positively charged with respect to the work. The AC welder's tip switches back and forth between positive and negative with respect to the work, so welding occurs only half the time. During the other half cycle, no material moves from the rod to the work. In fact, some material makes the trip back, in effect de-welding the work!

These cycles turn over sixty times per second in time with the power-mains cycles. This is too fast for a human to follow or the weld to respond,

but you can hear it as a loud hum while the arc is on. This sixty-cycle hum gives AC welders the name "buzz boxes."

While the cycling is hard to notice, it does make the arc harder to control. It is harder to maintain the arc near the low-current end for a given piece. Sometimes, especially with thin metal, you have to use more current than optimal to keep the arc from dropping out. This can lead to overheating and holes burned through the piece.

DC machines are more expensive because of the additional circuitry. It is also very difficult to build electronic components that can handle the extremes of high voltage sometimes and high currents at others. The DC welder's superior controllability, however, makes it a lot easier to make high-quality welds.

From the welder, you have a hefty cable with a clamp on the end. That is your ground cable and you electrically connect it to the piece you are going to weld.

There is a second output cable from the welder that goes to a handle that holds the welding rod. The welding rod itself has a metal core surrounded by a flux sheath that looks like dried mud. The flux melts in the arc, releasing a gas that displaces oxygen in the air that would other-

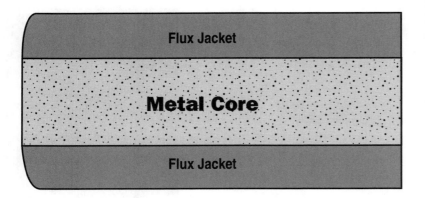

Rods for arc welding have a metal core surrounded by a jacket of flux material.

Table 18.2
Arc Welding Equipment

- Arc welder
- Welding rods
- Protective clothing
- Welder's helmet
- Scrap angle iron for building jigs
- Assorted C-clamps
- Steel-topped workbench (optional)
- Bench vise
- Framing square
- Square
- Steel tape measure
- Vise grips

wise burn away the metal you are supposed to be welding. The melted flux rises to the surface of the weld puddle and then cools to form a protective coating over the weld area. It serves essentially the same purpose as the paste flux used in gas welding: controlling oxidation. This is critical, not only because you want to fill the joint with solid metal rather than rust but because iron oxide is a non-conductor that will block the arc. If you let the surface oxidize while you are welding, your arc will simply sputter out.

That is the arc welder portion of arc welding. Another consideration is how you're going to hold your parts to be welded. You have two problems to worry about: alignment and rigidity.

Unlike gas welding, your parts don't overlap. In fact, they are barely in contact before you start to weld. You can't just lay them next to each other and expect that they'll stay in place. So,

you have to set up some kind of jig (support structure) to hold the pieces in perfect alignment during the welding process.

The jig has to be very rigid because from time to time, you're going to accidentally touch the welding rod to the piece and it will stick. Then, you have to wiggle the handle around to break the rod free. If your jig isn't rigid, you'll mess up your perfect alignment while yanking the rod free.

Use steel for jig components. Don't use wood. The pieces you are welding will heat up very fast and burn the wood. Then, you no longer have a jig!

Since the jig is temporary, you can use any sort of scrap steel to make it. Jigs can be bolted, welded, or clamped together. To fabricate jigs, you'll need scrap angle iron and a hacksaw. To prepare the metal to be joined, you'll need a portable grinder, a wire brush, and some fairly substantial files suitable for finishing steel. After you've made your joint, you'll find it covered with a hard brittle coating (what's left of the burned flux). Before you paint or chrome the weld, you need to chip that coating off with a hammer.

The most obvious features of a well-equipped welding shop, beside the welder, are a big workbench with a steel top, lots of scrap steel, and a generous assortment of C-clamps. The best welding bench is a big ol' sheet of boiler plate at least a quarter-inch thick supported on a steel frame. C-clamps come in a variety of sizes from little ones that don't open more than an inch to big mothers that may open six inches or even ten inches. For motorcycle work, you're unlikely to need anything opening more than six inches.

I've found that vise grips are really convenient for clamping metal pieces together temporarily. They clamp securely. They take only one hand to operate, leaving the other hand free to position the pieces to be clamped. They clamp and unclamp quickly. Welding rod doesn't seem to stick to the metal they are made from. Most of my vise grips now have scars from accidental arc strikes because I use them so much when welding.

Another item that gets a heavy workout during welding sessions is your bench vise. You will

It's More Than Just a Pretty Flame

There are very definite health and safety concerns with arc welding. The light from a welding arc is much more intense than sunlight. If you look at it without some pretty serious eye protection, you'll walk around with little blind spots on your retinas for the rest of your life. It doesn't happen instantly, but permanent damage can happen in less time than it takes for you to make a weld.

That's the obvious problem that everyone knows about. The danger few non-welders seem to know anything about is the sunburn. A welding arc is considerably hotter than the surface of the sun. The sun is only yellow-hot. That arc is blue-hot. If you think it's bright in visible light, you ain't seen nothin' compared to how bright it is in ultraviolet! Wear a long-sleeved shirt. Roll the sleeves down and button them. Button up the neck. Wear gloves—in fact, wear gauntlets! By the way, sunburn protection is the reason those welder's helmets cover your whole face rather than just your eyes. If you wear shorts and sandals while welding, you're outta your mind! ■

An arc-welder's helmet features an opaque full-face shield. It's not there for show—the bright light from a welding arc will give you a killer sunburn in no time flat! *Photo courtesy of Lincoln Electric Co., Cleveland, Ohio.*

also need some equipment normally associated with carpenters: a framing square, a square, and a steel tape measure.

You have to rustproof any welded components, of course. To get a good electrical contact for welding, the metal has to start out clean and bare, so part of the preparation is degreasing the parts and removing any oxide. Such bare metal will rust almost instantly in any climate. Plan to paint or chrome any welded parts right away.

I'll talk about setting up for painting in another chapter. I will not, however, tell you how to set up for chroming. Amateurs don't do that. Even professional motorcycle mechanics don't do that. Find a plating shop and pay them to plate your stuff. The equipment is very specialized and the process is very dangerous—involving tens or hundreds of gallons of very nasty acid. Given a choice, I try not to even step into plating shops, never mind setting one up in my basement! Platers charge a lot of money, and they earn every penny of it.

Table 18.2 lists a whole gamut of stuff you'll need for your welding setup. The welder itself is only a small part of the necessary equipment.

When I first started welding I wasn't careful about ventilation. I couldn't understand why I always felt cruddy—headachy, nauseated and exhausted—on Monday, Tuesday and Wednesday. By Thursday, I'd start to feel a little better. Then, I'd be sick again the following Monday. After a couple of weeks I realized it was from welding in a closed garage on Sundays. Be sure the space you weld in has lots of ventilation.

Inert Gas Welding

Just about everything I've said about arc welding goes for inert gas welding as well. The welding process itself is the same. What you're trying to accomplish is the same. High temperatures are still generated by converting electrical energy into heat in an intense electric arc.

There are two differences: how atmospheric oxygen is excluded and how the welding rod is delivered.

The arc-welding rod has a metal core surrounded by a solid sheath of flux that burns to use up the oxygen in the air surrounding the joint. Inert-gas welding does away with the need for flux by blowing a stream of inert gas over the

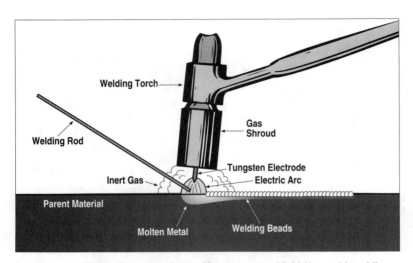

Inert gas welding relies on a cloak of inert gas to shield the weld puddle from the atmosphere, thereby inhibiting oxidation during the welding process.

arc. Inert gases, such as argon and helium, simply don't react with anything—that's why they're called "inert." Blowing a stream of inert gas over the welding area excludes atmospheric oxygen by simply elbowing the air out of the way. No air means no oxygen. No oxygen means no need of flux.

Doing away with that crumbly sheath of dried mud—I mean flux—makes the welding rod flexible. Well, it makes the rod as flexible as a solid steel wire can be. This flexibility lets you wrap the wire around a spool and feed it continuously into the arc.

As you lay down a welding bead, the arc deposits material from the welding rod into the joint. That means the rod gets shorter. To maintain the arc in stick welding, you have to keep moving the rod closer as it gets shorter. It'll start out about a foot long. By the time you've run a bead about six inches long, it has burned down to a nub. The metal from the rod is now in the joint. Once you've burned up the rod, you have to stop, fish another rod out of your little stash of welding rods, and start again. Then you lay down another six inches of joint, and stop again to get another rod.

Inert gas welding does away with all that. Because the rod is now only a piece of wire fed from a spool, you can install a little motor to feed the wire into the arc at the same rate it burns up. Now you can turn on your inert gas flow, strike

an arc, depress the little trigger to feed the wire in, and weld to your heart's content.

Inert gas welding wire can be (in fact, works better if it is) smaller in diameter than welding rod cores usually are. The welder (machine) likes that because the thinner wire is more flexible, so it feeds more easily. The welder (human) likes that (sometimes) because thinner wire makes a smaller arc that is more controllable. Expect to be able to weld thinner material than you could with a simple arc welder.

A word about selecting welding rod or wire. You want the diameter of the rod core or wire to be no larger than the thickness of the metal you're welding. You can weld, say, sixteenth-inch sheet metal with an eighth-inch rod (I know because I've done it), but it's a real pain in the butt. When the rod's too thick, the arc gets too big and it burns great gaping holes in the sheet metal. Then you have to fill in the holes. But, while filling in the holes you make more holes! There's a trick to doing it successfully, but I'm not telling. Better to use the proper size rod than to fiddle around with it.

On the flip side, the welding rod should be no smaller than half the thickness of the hole you're trying to fill or you'll end up spending your life filling in the hole! It'll take forever. You'll think it's a career.

Even worse, if the rod is too small, you won't be able to get the steel up to temperature. In order for the welding rod material to fuse into the joint, the surface of the joint has to reach melting temperature, too. Metal conducts heat. Thicker metal conducts heat faster. If what you're welding is some amazingly thick chunk of steel that conducts heat like gangbusters, and you're trying to run a bead with an itty bitty little wire, you'll end up with molten drops of welding wire tacked onto a cold steel surface. It's what welders call "no penetration." You might as well try to hold the thing together with Scotch tape.

Most of the welding you do on frames can be done with 1/8-inch rods. (Remember, that's the thickness of the core, not the outside diameter of the rod when covered with flux.) For fenders, tanks, and other sheet metal, use a much thinner wire in an inert gas welder.

Compressed Air

A compressed air system is extremely useful in any workshop. How big it must be and what accessories it includes depend on what you're going to do with it.

Jobs you can use compressed air for:

• Inflating tires

• Blowing dust, dirt, filings, and bits of crud off parts

• Spray painting

• Running air-powered tools

• Raising motorcycle lifts

• Running a pressure washer

These are listed in increasing order of how much strain they put on your air compressor. Most of the use motorcycle mechanics have for compressed air falls into the first three categories. In fact, number two is the most common use for compressed air around a motorcycle shop.

Inflating tires doesn't demand much. Many little portable compressors, even the 12-volt jobbies, can pump out 200 psi, which will blow up a motorcycle tire like a cherry bomb in a condom. Those little guys may take a while to fill a tire, but they'll do it. That's basically all they are good for.

Cleaning off stuff takes a fairly short blast of compressed air. You don't have to sustain it long, but you need a lot of airflow for a few seconds. Even a big shop air compressor can't provide that kind of airflow on its own. To do it, you need an air storage tank.

The tank acts as a reservoir for high pressure air. It's like if you wanted to dump a whole lot of water over your big brother's head—really get him soaked before he has a chance to run away

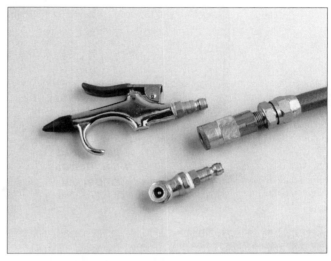

Compressed-air fittings are designed to automatically seal off the air flow when disconnected.

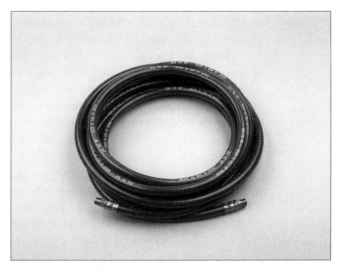

Compressed air hoses have heavy, reinforced walls and airtight high-pressure fittings.

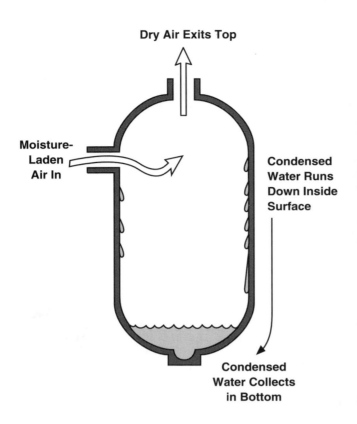

Dry Air Exits Top

Moisture-Laden Air In

Condensed Water Runs Down Inside Surface

Condensed Water Collects in Bottom

A water trap removes moisture that condenses as compressed air is released from the holding tank.

Compressed air systems range from small units designed to inflate tires to this full-sized unit consisting of a 5-hp compressor and a 60-gallon tank.

(or hit you)—you wouldn't start dragging out the garden hose. You'd get yourself a big bucket, sneak over to the sill cock behind the house, fill the bucket, then sneak up behind your big brother and dump it on him all at once. A garden hose on full can dump out on the order of 100 gallons per hour. Sounds impressive, huh? Well, upending a five-gallon bucket will drop the whole five gallons out in less than a second. That works out to 18,000 gallons per hour!

The principle is the same for a compressed air tank. You let the compressor run for maybe ten minutes and pump up the pressure in the tank to a couple hundred psi. Then, when you want that blast of air, you open a valve in the tank. The tank can empty itself out in a minute or less (depending on how big the tank is), but you don't need that much air. You can get a whole lot of

two- or three-second blasts before the pressure in the tank drops off. By that time, the pressure switch in the tank turns the compressor back on, pumping the tank up for the next series of blasts.

On a big system you also need to install a cooler between the compressor and the tank. That's because whenever you compress a gas it gets hot. You don't want your compressed air tank getting hot, so you cool the compressed air before it gets to the tank.

Small systems don't need an intercooler because the air loses enough heat while going through that little metal tube to the tank. As the compressor and tank get bigger, the little tube gets longer, turning into a loop, then a coil, then sprouts fins and becomes an intercooler.

Painting is a little more demanding on your compressed air system for two reasons. First, although it doesn't use air as fast as cleaning parts, the flow is sustained. You can spend as much as five or ten minutes shooting one coat of paint on two fenders and two tanks. Second, the air has to be absolutely clean. Not only does it have to be absolutely free of bits of dust, dirt, rust from inside the tank, and wear particles from the compressor, but it has to be free of water.

Where, you might ask, does the water come from? It's in the air all the time, of course. When you suddenly decompress air, its temperature drops like a stone. That's the principle air conditioners work on. You've seen water dribbling from an air conditioner on a muggy day. Well, shooting air from a compressed air tank does the same thing.

If muggy, or even normally humid, air goes in at the compressor, water drops come out of the tank. You don't want to spray water drops onto your sheet metal along with the paint, do you? That's what a water trap is there to prevent.

A water trap is simply a metal or glass canister attached to the tank outlet. Compressed air blows into the canister from one side. Any water droplets splatter on the opposite side and run down to collect in the bottom. The compressed air, on the other hand, doesn't collect anywhere. It swirls around and comes out the top, minus the water.

In small systems, you don't get enough liquid water collecting in the trap to cause problems. As the air warms up again between shots, the water in the trap evaporates and comes out as vapor with the next shot. In big systems, they use glass water traps so you can see if too much water collects in the trap.

Of course, you don't actually have to buy all these components and put them together yourself. Myriad vendors put together packaged systems where all the components are well matched to each other. A five horsepower system will have a bigger tank than a two horsepower system. All you have to do is pick a system, bring it into your shop, plug it in, and turn it on. I've gone into all the different parts and how they work together so that you'll know what you're buying and why.

The last item to think about with compressed air systems is the fittings. Notice that when your

This control unit combines air regulation and filtration in a compact system. The gauge you see controls air pressure for smooth and consistent air flow, just what you need if you're thinking of painting.

Once you have an air compressor, you'll find many tools that you didn't know you couldn't live without, like an air sander.

friendly neighborhood scooter mechanic takes a dingus off the end of his compressed air hose, the hose doesn't leak. That's because standard air-hose fittings have a valve system that automati-

One important use for compressed air is to raise motorcycle lifts.

cally shuts off the air flow unless you've got a dingus attached to it. You don't have to think about it as long as you use the standard air-hose fittings throughout the system in the first place.

How big a compressor do you need? It's a matter of how much air you use at once. If the most you do is painting, you don't need a very big system. A motor developing a couple of horsepower and a tank holding a few gallons will be plenty.

As you become more compressed-air dependent, you'll find that your compressor will run more often. As the compressor spends more time on and less time off, it will start to get hot. That's what eventually burns the things out. When you find that your compressor runs most of the time, it's time to get a bigger system.

If you're planning a good-sized shop that will require a lot of air, the best thing to do is to consult with the folks you plan to buy your compressor from. Tell them exactly what things you are using air for and how often and for how long you will be using it. If you give them an accurate picture of what you'll be doing with the compressor, they'll be able to steer you to the right system for the job.

Chapter

20

Painting Equipment

Painting is its own worst enemy. Everything you do to paint motorcycle parts screws up your painting of motorcycle parts. For example, to get a good paint job, everything from the parts themselves to the space around them has to be absolutely clean. Yet, the painting process itself creates an ungodly mess.

Most of your painting effort goes into preparing your workspace and your parts to be painted, and controlling the mess you make in the process. Everything becomes a lot easier if you can set aside part of your shop for painting—kind of a paint shop within your workshop. Very few people, however, do enough painting to justify setting aside two or three hundred square feet of shop space, installing the partitions and ventilating system needed, and then putting a lock on the door to keep mechanics, visitors, and (the worst) parts storage from invading it. For most people, their paint shop is a temporary affair using space borrowed from other activities.

You need four areas for a paint shop:

- A preparation area, which doesn't need to be all that clean. In fact it'll get pretty dusty and dirty. As long as it doesn't have a fog of dust particles in the air, it'll be OK.
- A mixing area that is essentially about ten square feet of *clean* workbench space.
- A spray booth where you do the actual shooting of paint onto parts.
- A drying area adjacent to the spray booth, but protected from overspray.

Prep Area

Preparation activities include washing parts with detergent, stripping old paint, coarse sanding to get down to bare metal, and fine sanding to get out the grooves created by the coarse sanding. So, you'll need a supply of hot water available nearby, an area where you can deal with paint stripper without ruining what the parts rest on

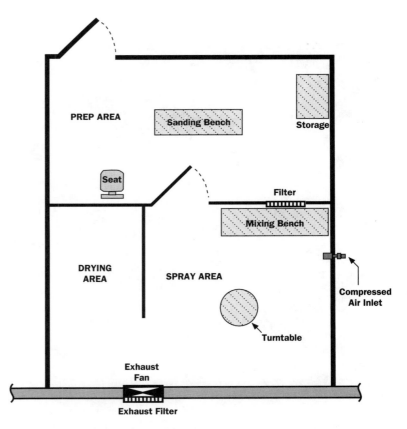

You need four areas to have a proper paint shop: preparation, mixing, spraying, and drying.

(the dining room table is absolutely off limits!), a bench to rest parts on while sanding them, and a chair (without arms) to sit on when your legs get tired. You'll end up sitting in the chair sanding away at a fender on your lap—guaranteed!

The workbench can be a small bench with a stainless steel top about two feet high. It's a good height for sanding or spraying paint stripper. The stainless steel top is impervious to paint stripper.

Besides the consumables like paint stripper and emery paper, you'll need a generous supply of rags, at least one old bath towel, and a dust mask. Goggles are a nice touch, but not really necessary unless you break down and pull out an electric sander.

Most of the rags can be terry cloth or some such fluffy cloth. Use them to dust off the parts after you've sanded them. The bath towel is to drape over your lap when you sit down with a fender in your lap.

Now that you have your parts prepared, you need to set them up for painting. The last thing to do just before painting is to degrease the parts.

An ordinary 24-inch box fan makes an ideal spray-booth exhaust fan.

You absolutely must have all grease, oil, and fingerprints off the metal. Paints, especially the newer acrylic paints, won't stick to fingerprints.

Spray Booth

Awright, now you've got your parts in your spray booth! The spray booth has to be completely dust free. But, it also has to be well ventilated. Unfortunately, if you blow air in to ventilate the place, you'll also be blowing in dust as well. If you use an exhaust fan to blow air out, the air has to come from somewhere, and that will suck dust in with the air.

Another major problem in spray booths is overspray buildup. I've seen spray booths where overspray buildup reached a half-inch thick or more. That much buildup occurs more in factory paint shops, where spray booths are operating for two or three shifts every day and have to be cleaned at least once a week.

For a spray booth you use only occasionally the problem tends to be that paint ages on the walls and ceiling, then flakes off. Of course, when nothing is going on in the booth, the particles just sit wherever they happen to be. Then, when you turn on the airflow, the vibration from the fan, closing the door, and so forth makes those loose particles rain down all over the place.

Don't imagine that you are dealing with large paint flakes, such as those you get when your house paint starts to peel. Overspray doesn't coat the booth in an even layer. It lands as individual spatters that are often partially dried when they land. Thus, the material you have to deal with is fine dust-sized particles. When I talk about dust in a spray booth, I'm mainly talking about paint particles that are generated in huge quantities within the booth itself.

The only way to control this dust is to clean the booth each time before you use it. Remember: dust falls down. Start by wiping down the ceiling and any hooks or fixtures attached to the ceiling first. Then wipe the walls and any benches or tables at work height. Finally, thoroughly clean the floor. The best thing to use is a vacuum cleaner with a dust-brush attachment.

If you want to build a really super spray booth, start by partitioning off an area 10 feet by 15 feet. The only openings should be a doorway,

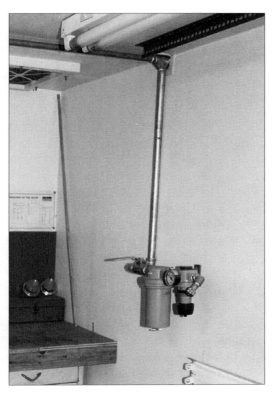

Pipe compressed air right into the booth through the wall.

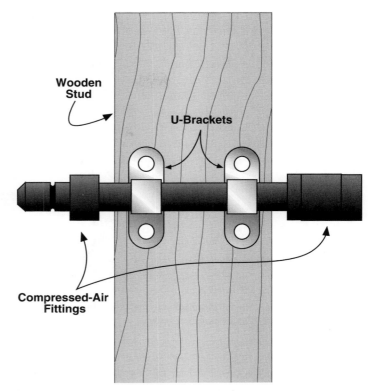

One way to pass compressed air through the wall into your spray booth is to mount fittings to the studs when you build the walls.

a 2-foot by 2-foot air inlet, and a similar opening for an exhaust fan.

The exhaust fan should blow directly outside the building. You'll need some sort of shutter system to keep weather out, especially when the booth is not in use.

Line the walls and ceiling with sheet aluminum. It's cheap, sheds dust, and is easy to put up. You can butt the edges together, just make sure there are no air leaks or spaces for dust to collect.

Of course, you'll have to line the ceiling with aluminum sheet, too. Your lighting should come from recessed overhead fixtures with translucent panels over them. Avoid putting anything overhead that could become a dust reservoir. It'd be pretty dumb to go through all this trouble and then hang fluorescent fixtures from chains. If you want to know why, just climb up on a chair and look at the dust on the top of any free-hanging fixture.

Paint the floor, and keep the floor paint in good condition by repainting it whenever the paint starts to wear through. Remember that un-

coated cement is a tremendous dust generator. Just the friction from your feet walking across a cement floor can generate enough dust to ruin a paint job. Sweeping a raw cement floor will fill the booth with fine particles.

Of course, don't forget to install a couple of electrical outlets. You shouldn't need 'em, but you will. Use aluminum trim plates.

You're also going to need compressed air in the booth, but you don't want to drag your dusty, dirty compressor in there. Install a compressed air outlet in the wall. The illustration shows one way to set it up. You can go one step further by installing an air-pressure regulator inside as shown in the photo, so that you can control the pressure without leaving the booth.

The door should be about three feet wide and be completely weather stripped. Your best bet is to install a decent quality outside door and frame. Don't forget to put sheet aluminum on the inside surface. If you go all out and buy a metal-sheathed security door, you don't have to worry about sheathing the inside. Just make sure the

The rotating table is just a platform with a lazy Susan mounted on top.

door doesn't have any sort of ornate dust-collecting pattern on the inside.

Mount an air filter of the type used in central air conditioning systems over the air inlet. This is supposed to be the only way air can get into the room, and putting a clean filter over the opening will ensure that the only dust you'll have to contend with is the dust you generate in the booth.

For an exhaust fan, all you need is a two- or three-foot boxed fan. Mount it in the outlet opening pointing out. Make sure it fits snugly in the opening. If you need to, use some of the aluminum sheet to make a shroud so air can't backflush around the fan. Set up your electrical wiring so you can turn the fan on and off by a wall switch. Finally, mount another air filter over the inside of the exhaust fan opening. No matter what you do, that exhaust fan will collect dust. A filter will make sure it sheds that dust outside, rather than into your spray booth.

Unlike other motorcycle workshop operations, painting requires temperature and humidity control. The air in the spray booth will be the same air that is outside the spray booth *without* the dust. If your shop gets unacceptably hot or cold, think about how you'll control the temperature in the spray booth. One way is to heat and air condition the prep area, and let that be what's on the other side of your air inlet. Just putting a recirculating air conditioner in your spray booth won't work at all because the air in the booth changes so rapidly.

I heard of one guy in Las Vegas who checked the weather records to find out what the average high for the year was at his shop's location. Since it was a bearable (for a native Nevadan) 105 degrees, he decided to do all of his painting at that temperature. He installed thermostatically controlled heat lamps in his spray booth to maintain a steady 105 degrees all year long. On the few days that the outside temperature climbed over 105 degrees so his heater-only system wouldn't work, he simply took the day off.

Drying Area

You ain't done yet. Remember that I told you to partition off an area 10 feet by 15 feet? You really only need 10 feet by 10 feet; the extra five feet is for your drying area. You *can* dry your parts in the spray booth, but that means you can't use the spray booth until your parts are completely dry. Additionally, some paints, such as acrylics, like to be force-dried at high temperatures—like 140 degrees. You don't want to be running the temperature of your spray booth up that high because at over about 115 degrees, the paint will dry to powder before it even reaches the parts!

To form a drying area, add a partition between it and the spray booth. The main use of the partition is to keep overspray from your booth from reaching the drying parts. This partition can be as simple as a shower curtain! Just make sure it doesn't collect dust.

The diagram shows a usable floor plan for laying out a spray booth, prep area, and drying area. It includes a solid, insulated partition between the spray booth and the drying area to accommodate force-drying. Remember that the whole reason for keeping air flow through the spray booth is to remove paint fumes. You don't need a lot of air flow through the drying area, but you still need some. Fumes in the drying area will diffuse out to the spray booth and then be pulled out by the exhaust fan, but only if you keep the exhaust fan running throughout the drying process.

Finally, you need some means of supporting your parts while spraying them. There are two ways of doing this: ceiling hooks and a rotating table. You'll need both. Install a few screw eyes in the ceiling from which you can hang small parts by wire hooks. Do the same thing in your drying area. You should hang all parts for drying.

Your rotating table is just a platform with a lazy Susan mounted to the top. This table should be fairly rugged and the lazy Susan on top should be about two feet in diameter. You can buy lazy Susan bearings at most hardware stores and lumber supply houses. This table should be about two feet high and both rugged and stable. It should also be portable.

Prop your parts up on the lazy Susan using wooden blocks, small cardboard boxes, or even wooden frames made specially for the purpose. Anything that will hold the parts off the rotating table without shifting when you turn the table. If you do a lot of painting, you'll end up making a bunch of frames to hold specific parts in specific orientations. For example, you might have one frame to hold rear fenders upside down (to paint the insides) and another to hold them right side up (to paint the outside).

Mixing Area

Other items you'll need are for paint mixing and cleanup. You can do your mixing in the prep area, or you can set up a table in the spray booth. Doing the job in the prep area keeps the mess out of your booth. Doing it in the booth keeps dust out of the paint, gets rid of paint fumes, and saves steps when changing colors or reloading the spray gun.

For mixing you'll need at least one container for measuring the paint. If there are graduations on your spray can's reservoir, that's all you need. If not, you'll need a separate container marked off in fluid ounces (or some other fluid measure). It should have a capacity of at least one cup. Two cups would be a whole lot better.

Don't try to pour paint out of the can into the reservoir. Get a small cup, preferably metal. You can find good measuring cups in most grocery stores among the cooking utensils. Buy a cup with graduations, to help with measurements. Some people have successfully used the small paper cups you use in bathroom dispensers, but because those cups are coated with wax (to keep them waterproof) some kinds of paint may dissolve the wax and cause *big* problems with your painting. I wouldn't trust them. There are also uncoated paper cups, which work fine. Dip the cup into the paint can, wipe off the bottom so it won't drip, and pour the paint slowly from the cup into the measuring container. Keep dipping and pouring until the paint reaches the appropriate mark.

If, for example, you want 2 oz. of paint, 3 oz. of thinner, and 1/2 oz. of hardener, pour thinner until you reach the 3 oz. mark. Always start with the thinner. Then add paint until you reach the 5 oz. mark. Finally, pour in hardener until you reach 5-1/2 oz.

If you're going to do a significant amount of painting, plan to invest in a spray gun. This "detail gun" is an ideal size for motorcycle work. Note the final filter and pressure control.

Those who paint only occasionally can pick up an inexpensive spray outfit. The aerosol can is filled with the propellant used in spray cans, but no paint. As the propellant shoots out of the can, it draws paint out of the paint reservoir.

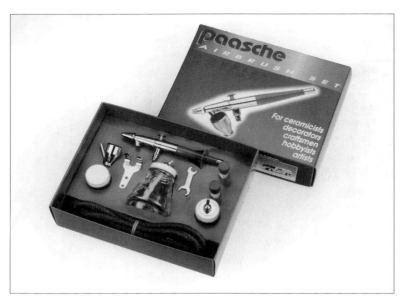

When you start wanting to get into fancy graphics, you'll need to add an airbrush to your painting toolkit. *Photo courtesy of Paasche Airbrush Co., Harwood Heights, Illinois.*

Spray Guns

Now that you have a place to do your painting, you need some equipment. Specifically, you need a spray gun. I'm ignoring spray cans because I've never found any paint from a spray can that will stand up to gasoline. It's all right to use spray paint from a can to touch up your frame. You can also use canned spray primer everywhere. But don't bother to shoot a finish coat on a tank from a can. Use freshly mixed paint with a separate hardener for that. Of course, you should use the same paint on your fenders that you use on your tank so they'll match. If you're gonna do any *real* painting, plan to invest in a spray gun.

There are three basic styles of spray guns: the big ol' jobbies you use to coat a whole fender at once, "detail" guns (also called "jamb" guns in auto body shops), and airbrushes. The effective differences are speed and control.

Airbrushes let you make fine graphics with tremendous control. If you try to cover a whole fender or tank with an airbrush, however, you'll think it's a career.

The big ol' spray guns, on the other hand, blow paint over everywhere at once. You can do an entire fender in three passes.

Detail guns are a nice compromise for motorcycle parts. They have enough flow to complete jobs in a reasonable time, yet they are small enough to offer good control.

If you're just going to do solid colors, or a lot of masking, a detail gun is all you'll need. When you become adept and want to get fancy, think about adding an airbrush to your kit.

If you use a separate measuring container, use a *clean* popsicle stick to mix the paint up thoroughly. If you're using the spray gun's reservoir, attach the reservoir to the gun and mix the stuff up by rotating the gun in a swirling motion.

Cleanup should be done in the booth. It involves wiping everything down thoroughly with paint thinner. Take apart the spray gun and clean all the parts. Clean out measuring containers, wipe up spills, and throw away trash. Use lint-free rags and paper towels. You'll also need those lint-free rags for a final degrease (using thinner again) and dust-off just before you shoot your paint.

Chapter 21

Metal Fabrication Equipment

Metal fabricating equipment in a motorcycle shop is used for customization. If you restrict yourself to unbolting stock parts and replacing them with stock parts on a fairly new motorcycle, you won't need much in the way of metal fabricating equipment. If you build completely custom motorcycles, you may need to set yourself up with a complete pattern shop.

Pattern making is the construction of one-of-a-kind items of a quality that is at least as good as mass-produced items. All products start out as prototypes made one at a time in a pattern shop. Harley-Davidson started out as a couple of guys working in a pattern shop to build one motorcycle from raw stock. They kept on building them one at a time in that pattern shop until their sales volume got high enough to justify mass producing the things in a factory. The quality of work coming out of the pattern shop and out of the factory had to be the same, but the production methods were different.

Industrial engineers talk in terms of "process." They'll spend a ton of time and effort, not to mention filling a lot of dumpsters with rejects, to get their process just right so that the 10,000th unit comes out exactly the same as the 9,671st unit did. Since there are an infinity of ways to get something wrong, and only one way to get it right, every unit has to be right. Sheet metal parts that don't fit, for example, are even more of a pain for the factory manager than they are for the consumer, so factory managers spend their lives trying to make every item come out perfectly.

One-offs, however, don't come out of a process in the same sense. If you make your own fender, for example, you end up hand fitting it. If it's a little off, you modify it. It takes a lot longer and is much, much more expensive. The only advantage for the consumer is that this item is different from any other.

The deeper you get into building custom bikes, the more metal fabrication equipment and skills you'll need. You will, of course, need all of

A press is good for everything from reshaping kickstands to squooshing rivets.

Do You Have the Custom Bike Bug?

In 1988 I bought a Harley-Davidson Heritage Softail Custom with the standard black-and-cream paint job. I bought it right off the showroom floor and all I had done to it was add an oil cooler. The only problem was that so many people bought that model and paint scheme, it was sometimes hard to pick my bike out from all the other black-and-cream Heritage Softail Customs in the parking lots at rallies. However, I resisted the urge to repaint it and six years later, when everyone else had customized their bikes to Hell and gone, mine was the one that turned heads.

There's an old saying: "I want to be different, like everybody else!"

You pay for being distinctive by spending a lot of money for stuff that is no better than stock—only different.

The only way out of spending idiotic amounts of money for custom motorcycles is to get good at building them yourself. That way, you spend *time* instead of *money,* and instead of going to a rally and saying "This is a custom bike built for me by [insert somebody else's name]," you get to say "I built this bike last week." It's not pride of ownership anymore, it's your own creation.

It's funny. When you start building custom bikes, you stop caring who owns them or what anyone else thinks of them. It is no longer transportation, or the key to a lifestyle or even a motorcycle *per se,* it is your creation. Whatever happens to it afterward, whether you sell it, crash it, dismantle it, burn it, or just ride it around, you will always have created it.

In fact, I don't even take pictures of the things anymore. The act of creating them is what's important. After that, who cares? ∎

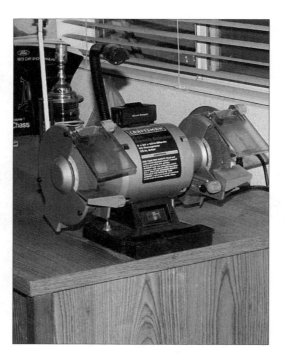

You pay for greater precision by getting limited flexibility.

the equipment and skills I've described so far. In addition you'll need specialized cutting and forming equipment.

I'm not going to go into any detail with this stuff because the skill to use most of it is more important—and harder to get—than the equipment itself. I'm just going to show you the types of metal fabricating equipment that are available for anyone with the money to spend on it and the time to learn how to use it.

Cutting Equipment

Cutting equipment starts out with tin snips, hacksaws, files, and hand drills. You hold the tool in your hand and the work in a vise.

The next level takes these simple tools and mounts them in a way to give you much more precise control. You no longer hold the tool in your hand, you just "operate" it with your hand. That's how you get drill presses, band saws, and lathes. These tools are now "machines." You pay for the greater precision by getting limited flexi-

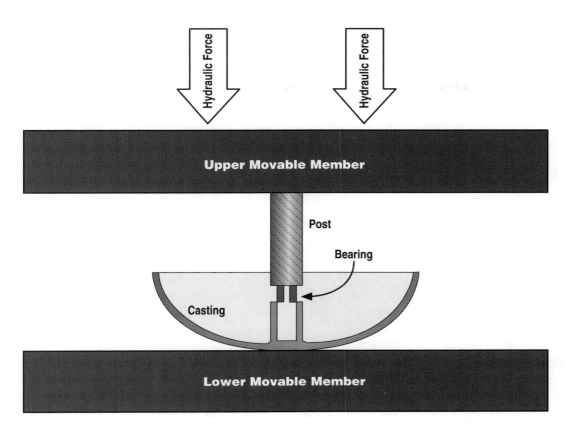

Pressing a bearing is a typical job for a hydraulic press.

bility. With a drill press, you can now drill a hole in just the right place and at just the right angle and get it perfectly round. But, that's about all you can do with it.

Machinery designers developed the next level of equipment by adding flexibility and automation. A milling machine takes the place of (at least) a drill press. But instead of just cutting holes, you can create complicated forms with equal precision.

As you graduate to different levels of equipment, the skills you need change from eye-hand coordination to planning and setup. Eventually, with modern automated milling machines, you stop being an operator and become a programmer.

Forming Equipment

There is a similar progression in forming equipment. You start out with a vise and a hammer to bend simple brackets, and go on to sheet-metal brakes that can make simple straight bends in much larger sheets with much more precise control.

Pounding out round shapes with an anvil and ball-peen hammer progresses to wheeling machines and roll formers. The ultimate in sheet metal forming equipment is, of course, the stamping machine used by factories to form entire panels (such as fenders) with one big ka-chunk. Of course, you need to put a lot of effort into creating the forming die in the first place. It's an example of how factories can mass-produce things that pattern shops have a devil of a time with.

One machine that appears in many small workshops is a press. I'm covering it in forming equipment, but it is actually pretty general in purpose. You can use it for everything from re-shaping kickstands to squooshing rivets. Its main purpose is for installing and removing press-fit items, such as bearings.

An arbor press is a (relatively) small, hand-operated unit, consisting of a C-shaped frame

In the hands of a skilled operator, a milling machine combines the capabilities of a mill, a drill press, plus a lot more.

"rack and gear." Arbor presses come in various sizes and strengths, typically producing maximum forces in the neighborhood of one or more tons.

A press consists of a large frame with two movable members. You move the lower movable member by hand. Actually, you set its position, then lock it into place. You use a hydraulic ram (essentially a hydraulic jack) to push the upper movable member down toward the lower member (which you've already locked in place).

The work piece fits between the two movable members. As the hydraulic ram pushes the upper member down, it squeezes the work piece until it cries "Uncle!"

Say you're trying to press a bearing insert into a casting. You set the lower movable member so that there's room enough to position the casting solidly on the lower member. You then position the bearing insert in the appropriate hole in the casting.

You'll need a post-like dealie to concentrate the force on the top of the insert. An assortment of such dealies came with the press. Select one that will do the job and fit it into the appropriate hole in the upper member, then jack the upper member down until it just starts to press on the top of the bearing insert.

Make sure the whole stack lines up properly to push the insert straight down into the casting. Finally, you get your fingers out of the way and jack the upper member down. As it comes down, it will press the insert into its hole. Stop jacking when the insert bottoms out in the hole. You're done!

with a ram passing through the top end of the C and down onto a flat table at its base. The mechanism consists of a crank turning a shaft let through the top end. A straight-cut gear (also called a pinion gear) rides between teeth cut into the ram. The teeth cut in the ram form a "rack," making the mechanism a "rack and pinion" or

As I pointed out at the beginning of this book, most motorcycle workshops are either owned by professional mechanics who must clearly and loudly announce their presence to the world or by amateurs, who are relatively discreet and anonymous. The difference is that amateurs generally get to choose who they want to have visit their shops. Professional mechanics, on the other hand, have to bring everyone they can into their shops. The more the merrier!

Yoshimura Research and Development of America in Chino, California, on the other hand, is a professional shop that *doesn't* cater to the public. In fact, if they don't invite you in, you ain't a gonna find 'em.

Don Sakakura, Yoshimura's race team manager, gave me detailed directions that led me right up to their door, and I still wasn't sure I was in the right place! I went to the address Don gave me, which was blazed in numbers several feet high near the top of the building. I found their driveway all right, too. Then I hunted for the entrance. I finally found it hidden behind a big bush. Once I saw the door, it was clearly the "public" entrance, but to what? After searching carefully, I found the company's logo picked out in small letters a couple of inches high near the bottom of the front window!

Inside, I found what looked like a receptionist's desk, but no receptionist was in evidence. I found Don by peeking into the nearest open office door and asking the first person I saw where to find him.

Why would Yoshimura make their shop so hard to find? Because they aren't catering to drop-in trade. Of course, finding a salesperson who will sell you their performance products isn't at all hard. Getting in to pester their racing mechanics and development folks is another story, as it should be.

Racing and Performance Development

Yoshimura's main business is design, development, and manufacturing of aftermarket motorcycle exhaust systems varying from fully street-legal EPA certified exhaust systems through their ZRS system (Zyclone Reduced Sound—"for the person who wants a little better sound, but doesn't want to offend anybody"), to all-out racing exhaust systems. They also manufacture

Workbenches in the engine-building area have to be made more solidly to carry the weight of complete motors.

camshafts, rear sets (racing footage mountings), triple trees, and various other aftermarket engine and chassis performance components. Of course, Yoshimura will be happy to sell you a completely race-ready AMA-legal superbike. All you have to do is come up with the bucks!

To maintain their position as a leader in state-of-the-art performance products takes a deep in-volvement in motorcycle racing. Yoshimura runs the American Suzuki factory teams in the AMA Superbike and 750 Supersport racing series and also sponsors other racing efforts, such as Smokin' Joe's Honda Race Team.

"Yoshimura R&D pretty much started Superbike racing and has maintained it and developed the state of the art to where it is," boasts Brad Dixon, Marketing Manager. That's a big claim, but one that history backs up. Superbike racing grew out of Yoshimura's active involvement with Suzuki, and, prior to that, Kawasaki, factory racing efforts.

Setting the workbenches parallel to the motorcycle makes it easier for chassis builder Reg O'Rourke to install systems, such as wiring, that consist of a lot of small parts individually mounted.

The diagram shows the racing shop layout. Yoshimura's racing workshop shares a building with the manufacturing facility's shipping and receiving area. The racing shop includes an engine-building area, a chassis area for working on whole motorcycles, a machine shop (including welding), two dynamometers, a carburetor development facility, and lots and lots of storage.

The part of the building devoted to R&D is two stories tall and roughly 40 feet long by 30 feet wide. The chassis area—where complete motorcycles are moved around—is on the ground floor. They put the engine area on the second floor. The dynamometer rooms and a carburetor analysis facility (which are not shown in the figure) are set up in adjoining parts of the building.

Chassis Area

The actual entrance to the racing workshop is in an alcove near the shipping dock. That door leads immediately to the chassis area.

The chassis area has five workshop bays. Two immediately to the left as you enter the shop, and three on the right. Four of these bays are equipped with electrically operated scissors-type lifts for elevating complete motorcycles. You just roll a bike onto the lift, strap it down so it's stable, and up she goes.

The photo shows two of these lifts. To support the rear end, they, like most racers, use a modification of the simple lever affair I talked about in Chapter 17. Instead of picking the bike up by the frame itself, these lifts hold the bike at specific suspension points. The one on the left hooks onto special pivot points attached to the swingarm near the rear-wheel axle. When the

Workstations in the chassis area have electrically operated lifts.

swingarm isn't installed, however, they use the version on the right, which holds the bike at the points where the swingarm bearing mounts.

These lifts have the advantage of holding the bike much more securely than the type that just sits under the frame. The disadvantage, however, is that they have to be fabricated to fit a specific motorcycle. That's not much of a problem for Yoshimura (or any racing team, for that matter), since they support only a limited number of specific bike models. For most bike mechanics, who have to deal with many different models and custom variations of street bikes, that could run into big bucks. Besides, very few street bikes have the pivots installed on the swingarms, anyway.

It's a lot harder to make that same lift system support the front end, however. The front axle is too short to provide a wide, stable base. The fact that the front forks pivot around the steering head gives an extra measure of instability. It's a lot better to pick the front up by the frame. Notice in the picture that the fronts of both bikes are supported on tall jackstands.

Every bike workstation has, of course, its regulation six-feet of workbench space, with plenty of storage all around. Lighting over the bench and the white back wall surface provides even illumination. In chassis building, relatively little of the actual work is done at the workbench. The main use for workbenches in the chassis area is to provide a place to put parts awaiting their turn to go onto the bike and to give the mechanic a place to put a screwdriver or wrench. Since they don't generally have to support heavy components, they don't have to be especially solid.

Their workbench has a couple of neat storage features. You generally expect to see storage under the workbench, although doors under the bench are an unusual feature. Doors on storage spaces have the advantage of helping keep things a lot neater and cleaner. The disadvantage is that doors make it harder to find parts and a bit harder to get them in and out of the storage space.

The neat storage features here, however, are the overhead storage space and the shelf for back-of-the-bench consumables. The fairly tall ceiling height in Yoshimura's chassis area makes it possible to put in over-the-bench storage and still have adequate overhead clearance on the

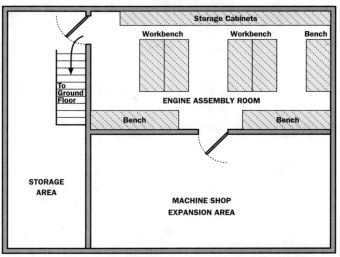

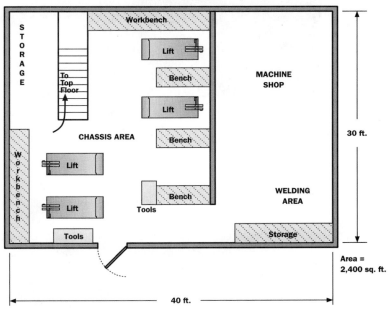

Yoshimura R&D prepares motorcycles for the Suzuki Superbike and 750 Supersport factory racing team in this two-story facility.

bench. The shelf at the back of the bench organizes the consumables and keeps their clutter off the work surface.

The second photo shows three bays set up differently. The big difference is that the workbenches are set up parallel to the bike's long axis. That arrangement is particularly convenient

The engine dynamometer is used for testing complete engines out of the motorcycle.

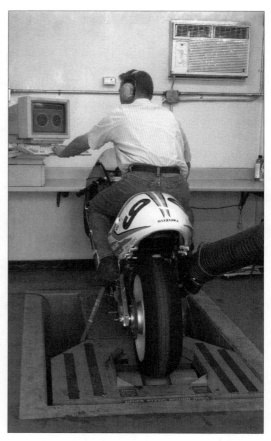

Rob Little shows how an inertia dynamometer provides a realistic test of engine/drivetrain performance under acceleration.

when a mechanic is putting a lot of small parts on a bike, such as installing wiring or plumbing. You can stand between the bench and the bike, pick up a part, turn around to bolt it onto the bike, then turn back for the next part.

Machine Shop

"Fabricating special parts is important for a chassis builder," says Don. Yoshimura's racing mechanics have access, of course, to the machine tool facilities in their manufacturing division. However, they have their own shop adjoining the chassis area, which is equipped with several lathes, milling machines, drill presses, sheet metal forming equipment and, of course, tire changing and balancing equipment. They also have a welding bench set up in one corner.

Engine Assembly

Yoshimura has three people whose sole jobs are to build engines. Engine innards need to be kept absolutely free of dirt particles, so the engine area is set up to be even cleaner than the chassis area. The floor is surfaced with linoleum tiles, which wouldn't last long in the chassis area with complete motorcycles rolling around on them.

Yoshimura builds engines on two long workbenches that provide plenty of space for arranging parts. These benches are built solidly to support heavy, water-cooled motorcycle engines.

About fifty inches deep, these benches are also wider than a standard workbench and divided in two. Effectively, each is two workbenches back-to-back. The dividers down the middle of each bench keep parts of a motor being assembled on one side of the bench from sneaking over to party with parts of the motor being assembled on the other side.

Note in the photo how they've set up the near bench for assembling a cylinder head. The head itself is set up on a stand that gives the engine builder access to both the top and bottom of the head at the same time. Trays and small containers keep small parts from going walkabout while awaiting assembly. Larger parts are laid out on paper towels, which help control dust, sop up oil used to coat parts as they're assembled, and incidentally defines the temporary on-bench storage space. Any part caught inching off the towel is clearly trying to escape!

Engine blocks are assembled on engine stands that, again, provide access on all sides, top, and bottom of the motor. Just to the left outside the picture and on its own little engine stand is the block that the head mates to. The workbench is just the right size on which to arrange the pieces for one engine. A builder starts with parts spread out in neat little groups all over the bench, and consolidates them into one compact engine.

Engine Dyno Room

Yoshimura doesn't just build an engine, drop it into the bike, and hope it goes fast. They test it and tune it on a dynamometer before it ever gets near a motorcycle.

The engine dyno room centers around the dynamometer, with its shaft leading to where the motor mounts in an engine stand. On the right is an overhead crane that makes weight lifting prowess less of a requirement for mechanics when positioning and mounting the engine. The large glass cylinder is for measuring the amount of fuel used during the test.

Suzuki's 750 engines, which are the basis of the Superbike and 750 Supersport class machines, are water-cooled. The tank on the floor to the right contains a standard bike radiator, plumbed into the motor's cooling system by ¾-inch hoses. The tank is filled with water that sucks heat out of the radiator, then carries it away to a cooling tower outside.

Not shown in the photo is an air-induction box that pipes air to the carburetors. The pressure in the induction box can be varied to simulate the ram pressure a bike generates at different track speeds.

So, a Yoshimura engine builder can control everything that might affect a motor's performance. What isn't obvious is the sophisticated computer control coordinating all these inputs and logging all these measurements.

For a particular test run, technicians program the computer to set up a test profile that will include warming up the engine, then setting up various conditions and monitoring engine performance. For example, automatically setting the throttle and adjusting the dynamometer load

Ever Wonder What Parts Do at Night?

Why, you ask, all this effort to keep parts from sneaking off and escaping or mixing with parts from other motors? They're inanimate objects, right? They just sit there, don't they?

Modern religious thinkers look down their noses at "primitive" people who imagine spirits inhabiting rocks and trees. Those of us who work with inanimate objects, like motorcycles, know that while there may not actually be a spirit inhabiting, say, a carburetor float spring, the dang thing sure *acts* like there is. If you've ever dissassembled a carburetor, you know that an escaped carburetor float spring is as hard to capture as a cockroach with the lights turned on!

Small motorcycle parts may not have minds of their own, but it's absolutely necessary to treat them as if they do. If you don't, they'll escape, party with their friends, and go off to explore the farthest nooks and crannies of your workshop. You'll spend more time hunting for them than assembling your motor. ■

yields the power output at a given throttle setting and engine speed.

Considering that the variable parameters of an engine test include engine temperature, throttle setting, ram air pressure (which varies with simulated ground speed), and engine speed, you can see that it takes a lot of data to fully characterize an engine. Every time Yoshimura tries something new—a slight change in the muffler, or a different carburetor jet setup—the engine has to be completely retested because any little change affects every aspect of the engine's performance.

"Dyno testing allows us to make modifications to the engine," Don points out, "and actually see the performance improvements it makes, or a lot of times it goes the other way!"

The point is that there's no way to know whether what seems like a good idea on paper may actually do more harm than good in a race. The time to find that out is in the dyno room, not on the track.

"It's very important to have access to a dyno if you're going to go racing," Don insists. "Everybody wants to change everything, but nowadays the motorcycles are very good the way they come. A lot of things don't need changing."

Inertia Dyno

"I think an inertia dyno gives a much more lifelike test," Don says.

An inertia dynamometer, which is what you sometimes see mounted in the back of a truck at some big rallies and races, tests the power actually delivered through the drivetrain to the rear wheels. In essence, it is a massive steel drum on which the bike's rear wheel sits. The drum is very heavy—comparable to the weight of a complete motorcycle plus rider.

The inertia dyno simulates the dynamic load on the engine as the bike accelerates. On the track, engine power goes into making the bike go faster. At any given moment, the power delivered is equal to the bike's mass times the acceleration rate times the track speed at that moment, all of which (except the mass) change very rapidly. And, of course, there is no reason to expect an engine to operate exactly the same way under rapidly changing conditions during acceleration as it does under the constant conditions set up by the engine dyno. On the inertia dyno, the drum's mass simulates that of the bike and rider, its rotation speed simulates the bike's velocity on the track, and the rate at which the drum accelerates simulates the bike's acceleration.

The problem for anyone trying to test with an inertia dyno is how to measure all the things that are happening while they are changing so fast. The answer is, of course, to let a computer log all the data as it streams out. Sensors automatically monitor the throttle position, engine speed, drum speed, wheel speed (which should equal the drum speed, but how do you make sure?), and so forth. The computer jots down all these numbers thousands of times per second in its little random-access memory, and proudly displays the results for you in the form of little graphs and tables.

So, if you think the new super-whiz-bang, advanced-gimcrack spark plugs you saw advertised on ESPN are gonna give you 25% more horsepower, just pop in a set and twist the throttle. Your inertia dyno will tell you exactly what results you'll really get.

"An inertia dyno is not something you want to take to the track," says Don. "It's not that portable! There are racers who do that, but . . . Just before you go to the track, though, it's a good idea to use one to see where you are. Then, go out and race. When you come back to the shop make your improvements. Without graphs and numbers of what your machine is really putting out, it's very difficult to be competitive."

Carburetor Testing

To set up a carburetor, you put it on a motor and try it out, right? Not if you work for Yoshimura R&D. They have a special test stand just for carburetors, shown in the photo.

The system consists of a vacuum pump (to simulate the engine's suction), a fuel delivery system, and all of the gauging needed to run a carburetor through its paces while metering its performance. Gauges indicate fuel flow, air flow, fuel pressure, and vacuum at various points.

To set up a test, you set the throttle position and airflow, then monitor the results. The important thing you are looking for, of course, is the fuel/air mixture ratio, which is calculated from the amount of fuel delivered and the airflow rate.

The test stand is great for developing new carburetors or for preparing any carburetor block for racing. Balancing carburetors is a whole lot easier when done on this machine than it is on a motor. And, replacing a carburetor block trackside in an emergency is a whole lot easier when the spare was set up ahead of time at the shop.

Don's Advice to the Race-Worn

Don says, "One thing I stress to all the guys here is to make sure we get prepared at the shop so that when we unload a bike from the transporter at the track, we're ready to race. If you do that, you can stay a step ahead of everybody else. It really shows in the results."

There's no way to predict emergencies, of course. You just have to be prepared for when they happen. You have to have complete engines, fairings, and whatever you might need. That is one reason for so much engine dyno testing. Spare engines have to be tested, tuned, and broken in so that if evilness happens to the number-one motor, there's a spare ready to go.

A well-equipped machine shop is a necessity for serious racing teams. This one includes lathes, milling machines, and a variety of other useful metalworking equipment.

Good preparation also calls for teamwork. One of the problems privateers have is needing to do too many jobs at the same time.

Don continues, "If you're a rider, I think it's very important to have somebody other than yourself working on your motorcycle. If you're going to go through the effort of running an entire series, or even just selected events, you should have somebody else working on the motorcycle for you—somebody you can work with and have confidence in. Otherwise, you'll be riding the machine, then getting off and worrying about changes you need to make. As a rider, you need to concentrate on riding only."

The experience of Aaron Yates, who joined the Suzuki team in 1996, shows the importance of having a tuner. The previous year, Yates was one of the Suzuki support riders, and he worked on the machine a lot on his own. He had some good results and a lot of not-so-good results.

"In Aaron's case," Don recalls, "he had to do his own wheel changing, mounting his own tires, and all that. And, I believe his equipment wasn't quite up to par all the time either. He was having to ride over his head to try to make up for deficiencies in the bike, a tire, or whatever. As a result, he fell down quite a bit last year. Before he fell, however, he'd usually be running right up front."

Aaron says that it's completely different for him now because he doesn't have to worry about setting up the motorcycle, going back to the shop after the event, tearing it all apart, and preparing it for the next event. Now, he goes home and trains full time to get into physical and mental shape for the next event. It makes a big difference.

"I think a lot of his problems last year occurred just because it takes a full-time mechanic to maintain the bike and a rider concentrating only on his or her riding and racing," says Don. "This year he doesn't have to worry about preparation of his motorcycle—only his riding—and he's doing really well."

High quality hand and power tools can found at just about any auto parts store or home improvement center. Listed below are companies who also sell tools and shop equipment for motorcyclists.

American Tool Companies, Inc.

701 Woodlands Pkwy
Vernon Hills, IL 60061
www.americantool.com
(847) 478-1090 | (847) 478-1091 (fax)

American Kowa Seiki, Inc.

13939 Equitable Road
Cerritos, CA 90703
www.kowatools.com
(800) 824-9655 | (562) 407-5870 (fax)

Dennis Kirk, Inc.

955 South Field Ave.
Rush City, MN 55069
www.denniskirk.com
(800) 328-9280 | (320) 358-4019 (fax)

The Eastwood Company

263 Shoemaker Rd.
Pottstown, PA 19464
www.eastwoodco.com
(800) 345-1178 | (610) 323-2200

JC Whitney

225 N Michigan Ave.
Chicago, IL 60601
www.jcwhitney.com
(800) 469-3894

Matco Tools

4403 Allen Rd.
Stow, OH 44224
www.matcotools.com
(866) 289-8665 | (330) 926-5323 (fax)

Precision Mfg. & Sales Co., Inc.

2140 Range Rd
Clearwater, FL 33765
www.precisionmfgsales.com
(800) 237-5947 | (727) 442-4025

Whitehorse Press

P.O. Box 60
North Conway, NH 03860-0060
www.whitehorsepress.com
(800) 531-1133 | (603) 356-6556

C.G. Masi, or "Charlie" to those who have to put up with him on a daily basis, was *not* born in a log cabin to poor immigrant farmers. He was born in Franklin, Massachusetts, to middle-class professional parents—both were school teachers. He was a middling student in high school, where he claims to have majored in "cars and girls." After a brief stint as an English major at Boston University's School of Education, where he says he really majored in "drugs"—it was, after all, the late 1960s—he quit to tour the country and has been somewhat of a gypsy ever since. He and his wife, Bonnie, have set up residence at 17 locations in five states. They have two grown children, who also live on opposite sides of the country.

Along the way, Charlie picked up a Bachelor's degree in Physics, a Master of Science degree in Astrophysics, and a Master's in Business Administration. He has worked as a college professor, scientist, engineer, and journalist. His journalistic credentials include well over 100 articles published in scholarly, trade, and consumer publications, and launches of three successful magazines: *Test & Measurement Europe, Motorcycle Tour & Travel,* and *Cal Lab.*

Charlie writes articles for numerous science and technology publications, including *Vision*

Systems Design, Drug Discovery and Development, and *R&D*. He is the Editor of *R&D Magazine's Micro/Nano Newsletter* and fills in with various other writing and editing projects. In between, he teaches Astronomy at Mohave Community College and studies for his Ph.D. in Aerospace Engineering at Arizona State University.

All this activity has started to cut into Charlie's motorcycling time. "I've had to limit myself to two bikes, a chopped Harley, and a Suzuki tricked out for touring," he admits. "It just takes too much time to keep up with the weekly maintenance on any more of them!"

Other Tech Series Titles by

![Whitehorse Press logo] **Whitehorse Press**

the motorcycle information company

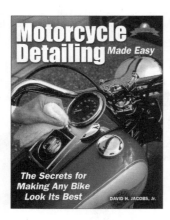

Softbound
8¼ x 10½ inches
144 pages
Approx. 300 b/w illus.

ISBN: 1-884313-35-3
Order Code: MDME
Price: $19.95

Motorcycle Detailing Made Easy

by David H. Jacobs, Jr.

Whether you want to return your bike to showroom condition, get it ready to sell, or prepare it for a custom show, this book will teach you what cleaning a motorcycle is all about. Learn the tricks that will help you keep your bike looking great.

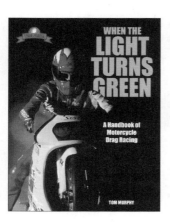

Softbound
8¼ x 10½ inches
176 pages
Approx. 300 b/w illus.

ISBN: 1-884313-29-9
Order Code: WLTG
Price: $19.95

When the Light Turns Green: A Handbook of Motorcycle Drag Racing

by Tom Murphy

From engines, carburetors, and fuel injectors to ignition systems and clutches, this is a complete guide on how to build and operate a drag machine, with tips to help you prepare mentally for drag racing, as well as an illustrated course in racing techniques, correct form, and positioning.

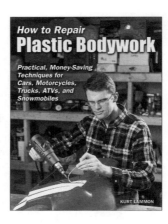

Softbound
8¼ x 10½ inches
160 pages
Approx. 200 color illus.

ISBN: 1-884313-37-X
Order Code: PLAS
Price: $19.95

How to Repair Plastic Bodywork

by Kurt Lammon

This book gives invaluable tips for making structural and cosmetic repairs, rebuilding broken tabs and bolt holes, and fixing stripped threads. Learn what tools and materials are necessary to fusion weld plastic or perform repairs using hot-melt adhesives. Finally, to make getting started even easier, a comprehensive Resource Guide puts dozens of suppliers at your fingertips.

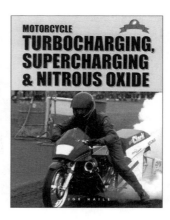

Softbound
8¼ x 10½ inches
198 pages
Approx. 280 b/w illus.

ISBN: 1-884313-07-8
Order Code: HAIL
Price: $19.95

Motorcycle Turbocharging, Supercharging & Nitrous Oxide

by Joe Haile

Written by the master himself, this book will give you a thorough understanding of the principles of forced induction systems and the practical matters involved in putting these principles to work to boost power. Helpful tips on what equipment to buy, how to use it, and much more.

Request a free copy of the Whitehorse Press Motorcycling Catalog, which features thousands of books, videos, tools, shop supplies, accessories, software, maps, posters, and T-shirts for the enthusiast.

Phone: 800-531-1133 or 603-356-6556
Fax: 603-356-6590; Web: www.WhitehorsePress.com
Email: CustomerService@WhitehorsePress.com